# Henry W. Blair's Campaign
# to Reform America

# Henry W. Blair's Campaign to Reform America

*From the Civil War to the U.S. Senate*

GORDON B. MCKINNEY

UNIVERSITY PRESS OF KENTUCKY

Scholarly publisher for the Commonwealth,
serving Bellarmine University, Berea College, Centre College of Kentucky,
Eastern Kentucky University, The Filson Historical Society, Georgetown
College, Kentucky Historical Society, Kentucky State University, Morehead
State University, Murray State University, Northern Kentucky University,
Transylvania University, University of Kentucky, University of Louisville,
and Western Kentucky University.
All rights reserved.

*Editorial and Sales Offices:* The University Press of Kentucky
663 South Limestone Street, Lexington, Kentucky 40508-4008
www.kentuckypress.com

17  16  15  14  13     5  4  3  2  1

Library of Congress Cataloging-in-Publication Data

McKinney, Gordon B., 1943-
  Henry W. Blair's campaign to reform America : from the Civil War to the U.S.
Senate / Gordon B. McKinney.
      p. cm.
  Includes bibliographical references and index.
  ISBN 978-0-8131-4087-2 (hardcover : alk. paper)—ISBN 978-0-8131-4089-6 (pdf)—
  ISBN 978-0-8131-4139-8 (epub)
  1. Blair, Henry W. (Henry William), 1834-1920. 2. Legislators–United
States–Biography. 3. United States. Congress. Senate—Biography. 4. New
Hampshire—Politics and government—1865-1950. I. Title.
  E664.B62M35 2013
  328.73'092--dc23
  [B]                                                        2012036169

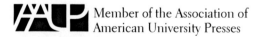

# Contents

# Preface

Seeking information in a small New Hampshire town inevitably leads the researcher to the clerk of the township. A brief visit to the office of Campton clerk Sterle A. Cheney revealed that he was working at home. A short ride to Mr. Cheney's typical New England farmhouse with attached barn opened the world of Henry Blair. Not only did Mr. Cheney know much about the early history of the township, but he also was able to give me the address of Blair's relative Robert Braeman. Although Bob Braeman was living on an island off the coast of Ireland, he wrote that his cousin Giles Low II still lived in Campton.

In June 1980, I visited Giles and Eileen Low for the first time to talk about Uncle Henry. During the first two visits, Giles showed me a huge trunk full of Henry Blair's letters that he had rescued from a family bonfire. Many of the rescued manuscripts dealt with Blair's public career. Unfortunately, few items relating primarily to Blair's personal life survived, and few public sources cover that part of his life. With the assistance of research grants from the National Endowment for the Humanities and the American Philosophical Society, I spent the next two summers photocopying the Blair manuscripts and conducting background research in New Hampshire. While there, I had an opportunity to talk with the Lows and learn much more family history that helped put their famous ancestor in perspective. Without their generosity, interest, and substantial assistance, this project would not have been possible. The Blair manuscripts are now housed at the New Hampshire Historical Society.

Many other individuals and institutions contributed to my research on Blair and his contemporaries. Stuart Wallace and Ruth Weeden Wallace at the New Hampshire Historical Society provided enormous assistance during my research trips there. Joy Trulock and the library staff at Valdosta State University actively sought materials for me, and the graduate school at Valdosta State University purchased newspapers on microfilm that greatly facilitated the research process. The library staff at Western Carolina University, including the Special Collections staff member George Frizzell, was extremely helpful and ensured that I never lacked necessary resources. Shannon Wilson and other historian/librarians at Hunter Library, Berea College, helped me acquire much needed research materials. Library staffs at Dartmouth College, the University of New Hampshire, Plymouth State University, Duke University, the New Hampshire State Archives, the Library of Congress, and the National Archives assisted my research with skill and diligence. Professor Lewis Gould of the University of Texas shared a Blair autograph letter with me. My biggest professional debt in this research is to Professor Daniel W. Crofts of Trenton State College. Dan wrote his dissertation, in part, on the Blair bill and published on the topic. He allowed me to use his work to the fullest extent of my need. This generous assistance added great substance to the two chapters on the education bill. Professor Robert Wiebe read the manuscript thoroughly and offered many interpretive suggestions that strengthened the manuscript. Finally, I am profoundly grateful to Anne Dean Watkins, Ann Malcolm, and Director Stephen M. Wrinn of the University Press of Kentucky for their professional support and keen awareness of the place of this and other works in the dialogue about the meaning of the American experience.

I owe a special thank you to Dr. Shamik Aikat and Dr. Chand Ramaiah of the Gill Heart Institute at the University of Kentucky. They diagnosed and corrected some major problems with my heart. Without their highly professional and compassionate care, I would not have been able to complete this manuscript.

Finally, I wish to thank family and friends who extended generous support when this project most needed it. Maynard Sundman and the Littleton Stamp and Coin Company made their photocopying facilities available to me for the early part of this project. My aunt and uncle, Mary McKinney Healy and William Healy, provided lodging and welcome companionship while I worked in Concord. Their generosity allowed me to extend my scholarship monies to cover the expenses of research far from home. To my wife, Martha McCreedy McKinney, I owe the inspiration for this long journey. Her support, affection, and sympathetic understanding, as well as professionalism in her own career, kept me writing despite the sometimes overwhelming time demands of other commitments.

# Introduction

"The fate of that noble party to which they all belonged, and which had a record that could never be forgotten, depended on their letting principle alone. Their principle must be want of principle."[1] Henry Adams's bitter assessment of the Republican Party's commitment to reform in the Gilded Age was one shared by many contemporaries and later observers. The party that had freed the slaves seemed to have abandoned them to embrace business interests and work solely for base political objectives. By the late nineteenth century, many Americans associated politics with despoiled state and national treasuries, unfit officeholders, purchased votes, campaign violence, and very few positive accomplishments. Politicians often were viewed as incompetent, untrained, unconcerned about corruption, and interested only in the results of the next election.[2] The idea that political leaders in the 1880s made serious attempts to deal with societal problems and that a viable reform tradition existed defied conventional wisdom.

The most sensational reform advocates in the Gilded Age confirmed the prevailing image. In almost every case, they seemed to be people outside the regular party lines and political discipline. Reformers who stayed within the two-party system, like the Liberal Republicans in 1872 and the Mugwumps in 1884, found they had little leverage with party leadership.[3] Despite the generally high social and economic standing of these party-affiliated reform groups, the political process seemed impervious to change. Their legislative accomplishments were often quite conservative in nature and did not threaten the status quo. For example, some contemporaries and later historians maintained that the Civil Service Act of 1883 and the creation of the Interstate Commerce Commission in 1887 did not represent important departures from previous practices.[4] In addition, these changes appeared to be forced on a reluctant Congress by an aroused public opinion.

Henry Blair's life offers important insights into the origins and applications of political reform in the Gilded Age. Blair was first elected to Congress in 1875 and left in 1895. Although he dealt with a broad spectrum of issues during his congressional career, he came to symbolize the moral reformer in politics in the 1880s. He, along with George F. Hoar and other members of an informal Senate leadership called the Half-Breeds, dominated the Republican Party throughout the 1880s.[5] They sought to complete many of the reform programs of the 1850s and 1860s while confronting some of the issues raised by industrialization and urbanization. Blair accepted racial classifications, the existing economic system, and the idea that individuals were personally responsible for advancing their position in society. Yet his identification with a tradition of political reform was deep and genuine. His presence in this circle of reformers was a product of the society in which he matured and the particular events of his early life. With a few exceptions, his ideas and experiences were typical of an entire generation, revealing a considerable amount about the way in which Americans viewed themselves.

Many of the people around Blair shared a belief in dynamic forms of Christianity that required them to improve or perfect the world around them. Led by northern men of Whig and Republican politics, their values and behaviors were shaped by industrialization, evangelical Protestantism, and middle-class status.[6] The result of this combination of ingredients was an earnest and optimistic individual who lived a moral home life, sought commercial success, was anxious about the increasingly unstable society around him, and viewed social respectability as a highly desirable goal.[7] For Blair, the Christian reformer's worldview became the most dominant force in his life. He faced a number of crises in his early life that could have challenged some of his assumptions, but their origin and final resolution tended to reinforce the ideals he had learned. This consistent pattern of beliefs and goals gave him enormous self-confidence in his self-worth and moral rectitude, enabling him to unceasingly pursue a program based on the platforms of the Whig and Republican Parties of the 1850s and 1860s.

The reform program in which Blair felt so much confidence was, like his personal value system, a product of the maturing United States. Soon after its formation, the Republican Party adopted the platform of the rising middle class, calling for equal opportunity through "free land, free labor, and free men."[8] For Blair, this platform became a lifetime program that he continued to pursue more than two decades after the reform period had ended. Policies aimed at equal opportunity were more than abstractions for him. First, they fit perfectly into the moral blueprint for human progress that he had accepted. But even more important was the fact that he had placed his life on the line for these ideals during the Civil War. Seriously wounded at the siege of Port Hudson, he never forgot the physical sacrifices he and others had made. Convinced that the Republican Party was the best vehicle for fulfilling his dreams, it was easy for him to see politics as a battle in which questionable electoral methods could be tolerated to keep the party of morality in power.

Throughout his career, Blair tenaciously sought federal funds for the improvement of public education. Starting with Horace Mann in Massachusetts in the 1830s, this crusade was concerned with much more than the acquisition of knowledge. Education was to be the means of transforming American society. Mann maintained that strong public education was necessary for the government to work properly. He asserted in 1848: "In a republican government, legislators are a mirror reflecting the moral countenance of their constituents. And hence it is that the establishment of a republican government, without well-appointed and efficient means for universal education for the people, is the rashest experiment by man."[9] Strongly agreeing with Mann, Blair often stated in the Senate debates of the 1880s that moral reform and leadership were impossible without an educated electorate.

While Mann worked to improve public education at the state level, Blair took his crusade to the national government. His high regard for Daniel Webster helps explain why he viewed public education as a national concern. Blair, who considered himself an heir of the Whig tradition, felt that Webster was the greatest man produced by his native state. So great was his respect for Webster that he purchased and preserved a building in which he thought Webster had argued his first court case. This romantic vision of Webster sensitized Blair to Webster's almost mythic reverence for the Union and the federal government.[10] Abraham Lincoln's rhetorical support of the Union further strengthened Blair's commitment to the idea, and his own Civil War experience confirmed its rightness.

Blair viewed public education as one of several reform initiatives that could solve the problems of racial and sexual discrimination. His proposal for federal aid to public schools was specifically designed to aid illiterate southern blacks. His attempt to carry out the unfulfilled promises made by the Republican Party during Reconstruction was not the only initiative that he supported on behalf of former slaves. He consistently backed black voting rights, introduced an antilynching bill in 1894, and worked as a lobbyist with the National Association for the Advancement of Colored People at age eighty. This stubborn insistence on greater opportunities for blacks during a period of worsening race relations demonstrated the depth of his commitment to his reform platform.

Blair also lent his name to proposals to grant more education for women. As with his program for blacks, this program went well beyond formal education. In addition to advocating greater legal and economic rights for women, he played a leadership role in the battle for women's suffrage.

These midcentury decades spawned another movement that had a profound impact on Blair's agenda for the reformation of American society. In the 1850s, Maine passed the first comprehensive prohibition law, and New Hampshire and other states followed with modified versions of that legislation. Prohibition, like education, was viewed as a broad-based reform that could improve many aspects of American life. Advocates argued that outlawing the manufacture and sale of alcoholic beverages would purify social relationships, save the family, free Americans from a kind of bondage, and spur the return of respectable behavior.[11] As a leader in this movement, Blair saw a positive role for the federal government to play in the establishment of a more moral America.

Throughout his political career in the 1860s and 1870s, Blair drew support from a large portion of the electorate—particularly within the Republican Party—that shared the same set of ideas and experiences. Those who fought for the Union established an enduring bond, and Blair certainly identified himself closely with that tradition. He was viewed as one of the champions of the soldier's widow and the veteran seeking a pension. More broadly, he appealed to those who believed that freedom of opportunity, access to education, respectability, sobriety, and nativism formed a coherent and important platform for action. Beginning in the 1880s, the forces behind industrialization began to dominate American society and politics. This change, which was not immediately obvious to contemporary observers, frustrated Blair's attempts to implement his reform program and brought him down to final political defeat.

Henry Blair was a composite created by the circumstances of his own life and the major currents of his time. The Christian reform culture of nineteenth-century New England provided a clear code of conduct and belief. The events of his early life reinforced the structured world in which Blair matured. Orphaned as a child, he lacked many of the formal credentials necessary to firmly establish himself as a member of the new respectability. Therefore, the earnestness commonly associated with the growing middle class was almost a compulsion with him. His sacrifice during the Civil War convinced him that he had found the best answers to the problems facing America. Secure in his commitment to just causes, he was usually magnanimous toward political opponents, direct and honest in dealing with political allies, not selfish or mean in personal relationships, devoted to his family, and able to laugh at some of his own foibles. Even when he was facing decreased respect in the Senate, his self-deprecating humor often evoked positive responses from his colleagues. He steadfastly defended moral reform in a hostile climate, affirming that the federal government had an important role to play in improving American society. This would be his enduring legacy.

# Chapter 1

# Early Years

The Beech Hill farm was a frenzy of activity. Richard and Sarah Bartlett were expecting a very important guest. William Miller and his followers had selected the next day—October 22, 1844—as the time that Jesus would return to Earth in his glory.[1] The Bartletts were not sure that the Millerites were correct, but they were taking no chances that the advent would catch them unprepared. At the same time, they wanted all their worldly affairs in order when the new era began. Richard directed their foster child, Henry Blair, to round up the livestock from the lower pastures and herd them into the barn. The Bartletts had many of the merino sheep so favored by New Hampshire farmers in this period and an old milk cow. The animals did not seem to understand the importance of haste, and young Henry struggled to make them obey. In the house, Sarah was busy stitching "glory robes" out of sheets so that they would be properly attired when the Lord appeared.

The final chores were completed as the autumn sun rapidly set in the foothills of the White Mountains. Henry sensed that it would be a cold night's wait as he crunched his way back to the house through the crimson and gold leaves that had recently decorated the landscape. After a fervent grace and a hasty meal, the Bartletts made final preparations. They were going to nearby Chandler Hill to await the Second Coming, with nine-year-old Henry staying behind to watch the animals, just in case William Miller was wrong. Midnight, dawn, and dusk came in slow procession as Henry watched across the valley. Concluding that all their concern was unwarranted, the Bartletts finally came home. Supper that evening was eaten in a somber atmosphere as all members of the family were lost in their own thoughts.[2]

When Uncle Henry told this story to his nieces and nephews and their children more than seventy years later, he related it with great humor and with an emphasis on the "practical" Christianity of his guardians.

This episode was more than a funny story, however. It highlighted two of the most important facts about Henry Blair's childhood. First, this dramatic encounter emphasized the deeply religious nature of the society in which Blair lived. Out of this pious background came the reform tradition that dominated his political life. Second, he was without any of his birth family at a time of crisis in his youth.

Equally important, this episode tells a great deal about the cultural milieu in which Blair was raised. The United States was experiencing a religious revival known as the Second Great Awakening. Reacting against the unemotional worship services in established churches, many Americans were searching for religious experiences that would be more personally fulfilling. In northern New England, that need was first met by the itinerant preachers of the Methodist Church. Membership in this denomination expanded rapidly and changed many Yankees' religious expectations.[3]

By the 1830s, religious experimentation had become an important part of northern New England culture. Among the new groups were the Shakers. These pacifist communitarians segregated the sexes, prohibited private ownership of land, and followed nontraditional worship practices.[4] Vermont natives Joseph Smith and Brigham Young founded Mormonism and proselytized in New Hampshire with considerable success before being forced to migrate west. Preaching from a new set of scriptures and offering a broader hope of redemption than the other sects, Mormons were most often associated with polygamy.[5] John Humphrey Noyes and the Perfectionists introduced an even more extreme religion. First organized in Putney, Vermont, this community was known for its outstanding craftspeople. However, the Perfectionists' claims of universal salvation and their institution of complex marriage alienated their neighbors. Complex marriage required every man in the community to be married to every woman and vice versa. Like the Mormons, the Noyes community was forced to relocate.[6]

William Miller and his followers were another part of the great religious leavening taking place in rural northern New England. Miller became a Baptist clergyman in the early 1830s, and like many of his contemporaries he was a millennialist. Convinced that the end times were rapidly approaching, he prophesied that Judgment Day would be October 22, 1844. In Sugar Hill, New Hampshire, a township north of Blair's home, a group of Miller's followers went to extremes. They harvested no crops and sold or gave away their livestock. They further prepared themselves by fasting and praying for six weeks. Their efforts to persuade their neighbors to join them generated little interest, as documented by the following incident: "On the day before the world was supposed to end, one man went into the field to give a final exhortation to some 'unsaved' neighbors. Worn out with fasting and prayer, he sat down on a haystack and went to sleep. The recreants then removed most of the hay and touched a match to what was left. The Millerite awoke with a start, shouting, 'Hell—just as I expected.'"[7] The religious upheavals of the time deeply influenced the childhood experiences of Blair and his contemporaries.

Some important secular ramifications developed out of these religious movements. For example, many of these groups revolutionized gender relations. The Shakers allowed no sexual contact of any kind, and women held leadership positions in their communities. The Mormons and Perfectionists cast traditional marriage relationships into new molds. The Millerites believed that women would be judged equally before God's judgment seat. As Blair matured, these challenges to the subordinate status of women became part of his intellectual and political framework.

Nonconventional religious groups shared the belief that control of the consumption of alcohol, a better diet, more education, and more rights for women would solve most of the nation's problems. Their conviction that American society could be greatly reformed or even perfected took root among many northern New England residents. Blair, like other young people growing up during this period, was deeply influenced by this way of thinking.

None of this drama seemed likely to occur when Henry William Blair was born on December 6, 1834, in Campton, New Hampshire. He was the third child and second son of William Henry Blair and Lois Baker Blair. Family members on both sides had roots deep in New England history and a sure sense of where they had come from and where they were going. The Blair family had left Ulster in 1718 and settled in Londonderry, New Hampshire. The coming of the Revolutionary War destroyed family harmony, scattering family members throughout eastern North America. William Blair, a first-generation American, supported the king. He was finally forced into a Canadian exile and died there.

William Blair's daughter, Frances, was one of the victims of this family disruption. She was forced to migrate to Holderness in Grafton County, where she bore a son, Peter, who would become Henry Blair's grandfather.[8] Peter established a new Blair clan in northern New Hampshire. He and his wife, Hannah Palmer Blair, had nine children that lived to maturity, and the family members became leaders in the rural township of Campton. After the War of 1812, Peter Blair helped reorganize the Congregational church in the community "in hope of obtaining [a] permanent, pious[,] regular, learned and Calvinistic Minister of the Congregational order."[9] Following in his grandfather's footsteps, Henry Blair viewed a strict moral code and an educated electorate as essential for societal improvement.

William Henry Blair, the oldest of Peter's sons, was born on December 1, 1805. Young William had a traditional family upbringing as a farmer and attended the schools in Campton. In addition to farming, he served as a teacher in the local schools, an officer in the local militia, and the director of the church choir. In 1827, he joined the Congregational Church by a public profession of faith.[10] The success of the Blair family and the church was clearly documented in 1829 when the congregation agreed to build a covered bridge across the Pemigewasset River in a section of Campton named after the Blair family.[11]

On February 18, 1830, William Blair married Lois Baker. Lois's family had moved from Candia, New Hampshire, to the Campton area after the American Revolution. Like her husband, Lois had joined the Campton Congregational Church before their marriage. She was also a schoolteacher and shared with William Blair an outstanding singing voice. According to her son, she had an unsurpassed knowledge of the Bible that she constantly shared with her children.[12] This union was quickly blessed with a daughter, Hannah Palmer Blair, and a son, Moses Baker Blair. Their third child, Henry Blair, was born on December 6, 1834. With questions of religion, education, and economic opportunity seemingly settled, Henry's future looked promising.

While helping tear down an old building in November 1836, William Blair was crushed by a falling wall. He never recovered from the resulting injuries and died on December 8, 1836.[13] Lois Blair was forced to try several unwelcome expedients in an effort to meet this domestic crisis. She placed the two older children in family homes in surrounding communities where they could provide labor to pay their upkeep. The pregnant thirty-year-old widow kept Henry with her, and she tried to sustain herself and her son by working on a farm owned by a relative. Her difficulties increased in May 1837 when a second daughter, Lois Esther

Blair, was born. Fortunately, there were a number of close relatives living in Campton who provided the struggling family with companionship and some financial support.[14]

Blair was something of a trial to his mother and a general discipline problem. He recalled that he and Pays Baker "liked to play in the great water-trough where the cows drank, and, as it was quite deep and danger-ous for our little bodies, Colonel David Baker strictly forbade our playing any more in it, but on the sly we did. Forthwith, the Colonel caught us by the neck, one in each hand, and baptized us by immersion head down-wards, until the life was half choked out of us, and we were released only upon our most solemn promise to sin no more."[15] Blair, a tall and rangy boy, engaged in many fights with boys his own age.[16] In addition, there were quiet moments of fishing in the creek that ran through the Baker property and the excitement of militia musters. Blair recalled: "I enjoyed beyond measure the pomp and circumstance (also the gingerbread) of glorious war. I have never seen anything since which compared at all with 'Great Training.'"[17]

Blair's reasonably typical rural boyhood was constantly interrupted by tragedy and hardship. At some time before he was seven, Blair became severely ill—perhaps with diphtheria—and family members were afraid he would die. After recovering, he remained physically weak for several months, suffering from emotional stress as well.[18] This illness became part of a pattern of youthful physical weakness and inability to deal with the accompanying pressures of an unsettled family life. Outside events soon came to have an equally severe impact on Blair's life. In 1841, in a des-perate attempt to reach financial self-sufficiency, Lois Blair placed Henry in the home of Samuel Keniston and went to work in the textile mills of Lowell, Massachusetts.[19] Taking her youngest daughter with her, the har-ried widow labored for a year before deciding that the wages did not com-pensate for the separation from her family. There is no indication of what Henry thought about this exile from his mother. On returning to north-ern New Hampshire, Lois Blair worked as a domestic in the larger town of Plymouth. For the first time, Henry realized that he was relatively eco-nomically deprived.

Unable to hold the family together with her limited resources, Lois Blair placed Henry with Richard Bartlett on May 1, 1843. That change of residence may have saved his life since his mother and younger sister contracted scarlet fever within a month of his departure. His older sister,

Hannah, returned home to nurse the two invalids, fell victim to the disease, and died in June. At the time of the funeral, Blair remembered, "Mother was very sick in bed. She sobbed and could only say 'I should have sent for you if I had thought Hannah would die so soon.'"[20]

Despite any negative feelings created by the Millerite incident, Henry's life with the Bartletts proved to be stable and satisfying. From the very beginning, they affirmed that he was needed and was making an appreciated contribution. The Bartletts apparently could not have children, and they needed someone to help with the many chores involved in running a family farm. Fifty years later, Blair's wife incorporated many of these work experiences into a novel that almost made the farm seem romantic.[21] Blair himself offered a more realistic appraisal of his early life, telling a correspondent that he doubted his friend could find "a man who knows more of the sorrows of the toughest sort of hill-farm husbandry than I did until my twenty-first year."[22] Nevertheless, he had a family to care for him when his mother was unable to provide support and after her death on July 10, 1846.

Blair's personal assessment of his relationship with the Bartletts indicated that he felt fortunate to be placed in their home. When in a much later recollection he explained how he came to leave his mother, he wrote that he went to "love" with the Bartletts—a most significant misspelling.[23] He described Richard Bartlett as "a good man and a good farmer," and a later observer noted: "Blair often speaks of his home with the Bartletts and always in terms of the highest respect, affection, and gratitude."[24] Still, Henry never forgot that he grew up not knowing his father and that his mother "died of overwork, grief, and poverty."[25] Even when he had won high political office and great personal popularity, he wrote: "I lived my whole life with a sense of orphanage & desolation."[26] These feelings motivated him to seek economic security and public recognition for the remainder of his life.

Taught to read by his mother, Blair recalled Josephus's *History of the Jews* as his favorite early reading.[27] Like Blair's parents, Richard Bartlett was thoroughly convinced of the importance of education. In addition to encouraging Henry to attend the district school in Campton, Bartlett became directly involved in the school program. Perhaps the clearest example of his commitment was his willingness to incur high taxes—reaching 30 percent of the district's budget one year—to ensure that there was adequate financing for the schools. From 1840 through 1851, Bartlett served as both secretary and treasurer of the District 6 school committee. Although Blair was encouraged to learn and received as good an education as was available in a rural district school, the ungraded schools offered less than three months of classes a year with teachers who usually had no professional training of any kind.[28]

At the age of sixteen, Blair decided that he wanted to pursue a career other than farming. In 1851 and 1852, he attended Holmes Academy, a college preparatory school in Plymouth, to prepare himself for college. During the next two years, he spent two terms at the New Hampshire Conference Seminary in Tilton, which offered both preparatory and collegiate courses. There, he probably took the following courses: arithmetic, algebra, Latin grammar, Caesar, English grammar, and Greek grammar.[29] In 1855, financial considerations forced him to return to Plymouth to finish his studies at the select school. He hoped that this schedule of study would allow him to enter Dartmouth and continue his education at a law school.[30]

To finance his educational ventures, Blair became a teacher in the local district schools. He taught at the Eastern Corner district school in Campton during the winter terms of 1852 and 1853. Two years later, he taught in the Plymouth village school. During the winter terms of 1855 and 1856, he journeyed to Randolph, Massachusetts—probably in search of a higher salary—and taught school there.[31] During the busy fall and spring seasons, he continued to work at the Bartlett farm. His driving ambition to get an education and the hectic pace he was forced to maintain finally wore him down, and in the spring of 1856 he collapsed. He appears to have had a severe case of the measles. Greatly weakened by this illness, he became convinced that his cherished goal of attending Dartmouth was unattainable.[32] His disappointment was so profound that he spent a significant portion of his public life trying to ensure that other Americans would not be deprived of educational opportunities.

Studies of childhood and adolescence in the nineteenth century indicate that Blair's experience was not that unusual. For most youths, including those living in a normal nuclear family, the years between ten and twenty-one were a time of semi-independence. Most young men had to remain on the family farm until at least their twenty-first birthday and could not pursue careers until after that time. In fact, those adolescents who suffered the loss of one or both parents often had an advantage because they were not restricted by family duties. Physical development also was much slower than at present, with puberty often coming at age six-teen and full growth not attained until age twenty-five.[33] In this particular case, there is evidence that Blair was still maturing physically at the age of twenty-six or twenty-seven.[34] Thus, few of his contemporaries enjoyed any real advantage over him except in the amount of formal education they had received. And, even in that instance, Blair was not unusually handi-capped. Of the twenty-six New Hampshire lawyers born between 1832 and 1836, thirteen did not attend college, and eight besides Blair attended neither college nor law school. When Blair passed the bar examination at the age of twenty-four, he was one of the youngest of his contemporaries to achieve that status.[35]

On May 1, 1856, Blair began his legal studies in the office of William Leverett of Plymouth. Leverett, a graduate of Yale University and Yale Law School, was admirably suited to provide Blair with the legal academ-ic background that he had previously missed. Because certain sessions of the Grafton County Superior Court met in Plymouth, an unusually large number of lawyers practiced in the town. While not a spectacular trial at-torney, Leverett was widely regarded as the leading lawyer in the commu-nity. Blair commented that Leverett was "remembered . . . for the strength of his mind, the accuracy of his legal knowledge, his elegant scholarship and gentlemanly accomplishments."[36] Leverett also seems to have been fi-nancially astute and owned real estate valued at $12,000 in 1860 (roughly $330,000 in 2012 dollars).[37]

Surviving documents suggest that Blair was directly involved in cas-es as early as January 1857 and was entirely responsible for some cases a year later.[38] He proved to be an adept student, and by May 1859 he had passed the bar and become his mentor's partner. In 1859, the Republican-dominated state legislature named him as one of the three justices of the peace for Plymouth, indicating that he was using his profession as an en-try into politics.[39]

Having established himself as a lawyer, Blair was now able to turn to other concerns. The most significant development was his marriage to Eliza A. Nelson on December 20, 1859. Educated in the Plymouth village schools and at the Newbury Seminary in Vermont, Eliza was an attractive and lively young woman who shared most of her husband's in-terests and values.[40] She was the daughter of William Nelson, the first regularly appointed Methodist minister in the Plymouth region. In this strongly Calvinist region, the Nelsons experienced considerable hostility and discrimination, something that Eliza deeply resented. Her decision to marry Blair suggests that he had not yet become a strong orthodox Congregationalist.

Blair's strong interest in political activities quickly remedied his need to have a secure income to meet his family responsibilities. As a junior partner in a small-town law firm, Blair had little opportunity to earn a consistent amount of money. Thus, when offered an appointment as solicitor for Grafton County in 1857 with assured income, he quickly accepted the offer. This appointment indicates that he had proved himself to be a competent attorney despite his inexperience. He also had demonstrated two attributes that would make him a powerful public speaker for the next forty years—a willingness to thoroughly research a case or topic and a powerful speaking voice that commanded attention.

Blair later maintained that the solicitor appointment was a complete surprise to him and came without his asking for it. He said that Judge Charles Doe—New Hampshire's most talented jurist in the late nineteenth century—offered the position to Blair because he was impressed by his court work.[41] While that assertion may be technically correct—Doe did approach Blair, and Blair did not formally apply for the position—the solicitor's office was a patronage appointment made by the governor. Given the high level of partisanship of that era and the fact that the Republican Party of New Hampshire was not in secure control of the state, the appointment could not have been just a stroke of good fortune. By this time, Blair must have been deeply involved in the township politics of Plymouth. Since Plymouth was a large Republican town in a Democratic county, the party leaders may have taken special note of his activities. Blair documented nothing of his own political activities in this period except to say that he was always a "radical" in his political outlook.[42] Nevertheless, this episode suggests that the close relation between the law and politics served as his primary motivation for studying and practicing law.

*Chapter 2*

# Colonel

Blair was one of many Americans whose lives dramatically changed during the Civil War. The election of 1860 was a crucial event that threatened his safety and the stability of the country. Like more than 60 percent of the voters living above the forty-first parallel, Blair cast his vote for the Republican candidate, Abraham Lincoln. Despite receiving few votes in the states that allowed human enslavement, Lincoln was clearly and legally elected.[1] The southern slave states—correctly perceiving a significant shift in the balance of national political power—reacted with fury and began taking precipitous steps to negate this perceived threat to their well-being. In December 1860, South Carolina seceded from the Union and was soon followed by six other Deep South states. Moving quickly, these revolutionaries created a new country with a capital at Montgomery, Alabama, and a new constitution that protected the institution of slavery.[2] While none of his letters from this period survive, there is every reason to believe that Blair was outraged by these challenges to the Union.

When Lincoln was inaugurated on March 4, 1861, the country was split into three sections, with the Upper South slave states undecided about their status. Making the situation even more unstable was the fact that the national government still controlled two fortifications on land claimed by the new Confederate government. These were Fort Sumter in the harbor of Charleston, South Carolina, and Fort Pickens off the coast of Pensacola, Florida. During his inaugural address, Lincoln promised to hold these facilities, and Fort Sumter, in particular, became a flashpoint.[3] Unable to purchase provisions locally, the Union garrison in Charleston informed Lincoln that it would be starved into surrendering by April 15, 1861. To prevent this, the president sent supply ships to Charleston and informed local and Confederate authorities of his intentions. Confederate leaders refused to accept this solution and opened fire on Fort Sumter on April 12, 1861.[4] The small Union force surrendered two days later, and

Lincoln called for seventy-five thousand troops to put down the rebellion. As a result of his action, four more Upper South states joined the Confederacy, which moved its capital to Richmond, Virginia.

Lincoln's call for troops generated an enthusiastic response in the northern states. In many locations, thousands more volunteered than the government was prepared to enlist.[5] Despite his desire to serve, Blair found it almost impossible to join the army. He had not completely recovered from his collapse in the spring of 1856 and was not considered strong enough to withstand the rigors of combat. In 1861, he volunteered to join the famous Fifth New Hampshire Regiment, but both his personal physician and an army surgeon at the state capital refused to give him the necessary clearance. With Blair watching from the sidelines, the Union raised large armies, and these undisciplined mobs headed south to confront equally poorly trained Confederate forces. The rout of the Union troops at the Battle of Manassas awakened everyone to the fact that this would be a long and difficult conflict.[6] The U.S. Navy countered the Confederate success on land with a string of victories that ultimately affected Blair.

Several of the naval victories took place on the Mississippi and adjoining rivers. A squadron of ships ascended the Mississippi from the Gulf of Mexico, survived passage by Confederate forts, and forced the surrender of New Orleans.[7] Further up the river, a joint army-navy expedition under the leadership of General Ulysses S. Grant and Flag Officer Andrew H. Foote captured Forts Henry and Donelson on the Tennessee and Cumberland Rivers. By June 1862, Union troops had captured Island No. 10 in the Mississippi and the city of Memphis.[8] These conquests reduced Confederate control of the great river to the strongholds of Vicksburg, Mississippi, and Port Hudson, Louisiana. Since both these Confederate positions were located on high bluffs above the river, naval forces were unable to force the surrender of either.

Other Federal armies failed to achieve similar results. The Army of the Potomac under General George McClellan was unable to defeat Robert E. Lee and his army in the Peninsula campaign in Virginia. Thomas J. "Stonewall" Jackson won a string of Confederate victories in the Shenandoah Valley, demonstrating that the Confederacy was a legitimate military power.[9] In the summer of 1862, Confederates began assembling a strong army in Tennessee that threatened Union control in that state and Kentucky. Recognizing that the Federal army was too small to handle all these threats, President Lincoln called for 300,000 three-year volunteers in July 1862 and 300,000 nine-month volunteers a month later.[10]

During the summer of 1862, Blair raised a squad of men and joined the Twelfth Regiment for a three-year term. Once again, the medical opinions were negative, and Blair was forced to turn his recruits over to a friend. Soon thereafter, the Union issued a call for more men, and the governor of New Hampshire, Nathaniel S. Berry, found that the state lacked sufficient volunteers to fill the state's quota. This was the opportunity for which Blair had been waiting. First, he went to the medical examiner for the state. As Blair later remembered: "[He] said he would accept me for nine months, as I appeared determined to go anyway."[11] Then Blair went to Governor Berry and received permission to raise a company of nine-month volunteers. This seeming compulsion to serve suggests that Blair viewed belonging to a military unit as more than a simple patriotic duty.

Finally able to swing into action, Blair started actively seeking men in August 1862. Drawing recruits from the Grafton County communities of Plymouth, Haverhill, and Piermont, he quickly filled the ranks. This recruitment process greatly speeded up after August 29, when the town of Plymouth offered a bounty of $200 to anyone who volunteered for nine months. Nineteen men from Plymouth, including Blair, qualified for this bonus.[12] When other units were slower to form, Blair found that he had a major problem. Writing to the state adjutant general, he reported: "The men are restive and as soon as you can be troubled with us at Concord please inform me and we will be forthcoming. We are greatly scattered and unable to drill to advantage as we are."[13] In early October, the units later known as the Fifteenth New Hampshire Regiment of Volunteers were called to Concord and mustered into the state militia.

Blair was able to take advantage of his earlier political prominence to secure a favored position in the regiment. On October 2, 1862, he enlisted as a private along with the rest of the regiment, but he was quickly selected as captain by the men in Company B. After the regiment was mustered into the service on October 8, however, he held the rank of major and was third in command of the outfit.[14] Since the governor appointed the top officers, this episode was another example of Blair's growing political influence. Sensing that he might be accused of seeking personal advancement, Blair offered the following unconvincing explanation: "Of the arrangements as to field officers I was ignorant, or rather had no part in them, until I was told that an arrangement was being made so that I would be made major."[15] Just as with his appointment as county solicitor, he was unwilling to acknowledge the role that political connections had played in securing him a position that he greatly desired.

For more than a month, the new major and the Fifteenth Regiment stayed in New Hampshire. As Blair slowly but doggedly learned his job, he began directing the regimental drill. Possibly owing to the "Great Training" of his childhood, he discovered that he actually enjoyed the exercise of military authority. Observing that his superiors were even less well trained, he began to feel "some relative confidence" in himself.[16] On November 7, 1862, the regiment was ordered to proceed to New York and join the force gathered under the command of Major General Nathaniel Banks. On November 12, the regiment marched to Concord and was mustered into the Federal army. The troops listened to a rousing speech by the governor, and the officers were presented with fine horses. Blair's horse was a handsome Morgan named Billie. The next day, the regiment boarded a train and traveled south through Massachusetts and Connecticut. On arrival at Long Island Sound, the men boarded a steamer for New York.[17]

Many of the new recruits had never been outside northern New Hampshire. For them and their officers, the next four weeks seemed like a great adventure. On November 14, they landed in New York City and then marched to join Banks's army on Long Island. Over the next few days, Blair and the other officers tried to bring some sort of order to the regiment. Driving rain and very cold weather often canceled part or all of this routine, leaving the Fifteenth Regiment remarkably poorly trained when it finally headed south. In addition, some serious morale and discipline problems surfaced for the first time. The poor weather left about fifty men in the hospital at all times, and, on November 22, the first member of the regiment died. At about the same time, the first of twenty-eight deserters from the regiment left camp.[18]

Both officers and soldiers probably were relieved when Banks's army was ordered south. On December 13, Blair left Long Island on the ship *Cambria* with the last companies in the regiment. The trip was relatively uneventful except for the inexperienced sailors' largely unsuccessful attempts to avoid seasickness. Two days into the voyage, Blair was called on to arbitrate a dispute between the troops and the ship's cook. This he managed to do while pacifying his men and preserving the dignity of the cook—a major piece of diplomacy. That night, he stayed up with the ship's captain as the vessel experienced difficulty in rough seas. On Christmas Day, the *Cambria* reached New Orleans, and the next day Blair and his detachment disembarked and marched to rejoin the regiment at the Carrollton, Louisiana, camp.[19]

Further up the river, General U. S. Grant renewed his campaign to open the Mississippi. After unsuccessful attempts to attack Vicksburg from the north and to divert the river through a canal, Grant employed a new strategy. He marched his army down the west side of the Mississippi until he was south of Vicksburg and crossed the river.[20] At this point, he expected to meet Banks's forces, which had been transferred to New Orleans. That army was delayed, however, because Banks became involved in the civilian administration of New Orleans.[21] Refusing to wait for Banks, Grant mounted a brilliant campaign that placed him between two Confederate armies—defeating one at Jackson, Mississippi, and then trapping the other at Vicksburg.[22] Belatedly, Banks brought his army north and prepared to capture Port Hudson, Louisiana.

During the more pleasant southern winter, the Fifteenth Regiment tried to prepare itself for battle. Colonel John Kingman and the second in command were either temperamentally unable or not competent to lead the drill.[23] An incredulous reviewing officer reported: "In one instance the lieutenant-colonel commanding [the] Fifteenth New Hampshire Volunteers admitted that he could not give the commands to pass his regiment in review."[24] As a result, most of the responsibility for making soldiers out of these raw recruits fell on Blair's shoulders. One soldier captured the essence of Blair during this period when he wrote: "Major Blair is tall and slight in form, precise in dress and bearing; his horse prances about like a centaur. He is red-haired, nervous, fiery, tireless—nothing escapes him. The blundering and awkwardness along the line, to him, are seemingly inexcusable. He would drill the boys interminably, but they should do better."[25] Blair maintained this vigorous pace despite the fact that he was sick at times with a malady called *swamp fever*. Apparently, most of the regiment suffered from this illness, which caused high fevers and sudden death, as they tried to adjust to the new climate and living conditions.

Blair soon received a tangible reward for his assiduous efforts. At the brigade review on February 14, General Thomas Sherman expressed outrage at the poor performance of the regiment and chewed out the officers in "the choicest 'West Point.'"[26] Shortly thereafter, Lieutenant Colonel G. W. Frost resigned his commission and returned to New Hampshire. Colonel Kingman immediately recommended Blair for the position.[27]

When Blair officially received his promotion on April 8, 1863, he was in no condition to exercise his authority. Five days earlier, the combination of great responsibility and a vigorous physical routine had led to his complete collapse. His illness prompted General Sherman to remark that the "Fifteenth New Hampshire was the damnedest regiment for sick officers he ever saw."[28] Sherman was actually incorrect in his assessment. The companion New Hampshire Sixteenth Regiment was even sicklier, suffering more deaths during its nine months of service than any regiment from the Granite State. Staying in the same locations as Blair and his comrades, this unit saw 30 percent of its members die—very few from combat-related injuries—before being mustered out.[29] As the army doctors in New Hampshire had recognized, Blair simply was not prepared for the rigors of army life. From April 3 until May 25, he was confined to a hospital in New Orleans. His condition deteriorated seriously, and, at one point, attending physicians thought he had died.[30] He recovered from this illness very slowly and remained quite weak.

While Blair convalesced in New Orleans, the Fifteenth Regiment prepared to go into combat. On May 20, 1863, the men traveled by ship to Port Hudson, Louisiana—one of the last two Confederate strongholds on the Mississippi. There they joined the other fourteen thousand men in Banks's army in besieging a seven-thousand-man Confederate force safely hidden behind the high slopes and strong fortifications of the city. As Banks prepared for a massive attack on the entrenched enemy, Blair returned to his regiment on May 26.[31] Apparently, he had heard that a battle was imminent and had rushed to the front to be with his men. The events of the next day would make that one of the most fateful decisions of his life.

Neither the men whom Henry Blair was ready to lead into battle nor the leadership of this Union army was well prepared. General Neal Dow of Maine served as the brigade leader for the Fifteenth Regiment. Dow had a national reputation as a temperance reformer, but he had no military training or experience. General Thomas Sherman served as the division commander over Dow. Sherman was a thoroughly trained military professional who had nothing but disdain for politician-soldiers like Dow. That attitude led to poor communications and misunderstandings with another political general, Nathaniel Banks, who was serving as commander of the expedition. Banks viewed the fighting around Port Hudson as a ticket to a successful presidential candidacy and hoped to win a quick and decisive victory.[32] Refusing to acknowledge the increasingly obvious fact that it was virtually impossible to storm a well-fortified position with available military technology, he ordered a coordinated attack by all units on Port Hudson on the morning of May 27, 1863. According to James G. Hollandsworth Jr., Banks's biographer, the commanding general's inability to coordinate his troops effectively led to needless slaughter and defeat.[33]

Serious errors on the part of their superiors made the May 27 attack a nightmare for Henry Blair and the men of the Fifteenth Regiment. At a strategy session on the evening of the twenty-sixth, Banks outlined his plans for a general assault on the city over the vehement objection of Sherman and others. The detailed orders that Banks issued the next morning were badly garbled, and Sherman either misunderstood or chose to ignore the call for an assault at ten o'clock. After the attack by the other divisions failed, Banks rode into Sherman's camp, furiously demanding that Sherman's division be immediately thrown against the Confederate works. Sherman recognized that this would lead to senseless slaughter, but he could not disobey a direct order. Sherman ordered Dow and another brigadier to form their troops into long narrow lines for the attack so that they would be less vulnerable to enemy artillery. Dow ignored this order and organized the companies into compact and deep units that proved to be easy targets for the enemy.[34]

Even under ideal conditions, the assault would have been most difficult. The Union troops had to march over four hundred yards of open fields where they were exposed to enemy artillery and sharpshooters. While covering that territory, the soldiers had to work their way through trees felled by the Confederates and over three fences around the Schalter House, which the regiment renamed the "Slaughter" House. After surmounting these obstacles, the soldiers had to cross through a deep ravine and charge up a heavily fortified system of earthworks.[35]

During the battle, the Fifteenth Regiment was supposed to serve as a support unit for the Sixth Michigan Regiment, which was detailed to lead the attack in Dow's sector. Overall, the attack was more successful than it should have been. Some Union troops actually reached the Confederate lines before being driven back. This result was achieved despite

Sherman and Dow being wounded and put out of action during the final phases of the attack. As a unit, the Fifteenth Regiment made almost no contribution. When it advanced on the enemy, the men found their path blocked by the burned remains of the Schalter House, and they were forced to break ranks to get around it. Much of the unit's organization was destroyed at that moment despite the frantic efforts of the officers. When the regiment sought to pass over the three fences in its path under increasingly heavy fire, all semblance of order was lost.[36] Many troops refused to advance beyond a sheltered position, leaving the few who continued the attack with insufficient support to perform the task assigned to them. One historian of the battle has concluded that, with greater support from the Fifteenth New Hampshire Regiment, the Sixth Michigan and the 128th New York would have succeeded in getting into the works of the Confederates.[37]

Despite the dismal performance of the regiment as a whole, Blair emerged as a hero. He led those members of the unit who continued to advance on the enemy works. Three or four times he directed a charge and yelled encouragement to continue the attack to the members of several regiments. During the next to last charge, he was hit in the right arm just below the shoulder and suffered a painful but minor wound. Putting his arm in a temporary sling, he grabbed his sword in his left hand—his scabbard had been shot away—and tried to rally his men for one last charge. When no one answered his call, he was forced to seek shelter behind an irregularity in the ravine. He soon lost consciousness and had to be assisted from the field under the cover of darkness.[38] The general failure of the regiment greatly magnified the reality of Blair's bravery. In the aftermath, all the men serving under him lived in the reflected glory of this lone officer trying to lead a hopeless charge. Blair retained some perspective on the events of the day. While proud of his exploits, he later remarked with some bitterness that the battle had been "hopeless" and that those who persisted to the front, like himself, were "fools."[39]

With Blair hospitalized in New Orleans, the soldiers had to adjust their thinking to the reality of battlefield wounds and possible death. Seventeen in the regiment had died of a total of seventy-seven casualties in the unit. While Blair was away, Colonel Kingman was placed under arrest for calling a general a drunkard, although his major crime appeared to be the regiment's failure on the battlefield. Blair claimed that at this point he "got sick" of the hospital in New Orleans and returned to Port Hudson on June 8.[40] The opportunity to assume direct command of the unit apparently was a significant lure.

After being driven back at Port Hudson by the Confederate troops, the regiment was ordered to begin regular siege activities. Under Blair's direction, the regimental volunteers began constructing a series of trenches to protect themselves against Confederate sharpshooters. The siege of Port Hudson placed the men and their officers under the constant pressure of enemy fire. Slowly, the more professional attitudes necessary for success in battle began to emerge. One soldier reported to his girlfriend: "There is hardly a minute but we hear the roar of artillery, or the report of musketry, the hissing shell, the rush of solid shot, or the whiz of the bullet. There have been many narrow and wonderful escapes, and yet the boys do not mind them so much now."[41] Blair's comrades described him as "busy everywhere" and "sleepless" during this period after the battle as he tried to shape the unit into a fighting force. His wound became very swollen as a result of the conditions: "He and the other officers live in the bushes with the rest, and fare on hard bread and salt pork. He is often seen with his sleeve down and pouring water on the wound."[42] On June 13, Blair's hard work seemed to be vindicated when a small group of regimental volunteers suffered thirteen casualties on a special mission but retained their composure.

This mission was just a prelude to a second major assault on the Confederate position ordered by Banks on June 14. On the night of June 13, Blair led the regiment on a five-mile march to a new position. The next morning, the regiment was ordered to the front lines. This time, the unit acted with precision in response to Blair's orders and executed several maneuvers under fire with skill. Blair was once again in the forefront of the charge and persisted until ordered to desist by a superior officer. The Fifteenth Regiment was fortunate to be partially shielded by natural barriers during part of the attack and lost no men. Blair tried to mount one last attack but was persuaded that the enemy's position was as strong as "the gates of hell."[43] At some point during this period, Blair was wounded a second time in the right arm with the shell also penetrating his side.[44] The general attack also failed, forcing the regiment and its twice-wounded leader to withdraw under the cover of darkness. Blair was ordered to report to the hospital, but he refused to leave his men while they were still under fire.

Blair remained in command for the next three weeks, trying to maintain morale at a high level during the dispiriting siege operations. On June 15, 1863, Banks sent out a request for one thousand volunteers for one last assault on the Confederate position, but Blair was unable to persuade many of his men to go.[45] This maneuver ultimately was abandoned because of a general unwillingness to try what appeared to be impossible. Blair was so weak at this point that he spent most of his time on a stretcher in the trenches.

On June 30, 1863, the regiment took part in a most unusual incident. After sunset, the regimental volunteers marched to a point along the river just below the fortress wall. From there, they were led by a Confederate deserter to a series of steps dug in the side of the fortifications. As they reached within twenty-five feet of the enemy position, Blair warned the guide: "On the least sign of treachery I shall shoot you down in an instant."[46] Just as the attack was about to begin, orders arrived from Banks calling off the entire effort. The regiment retired to its trenches without ever learning the particular circumstances that surrounded this order.

The rest of the regiment's stay in Louisiana was spent in the routine of camp life. The siege had become relatively bearable as the soldiers on both sides agreed not to fire on each other without warning. Then, on July 7, the news of Grant's capture of Vicksburg reached Port Hudson. Two days later, the Confederate garrison surrendered to Banks, and all fighting ceased.[47] Any elation that Blair might have felt at that moment was tempered by the death of Eliza's brother, Joseph. Blair's own condition had begun to seriously deteriorate. His arm was now badly inflamed, and on July 13 he was sent to the camp hospital. Three days later, he was sent to New Orleans to receive more intensive care. Blair remained there until July 25, when he returned to the regiment "absolutely helpless in body and delirious of mind."[48] The next day, he and the rest of the regiment started for home aboard the steamer *City of Madison*.

His military experiences, along with his perceptions of the combat roles of two other groups, had a major influence on the reform programs that Blair advanced two decades later. He was particularly impressed by the efforts of two free black regiments that helped lead the charge against the Confederate trenches on May 27, 1863. One Massachusetts soldier reported: "[Blacks] were placed in advance and nobly did their duty. They charged and re charged and didn't know what retreat meant."[49] Blair was equally impressed by the black soldiers, who showed far more courage than his own men. More than a quarter century later, Blair remembered: "I myself was in that charge upon the bloody walls of Port Hudson, . . . and among the dying and dead along the whole seven miles of slaughter none were nearer to the foe than the colored soldiers who there first fell in the uniform of their country."[50]

According to the historian of the black regiments, the valor of these troops was not uniform. However, the poor leadership provided by Banks and General William Dwight explains more of those troops' "failure" than any shortcomings on their part.[51] Blair attributed his commitment to full black citizenship to this war experience, but, since he actively opposed slavery, he might well have supported full rights for blacks in any case.

In addition to feeling sympathy for his comrades in the Union army, Blair also came to respect those who were his enemies. Reflecting on his Civil War experiences, he observed: "I know that all through the Northern army there was a prevailing sympathy for their Southern brethren, even in the fiercest days of the war."[52] Twenty-five years later, he translated this feeling into action by introducing a bill in the U.S. Senate to give wounded Confederate veterans preference for government jobs over Confederate civilians.[53] He even defended the lower-class southerner in a debate with a Texas senator. His defiant declaration — "I am one of those who belong to 'the mud-sills'" — demonstrated the distinction he made between the upper-class, undemocratic leadership of the South and the common people.[54]

The trip home was extremely difficult for all members of the regiment. Worn out by sixty days of exposure to the elements and forty-five days under enemy fire, eighty-six members of the unit died during the trip or shortly after reaching New Hampshire.[55] Blair was not conscious during much of this journey and had to be constantly attended. When the ship reached Cairo, Illinois, on August 3, 1863, the regiment was transferred to a train for the trip back to New Hampshire. The men arrived in Concord on August 8, and Blair was transferred through a driving rain to a room in the Eagle Hotel. Suffering from both typhoid fever and malaria, he stayed at the hotel for several weeks while the state government provided lodging and other assistance for Eliza.[56] While he lay helpless in bed, Blair was officially mustered out of the service on August 13. Early in the fall, he and Eliza returned to Plymouth, where he slowly regained his strength.

As Blair recuperated from his wounds, the Union war effort continued. Coincidental with the capture of Vicksburg and Port Hudson, the
Army of the Potomac confronted Lee's invasion of Pennsylvania at Get-
tysburg. The attacking Confederates were thrown back with heavy losses
and forced to retreat to Virginia.[57] A third Union army under William
S. Rosecrans maneuvered a Confederate army under General Braxton
Bragg out of the strategic city of Chattanooga, Tennessee, and into north
Georgia. On September 19, 1863, the Confederates turned and defeated
the Union forces at Chickamauga. The Federal army retreated back to
Chattanooga, where Bragg and his army besieged them. Stunned Union
officials sent General U. S. Grant and heavy reinforcements to assist the
beleaguered Union forces. In late November, the Union host attacked the
formidable Confederate defense and achieved a breakthrough at Mission-
ary Ridge, compelling the Confederates to retreat into north Georgia.[58]

Although the Union appeared to have the upper hand, the Confederates slowed their enemy's advances and inflicted large numbers of casualties. Grant was transferred to the Army of the Potomac, where he faced
Robert E. Lee and the Army of Northern Virginia. Grant advanced toward
Richmond by attempting to outflank his opponent. The wily Lee seemed
to anticipate Grant's every move, and the result was a series of confrontations at locations like the Wilderness and Cold Harbor, where thousands of soldiers in both armies were killed or wounded. Although Lee
was able to prevent Union breakthroughs, the numerical preponderance
of the Union forces pushed Confederate forces ever closer to their capital. By the middle of June 1864, Grant's host laid siege to Petersburg—
just south of Richmond—and required Lee to occupy one position for
nine months.[59] This fact limited Confederate options and allowed Grant's
army to apply increasing pressure to Lee's stalwart brigades.

At the same time, the other main Union army started advancing toward Atlanta under the leadership of William T. Sherman. The opposing
Confederate army, led by Joseph Johnston, prepared strong defensive positions every time Sherman's army approached. Unwilling to sacrifice his
men against these stout defenses, Sherman attempted to outflank Johnston, but the veteran Confederate leader anticipated his every move. Despite his inability to outmaneuver the enemy, Sherman's more numerous
legions were able to force the Confederates back to Atlanta. At this point,
Confederate president Jefferson Davis replaced the cautious Johnston
with the aggressive John Bell Hood. Hood attacked Sherman three times

in July 1864 and suffered significant losses in each encounter. By late summer, Sherman's army was able to sever Hood's transportation lines and then occupy Atlanta in early September.[60]

Sherman's victory at Atlanta was followed by a series of developments that brought an end to the Confederacy. First, this victory revived the political fortunes of President Abraham Lincoln, who was reelected president in November 1864 over the Democratic candidate General George McClellan.[61] At the same time, a series of cavalry victories in the Shenandoah Valley won by an army under General Philip Sheridan weakened the Confederates in the eastern theater of operations. Even more devastating to Confederate morale was the largely uncontested march of Sherman's army from Atlanta to Savannah and from there through South Carolina and into North Carolina. Part of Sherman's army under General George Thomas returned to Tennessee, where, on December 15, 1864, it destroyed a Confederate army under Hood. In late March 1865, Grant finally was able to cut Lee's supply lines and force the Confederates to abandon their capital, Richmond. Lee's surrender on April 9, 1865, effectively ended the Confederacy.[62]

The final success of the Federal forces had significant consequences for Blair. His active participation in the winning side of the conflict greatly enhanced his personal reputation. His connection with fellow veterans—a significant part of the electorate—provided him with a major advantage in postwar political contests. The war and the Reconstruction period that followed the fighting gave the Republicans a claim on the loyalty of a small but consistent majority of the electorate. Exactly how Blair would take advantage of these factors was unclear, but the Union's success laid the groundwork for him to introduce an ambitious agenda for societal reform.

*Chapter 3*

# Apprentice Lawyer and Politician

Even in a physically weakened condition, Henry Blair still possessed potent political influence. Captain Chester Pike appointed him the federal provost marshal for the Third Congressional District. Pike himself was from the district and had previously recommended Blair for Grafton County solicitor, suggesting that the two men were close political allies. By his own admission, Blair performed few duties and remained quite weak until the war and his job ended simultaneously. But this episode demonstrated both his continuing interest in politics and his willingness to try to make a contribution to the cause while greatly weakened.[1]

New Hampshire political traditions and legal boundaries shaped the structure and, to some extent, the substance of Blair's emerging political career. Many of these practices were established long before Blair entered public life, exerting an influence beyond the power of any individual to change. These traditions determined which offices he ran for, when, and for how long he held each position. During the decade after the Civil War, he served as an important part of the local political system. That work later allowed him to carry out programs relating to his childhood and war experiences at the national level.

As is the case in modern American politics, New Hampshire occupied a unique national role in the nineteenth century. The state held annual elections that served as sample public opinion polls for the national political parties. Because the New Hampshire elections were held on town meeting day in March, they started off the political year. Just as the New Hampshire presidential primary today assumes an importance out of proportion to the delegates selected, the early elections of more than a century ago attracted a great deal of attention. The change of a few hundred votes in New Hampshire could have a profound effect on the fate of legislation in Congress and campaign strategies in other states. As a result, nationally known speakers of all parties visited the most remote townships trying to attract the handful of votes that would influence national opinion. Because they had to spend three to four months every year campaigning, New Hampshire politicians became highly professional and developed organizations that were the envy of their counterparts in other states.

Until the 1890s, New Hampshire politics was highly personal in nature. The vast majority of the state's population lived in rural and sparsely populated farming communities where each person was identified with a particular family, location, church, and occupation. Political appeals often were made on an individual basis. Each party was careful to have local organizers who could serve as mediators between the party leadership and individual voters and assist with the delivery of government services. Political parties sought control of state or national patronage to build reward structures that would maintain party loyalties. Individual politicians had no real opportunity to create separate organizations. With the party serving as the primary means through which ambitious politicians reached voters, no political aspirant could afford to revolt against party constraints if he expected to gain nomination for office.

During the Age of Jackson, covering the years from 1829 to 1854, the Democratic Party dominated New Hampshire politics. Directed by creative and astute leaders like Isaac Hill, Levi Woodbury, and Franklin Pierce, the Democrats won every state election in that period except one.[2] The Democrats adopted and rigidly reinforced a rotation system that played a significant role in New Hampshire politics until the 1890s. In most cases, candidates for public offices and patronage holders were allowed to retain their positions for only two terms. The only exceptions were township positions, which could be held indefinitely, and U.S. Senate seats, which were limited to one term. The result was that even party bosses like Hill and Pierce spent relatively little time in any one public office. Hill was both governor and senator for a short time, but he was forced to use his position as a newspaper editor and chairman of the state Democratic committee as the basis of his power.[3] Pierce served as speaker of the state House of Representatives, congressman, governor, and senator for short terms before he was elected president.[4] The Democratic Party also made a conscious effort to distribute patronage positions to those who had rarely held elective office. Thus, aspiring politicians were assured of an open nominating system that allowed them access to power for a limited time if they abided by the rules.

To achieve party harmony, the Democrats were forced to subordinate the discussion of issues within the party. Divisive questions like railroad regulation, slavery, and temperance were avoided as much as possible. When controversy could not be evaded, the state party followed the lead of the national party. In general this approach was successful, but starting in 1840 the radical antibusiness spokesmen and those morally opposed to slavery split off into separate parties. Although these defections reduced the Democratic majorities, the weakness of the opposition parties in New Hampshire ensured continued Democratic success.

The rigid enforcement of party discipline completed the Democratic hegemony. Party members were expected to accept convention decisions about candidates and the party platform. Those who publicly challenged the party leadership were dealt with decisively. Two examples illustrate the machine's commitment to a united front. On January 7, 1845, Congressman John P. Hale announced his opposition to the Democratic Party's proposed annexation of Texas in a public letter.[5] Speaking for the Democratic Party, Franklin Pierce ascribed Hale's opposition to personal ambition rather than accepting Hale's claim that he was against the spread of slavery.[6] The Democratic platform accepted slavery as an institution sanctioned by the Constitution and therefore beyond public debate. By February 12, Pierce had succeeded in calling a special convention that replaced Hale as the Democratic candidate for congress.[7] Six years later, the Democratic gubernatorial nominee, John Atwood, refused to support a law passed as a part of the Compromise of 1850 that required the return of fugitive slaves. Pierce again engineered a special convention that replaced Atwood on the Democratic ticket.[8] Thus, the party leadership not only provided opportunities for the faithful workers; it also demonstrated a readiness to deal harshly with those who openly challenged the party's position.

In early 1854, the debate generated by the Kansas-Nebraska bill destroyed Democratic hegemony in New Hampshire. Many loyal Democrats refused to accept Senator Stephen A. Douglas's compromise, which could have opened western territories to slavery.[9] Because the opposition did not have enough time to organize for the March election, the Democrats were able to retain a precarious hold on the state government. On August 29, 1854, state antislavery groups formed a coalition at a mass meeting of two thousand in the town of Wolfeboro. Rather than becoming part of the new Republican Party, the New Hampshire antislavery alliance affiliated itself with the American or Know-Nothing Party. Playing on the popular disapproval of the Kansas-Nebraska legislation, the Know-Nothings won the state elections of 1855 and 1856.[10]

The developments in New Hampshire were part of a broader political upheaval that took place in the northeastern and midwestern states at the same time. The disintegration of the Whig Party as a national organization and the rise of the Liberty, Free Soil, and American political parties prompted the formation of different coalitions of these parties in each state. In addition, many Democrats deserted their former allegiance. This heterogeneous mixture adopted many names, including People's Party, Fusion, American, and Republican. While virtually all coalitions opposed the Kansas-Nebraska Act, some focused on stemming the flood of immigrants and others on ending the abuse of alcohol. In many cases, the conglomerate parties won impressive victories in the 1854 elections.[11]

The U.S. political system remained in flux as adherents of the American (Know Nothing) Party and the Republican Party sought control over the anti-Democrat coalition. The Republicans were most active and successful in the Upper Midwest, while the American Party held the advantage among Protestant voters in areas with growing immigrant populations.[12] In 1852, New Hampshire voters had rejected a referendum to allow Catholics to hold public office. The American Party took advantage of this anti-Catholic sentiment to build a strong party in the state. On the more positive side, it supported judicial reform and expansion of public education.[13] When the American Party became New Hampshire's majority party in 1855, its platform supported "a prohibitory liquor law, an extension of the naturalization period, an overhaul of the state's voter eligibility laws, repeal of the Nebraska Act, new laws curbing judicial expenses, large appropriations to public schools, and the funding of the . . . state reform school."[14] Party leaders kept many of these promises by funding the reform school, enabling cities to more easily establish high schools, increasing the share of municipal tax revenue allotted to support education, and enacting a law that largely prohibited the sale of liquor (exempting wine and cider).[15]

Henry Blair cast his first ballot in the spring election of 1856, voting for the Know-Nothing candidate. This vote indicated that he was actively opposed to the spread of slavery. At this time, Americans were strongly anti-immigrant and anti-Catholic. Although Catholics were not numerous in New Hampshire, Protestant intolerance was strong and nearly resulted in a mob destroying a Catholic church in Manchester.[16] Strong anti-Catholic statements made by Blair at a number of points in his career suggest that he shared many of these prejudices. Later, he admitted that these feelings were based on ignorance.[17]

Events in the spring of 1856 demonstrated that the antislavery reform element of New Hampshire's American Party platform was more important than its nativist prejudices. When the American Party's national leadership, reacting to southern pressure, refused to take a stand on slavery, the New Hampshire State Council voted unanimously to join the Republican Party. From that point until after the Civil War started, the Republicans held a small but safe majority in the state.[18] The new party leaders were young men who combined the idealism of the antislavery crusade with the lessons of political organization practiced by New Hampshire Democrats. Directed by Edward H. Rollins and William E. Chandler of Concord, the Republicans built a political machine as powerful as the Democratic machine previously established by Hill and Pierce. As the party organized itself, the leadership looked for promising recruits like Blair, offering them elective or patronage positions to gain their loyalty and to provide a safety valve for their ambitions.[19]

Although the new party did not change its name until after the election of 1856, the coalition supported the Republican presidential candidate and the party's national platform. Fifty-two percent of the New Hampshire electorate voted Republican in 1858. The Republicans retained that small majority for each succeeding election through 1865 except for the gubernatorial contest of 1863. In that election, popular opposition to the emancipation of the slaves and conscription threatened the Republicans with defeat. Republican strategists created a third party of War Democrats that attracted enough votes to deny any candidate a majority, thereby leaving the decision to the Republican-dominated legislature. Throughout this period, the issues most important to New Hampshire voters included the fate of slavery, conscription, war-related government debt, and soldiers' voting rights. These new issues virtually eliminated discussion of antebellum social and economic conflicts that had previously dominated the state's political campaigns.[20]

During this same period, Republicans were establishing themselves as the dominant party in the nation. In the 1856 presidential election, the party's candidate, John Fremont, won a majority of the nonslave states but lost the election to the Democratic candidate, James Buchanan. In 1858, the salience of the slavery expansion controversy helped the Republicans gain strength at the state level and in Congress. The Republican nomination of the moderate Abraham Lincoln and the division of the Democrats into southern and national factions brought the party to power in 1860. The subsequent secession of eleven slave states gave the Republicans even greater control of the national government.

Except for the congressional elections of 1862, a year when the Union armies suffered serious losses, the Republicans won national elections by a small but consistent majority. The party also built a strong record of accomplishments, including making homesteads in the West more available to farmers, establishing tariff protection for American industry, starting a transcontinental railroad, and providing federal support for land grant colleges in each state. In addition, Lincoln began to dismantle the institution of slavery with the Preliminary Emancipation Proclamation in 1862, the final promulgation of edict in 1863, the enrollment of 180,000 black soldiers in the Union army, and the introduction of the Thirteenth Amendment, which ended slavery. The emotional reaction of the voters to Lincoln's assassination and the collapse of the Confederacy reinforced Republican political dominance at the national level.[21]

It was in this political atmosphere that Blair resumed his career after the Civil War. The party had already recognized his importance by awarding him two patronage jobs, and he now had the added advantage of being a wounded war hero. Surviving correspondence suggests that he did not move immediately into politics; apparently, he had not sufficiently recovered from his war-related illnesses. By November 1865, he was able to resume a more regular legal schedule and to enter elective politics for the first time.[22] The Republicans of Plymouth nominated him as their candidate for the state House of Representatives. While no returns for that contest survive, Blair probably won the seat by the same 179–134 margin that the Republican gubernatorial candidate received in that era of straight ticket voting.[23] He then joined the approximately 280 other winners in the largest state legislative body in the United States.

During the summer 1866 session, Blair was appointed chairman of the Committee on Incorporations and established himself as a significant local leader among New Hampshire Republicans.[24] Because the rotation principle made it difficult for legislators to serve more than two terms, Blair's committee appointment was not extraordinary. However, his selection as a committee chairman suggests that the party leadership regarded him with great favor. The first important business of the session was the election of a U.S. senator by the Republican caucus. Since the Republicans had a majority in the legislature, their candidate's election was assured. Blair was actively involved in this battle as an organizer in the Third District (his home district) for Congressman James W. Patterson. The contest lasted four tense ballots, with Patterson winning over the incumbent on a close vote. Later, one of the defeated candidates gave Blair much of the credit for Patterson's victory.[25] While the two men were political allies before the caucus, Patterson's success and his resulting debt to Blair enhanced Blair's prestige and his ability to influence patronage decisions.

When the regular session of the legislature began, Blair proved himself to be a competent committee chairman and a member of the radical wing of the party. His committee reported out a number of uncontroversial local corporation bills that were handled with little debate. When dealing with issues generated by the Civil War, Blair was much more outspoken. Along with other Republicans, he voted for the resolution by which New Hampshire approved the Fourteenth Amendment.[26] He actively worked for the payment of state and local bounties to soldiers who had not received them during the war.[27] He followed up that action by proposing harsh amendments to a bill dealing with deserters and draft dodgers. One of his amendments required that these men "shall be incapable of holding any office of trust or profit, or of exercising the elective franchise in the State."[28]

In actions little noted at the time, Blair also took positions on some issues, such as federal aid to education, that would be important later in his career. He was a consistent supporter of the bill that established a land grant college in New Hampshire.[29] He also introduced a bill "in relation to the rights of married women" that was never reported from committee.[30] No details are available on the contents of this legislation. Although Blair strongly supported prohibition, the party leadership sought to avoid a divisive debate on this controversial issue. In an unexpected move, Blair voted to table legislation on the control of alcoholic beverages to avoid further discussion.[31]

On balance, the 1866 session was a very successful one for Blair. He cemented a political alliance with a U.S. senator that proved to be extremely useful over the next six years. His growing stature within the party was recognized when, in 1867, he received the Republican nomination for the Eleventh District state Senate seat. His campaign against his Democratic opponent, William W. Flanders, was completely overshadowed by the spectacular gubernatorial contest. The former War Democrat leader, Walter Harriman, was the Republican candidate, and the small-town businessman John Sinclair won the Democratic nomination. Both men were accomplished public speakers, and, when they agreed to a series of joint debates, thousands of voters turned out at each stop to hear them. The absence of a positive program proved to be a great burden for New Hampshire Democrats to carry, and Sinclair ultimately lost despite his brilliant canvass.[32] Blair carried his district with 3,499 votes to Flanders's 3,010. A close inspection of the returns indicates that, although Blair ran slightly ahead of the ticket, he owed his election to the general success of the party.[33]


In the much smaller state Senate, consisting of only twelve members, Blair made a less impressive contribution. However, he served on five committees and chaired at least two of them—Towns and Military. He soon resigned from the Committee on Towns because of a clear conflict of interest involving his native township of Campton. The reason for his failure to make a major contribution to the debates of this 1867 session was probably because of his membership on the special joint Committee on the Judiciary. Blair, two additional senators, and seven House members spent one-third of the session—ten of thirty days—studying the state's statutes. They worked six to ten hours a day, finally compiling a list of 154 amendments to the state law codes. Even the leading Democratic newspaper in the state applauded the efforts of this Republican-dominated committee.[34]

Blair also made a contribution in the area of financing and improving public education. On June 21, 1867, he amended a joint resolution dealing with the money obtained from the sale of state public lands to read: "and constitute a part of the literary fund, to be divided among the several cities and towns, and by them applied to the maintenance of common schools."[35] This amendment was accepted and became part of state practice. Blair had the good fortune that Republican leaders shared his concerns and that these programs were politically popular. His proposal was somewhat similar to the Morrill Land Grant College Act passed by Congress a few years earlier.

All Blair's activities took place in the momentous national debates surrounding Reconstruction in the former Confederacy. The ascension of former southern Democrat Andrew Johnson to the presidency after Lincoln's death ensured constant conflict with the increasingly radical Republican Congress. Congress seized control of the Reconstruction process and introduced a growing list of rights for southern blacks, including land ownership, legal marriage, education, and suffrage. The results were secured by passage of the Fourteenth and Fifteenth Amendments of the Constitution, the Reconstruction and Enforcement Acts, and military intervention in states where white southerners resisted the new regime. Despite the strong efforts of congressional Republicans, southern whites challenged the new local Republican leaders through economic coercion and terroristic violence. The opposition took its most organized form in the Ku Klux Klan, which acted as the militant arm of the Democratic Party. In Louisiana, Mississippi, South Carolina, and North Carolina, this pattern of electoral violence and fraud led to the contested presidential election of 1876 and the end of Reconstruction.[36]

The election of 1868 brought Blair into direct conflict with the New Hampshire system of rotation. Apparently, there was a movement to deny him a second nomination to the state Senate because he had already served two terms in the legislature. The state Republican leadership swung behind Blair and directed local leaders to aid him in any way they could. One local politician reported that he had secured two convention delegates for Blair "upon condition that their expenses should be paid": "Their fare and expense was some 10 Dollars but they will be satisfied with 8 Dollars. . . . The safest thing to do would be to fix it so they would not feel dissatisfied."[37] Blair probably paid the two men. The methods used to nominate him alienated a number of Republicans, and as the election approached he received a number of reports that many party members would not vote for him. The local leaders in his district carefully protected him from serious losses, and he defeated his Democratic opponent, Jewett D. Housley, by a 3,841–3,516 margin.[38]

The Republicans successfully carried the state in the 1867 spring elections. Blair's part of the state gave the Republicans some gains, and

Blair once again gained recognition as a powerful local politician. There was, however, one embarrassing result for him. His hometown of Plymouth voted Democratic for the first time in five years, and Blair lost there by a 178–169 vote.[39] The change in sentiment was caused primarily by local factors—particularly the location of a new road—but Blair had to carry the humiliation of this reversal. The partisan change also had profound political implications for him. He could no longer be assured of election to town offices or to the state House of Representatives. Two years later he explained: "I am not now a member of the legislature, our town is hopelessly gone to Dem't for the present. I am practicing law, and shall be of very slight consequence if any during the present contest."[40]

As a member of the majority party elected for a second term, Blair was one of several logical candidates for president of the state Senate. He declined to run, winning the gratitude of potential opponents.[41] The 1867 legislative session was a busy and generally successful one for Blair. Perhaps as part of a bargain not to seek the presidency of the Senate, he served as chairman of the powerful Railroad Committee. Since New Hampshire had joined the rest of the country in a frenzy of postwar building, Blair probably held the key committee position in the Senate. Most of the bills reported by the committee authorized the incorporation of companies that promised to build short lines to small towns not yet served by railroads.[42] As chairman, Blair was able to perform favors for elites in many rural communities that would be remembered in future political battles.

Even more significant for his political future was the role Blair played as Republican manager for half of Grafton County during the 1867 election. As was the case every four years, the New Hampshire spring returns were the first votes of a presidential year. Because Congress began impeachment proceedings against President Andrew Johnson during this campaign, the state election assumed greater significance than normal, and Blair was called on to direct the Republicans in a traditionally Democratic stronghold.[43] Probably the most exasperating task was scheduling speakers in an area where transportation was both difficult and uncertain. Blair had to juggle appearances by Congressman Ignatius Donnelly of Minnesota, Congressman William B. Stokes of Tennessee, and Governor George L. Woods of Oregon and then mix in local speakers.[44]

Just as in the two previous sessions, Blair devoted part of his time to the improvement of public education. In fact, his efforts began three months before the legislature convened. He served as one of the vice presidents of the Eastern Grafton Educational Association and presided over its annual meeting in Bristol on March 12, 1868. That meeting produced resolutions calling for a system of teachers' institutes and for a state normal school.[45] During the legislative session, Blair was an active supporter of the bill that created teachers' institutes in New Hampshire. Although the bill appropriated only $3,000, it called for each of the ten counties to have a teachers' institute lasting at least eight days.[46] Viewing this bill as a small step toward improving the quality of instruction in public schools, Blair was willing to wait for a politically more favorable time to press for a more permanent solution.

As noted by the historian Ward M. McAfee, the Republican drive to ensure universal public education represented an important phase of the Reconstruction period. Using the leverage of the Reconstruction Acts, congressional Republicans forced former Confederate states to institute statewide public school programs. Unfortunately, the lack of adequate state and local funding and the propensity of Klan-inspired mobs to destroy school buildings used by black children limited the effectiveness of these programs. When Congressman George Frisbie Hoar of Massachusetts introduced a bill "To Establish a National System of Education," many Republicans supported the bill despite opponents' claims that the legislation would require racially integrated schools. Even with considerable Republican support, the perceived radicalness of this social experiment doomed the bill to defeat.[47]

The national scope of Hoar's bill made it particularly noteworthy. In the northern states, its provisions were intended to reduce the growing influence of the Catholic Church in education. During the late nineteenth century, the church was particularly militant about educating all children of communicants in Catholic parochial schools. Starting with a Bible-reading controversy in Cincinnati, Protestant-Catholic conflict broke out throughout the urban North. Republicans eagerly capitalized on the anti-Catholic prejudice. Rejecting Catholic calls for public funding of parochial schools, they pushed for greater financial commitment to public education in the Protestant tradition. Deeply influenced by this movement within the Republican Party, Blair personally led this crusade after Reconstruction ended.[48]

The end of the state Senate session found Blair politically unemployed for the first time in almost a decade. He returned to the practice of law, but one of his major types of cases proved to be politically beneficial. Like other former soldiers who were both politicians and lawyers, Blair became part of an elaborate agent network that helped veterans process their pension claims. Unable to afford trips to Washington to do the necessary research, he worked with Lyman D. Stevens, a lawyer in Concord, who had excellent contacts in Washington. Blair identified veterans needing assistance and sent their names to Stevens. Stevens obtained information about each case from Washington officials, and then the two men plotted the proper strategy to be followed. The amount of work involved in each case determined how the two men split the fee. When clients needed the direct intervention of a member of Congress, Blair was able to make the necessary contacts. As a powerful local leader, his requests were always given prompt attention.[49]

Most of the claims were routine, with Blair simply expediting the application through official channels. Reasonably typical of the cases was that of Hannah Ladd. On May 24, 1873, Blair secured a medical opinion that her husband, Josiah Ladd, was not disabled before he entered the service. On January 7, 1874, Mrs. Ladd wrote to Blair asking whether he had secured the pension. Seventeen days later, Blair wrote to the U.S. senator Aaron H. Cragin, whom Blair had helped reelect in 1870, saying: "The woman is very Poor and it is a hard case if she is denied. Can't you help her in some way."[50] The slow pace of the federal decisionmaking process provoked three more letters from Mrs. Ladd in the next four months. In her last letter, she charged: "Every one that I have talked with say they don't think you have ever intended to get my Pension. And if you don't try & do something I shall get some one that will try."[51] Blair persisted and finally secured the pension for her. Still angry, she refused to pay him for all his work and complained to federal authorities when he asked for his fee.[52]

In the summer of 1872, Blair nearly lost his carefully groomed image as the soldier's champion. The War Department charged that he had received double pay for two months of service in Louisiana and had failed to repay the money.[53] Blair was angry and frustrated by this charge. He was also at a great disadvantage because a September 1870 fire had destroyed all his military records. He hired fellow New Hampshire Republican William E. Chandler to handle the case for him in Washington, a decision that led to a forty-year association between the two men.[54] Chandler was able to use some letters secured by Blair to persuade government officials that there had been no fraud on Blair's part.[55] From a political and personal point of view, Blair owed Chandler a great deal. Chandler's power and discretion kept the controversy from becoming public, sparing Blair the probably futile exercise of defending his record to his veteran supporters.

The aftermath of the 1870 election was a very significant period in Blair's political career. In June 1870, the New Hampshire legislature was scheduled to elect a U.S. senator. Recognizing that Blair had the ability to influence a large number of votes in the Grafton County Republican caucus, both of the leading contenders—the incumbent senator, Cragin, and the state chairman, Rollins—sought his support.[56] Despite the fact that New Hampshire parties rarely granted a second term to a senator, Blair endorsed Cragin. Part of the reason for this decision was undoubtedly that the senator was from the nearby Grafton County town of Lebanon and had helped Blair with pension and patronage matters in the past. As was the case in 1866, Blair had the good fortune to work for the eventual winner, further strengthening his position within the party. The senatorial vote was just the beginning of his endeavors during the legislative session. From his room at the Eagle Hotel just one hundred yards from the state capitol, he actively lobbied for several interests, working in concert with the legendary political manipulator Ruel Durkee.

Blair's greatest accomplishment during the 1870 session was again in the area of public education. He probably supplied some of the petitions introduced into the legislature in support of a bill creating a state normal school. There was strong support for this measure, which passed both houses by July 1, 1870.[57] On September 29, the board of trustees for the state normal school invited communities to submit bids for locating the school in their area.[58] Determined to spend as few state funds as possible, the board encouraged local groups to bid against each other and to assume most of the cost of starting the school. Blair, acting as the spokesman for the township of Plymouth, contacted the state superintendent of education requesting information about the application process. He was informed: "The more inducement you can hold out—the more influence it would undoubtedly have."[59] Blair and other local leaders in Plymouth took the advice to heart and carefully plotted their strategy. At the board

Holmes Academy, the first building at the normal school. Courtesy Plymouth State University Archives.

of trustees meeting, a participant remembered Blair as the dominant figure presenting Plymouth's case. The board apparently agreed, choosing Plymouth over Walpole by a 5–2 vote.[60]

A Blair family tradition maintains that there was an additional reason for Plymouth's success in attracting the school. After learning the details of the competing offers, Blair decided that the original Plymouth offer needed to be more attractive. With the informal consent of other town officials at the meeting, Blair added $5,000 more to the Plymouth proposal—probably the amount listed for repairs and equipment. Since the town meeting had not appropriated that sum, Blair loaned the money to the local government. Later, he complained to his family that it had been difficult to persuade the township to repay him the money he had advanced to the school.[61] Despite this seeming ingratitude, local officials acknowledged Blair's contributions to their efforts.

Democratic victories in the March 1871 elections had an important impact on Blair's career. Humiliated by their overwhelming defeat in 1870, the Democrats were determined to submerge their factional differences. They nominated James W. Weston, the popular mayor of the city of Manchester, for governor. The Republicans tried to appeal to followers of the Prohibition Party by nominating former congressman James Pike. As a minister and an outspoken proponent of prohibition, Pike had interests that coincided with the Republican platform. However, as a former member of the American Party, he was sure to lose votes among the growing Catholic population of New Hampshire.[62] His nomination also alienated Republicans who opposed prohibition, many of whom refused to actively campaign for the ticket.

The 1871 election provided the Democrats with their first victory in New Hampshire since 1854. After winning a slight margin in the legislature, they elected Weston as governor. Three Democratic congressmen also were elected. The Republican state committee became so concerned about the party's internal rivalries that it seriously considered adopting the direct primary system of nominating congressional candidates.[63]

With the Republicans suffering their worst defeat up to that time in New Hampshire, Blair emerged from the debacle stronger than ever. The towns under his direction had suffered no unusual losses in 1871, which once again marked him as a successful local leader. More important for his future was the role that he played in the battle for the Third District congressional nomination. A number of local leaders urged him to run for Congress and pledged their personal support.[64] Perhaps recalling the problems he had encountered when seeking a second state Senate nomination in 1868, Blair refused to challenge the rotation system. He backed Chester Pike at the convention, winning the gratitude of most participants for respecting party tradition.[65]

Before the next congressional nominating convention was held, Blair was forced to confront what was probably the most difficult personal decision he would make as a politician. From at least 1866 and probably earlier, he had formed a close and personal relationship with U.S. senator James Patterson. Patterson was everything that Blair wanted to be and more. The older man had overcome poverty to become highly educated and eventually a professor at Dartmouth. In addition, he was a highly polished classical orator who was one of the leading radical leaders in the national Republican Party.[66] He was a strong supporter of public education, eventually serving as New Hampshire's commissioner of education for more than a decade. He advocated direct federal aid to public education and was a firm believer in education as a means to solve the nation's problems.[67] Patterson also was an outspoken opponent of President Andrew Johnson and one of the architects of congressional Reconstruction. Thus, he and his backers, including Blair, were stunned when, citing the rotation principle, the Republican legislative caucus refused to send him back to the Senate in June 1872 and instead elected an obscure Milton attorney, Bainbridge Wadleigh, as his successor.

The friendship between Blair and Patterson was based on more than political expediency and shared commitments to specific reforms. Patterson was candid and informal in all matters and seemed to place great confidence in Blair. He ended one letter: "Remember, I write to you as a confidential friend in this matter & want my letters blotted forever from the record of time. Do not intimate that I have written you on the subject."[68] In another letter to Blair, he shared the many frustrations that went with his position, writing: "As for sitting down and writing a speech on agriculture or any other culture, during these holidays, worn and wearied as I am with work, I won't do it for money, office, or honor."[69] Patterson even teased Blair in a manner that only good friends would dare adopt. For example, the senator wrote to him: "Your views on Alaska, San Domingo, Sumner and the niggers, like poor whiskey, are best taken in small doses."[70] Blair affirmed his close friendship with Patterson when he named his son, born in 1867, Henry Patterson Blair. The older man was delighted by the compliment and was constantly concerned about his infant namesake. In one letter he informed Blair: "The earlier you can come over & see me the better *provided you bring your wife & that baby.*"[71] Another time he told Blair to "tell your Patterson to be good and he'll be great."[72]

Patterson's world, including his relationship with Blair, came crashing down on him in the winter of 1873. On January 3, Senate investigators accused Patterson of owning thirty shares of Credit Mobelier stock. He had received the stock from Congressman Oakes Ames, who had sought to use the securities to influence congressional votes on matters concerning the Union Pacific Railroad. In an effort to clear himself of the charges of illegal activities, Patterson testified before the Poland Committee investigating the controversy. Patterson's answers were at best evasive and self-serving. When Ames testified about Patterson's connection with the stock on January 29 and contradicted his account in detail, Patterson's friends deserted him in large numbers.[73] One Republican paper reported: "We in New Hampshire were completely overcome with shame and

Henry W. Blair, Henry P. Blair, and Eliza N. Blair ca. 1872. Courtesy New Hampshire Historical Society, Giles Low II Collection, F2201.

humiliation, so utterly was that confidence, the growth of ten long years, overthrown in an hour. That this man, whom we had so delighted to honor, whose eloquence had lifted us to nobler aims and higher purposes . . . should so forget his high station as a Senator . . . to prevaricate, falsify, and finally, to perjure himself, was appalling."[74] The editor caught the sense of betrayal that many of the senator's friends felt. Once viewed as a moral scholar in politics, Patterson now was perceived as more venal than the average ward leader.

Henry Blair was among those who drew back from Patterson. These events took place while Blair was actively seeking the Republican congressional nomination. His close relationship with Patterson was known to others, and he may well have recognized that it was a tremendous political liability. But his reaction transcended mere political expediency. He completely cut Patterson out of his life and refused to have any significant dealings with his mentor during the twenty years before Patterson's death. Bitter about this rejection, Patterson wrote to a Republican politician: "You are for Blair. He was one of my old friends & I can never forget the 'old guard,' though he turned a coward & like the rest, treated me like a leper at a time when . . . a friend should have stood by me."[75] Blair's reaction to this situation was extreme. Other Republicans of this period eventually accepted Patterson back into the party, and he once again became a respected public servant. Apparently, Blair's personal morality could countenance questionable political activities for a good cause but could not accept any individual breach of public morality.

Blair was too busy to brood over Patterson's political demise. He was deeply involved in the contest for the Republican congressional nomination when the Patterson affair was revealed. The leading candidate was General Simon Griffin, but there was significant opposition to Griffin on the grounds that he had been a poor candidate in 1871 and could not unite the party.[76] This situation created increasing pressures on Blair to become an active candidate. He consented to do so only after reaching some sort of agreement with his friend the former congressman Chester Pike. While excited about the opportunity, Blair retained a realistic estimate of his own chances. He explained to William E. Chandler: "Tom is running me a little for member of Congress—or candidate rather—Hope to get some votes—but chances are in Griffin's favor."[77]

| Table 1. 1873 Republican Congressional Nomination, Third District | | |
|---|---|---|
| | **First Ballot** | **Second Ballot** |
| Simon G. Griffin | 104 | 126 |
| Henry W. Blair | 49 | 113 |
| Others | 87 | 2 |
| Source: Manchester (NH) Union, January 16, 1873. | | |

The Republican congressional nominating convention held on January 15, 1873, proved to be a much closer contest than Blair expected. The voting narrowed down to five major candidates, and the nomination was determined after two ballots (see table 1). Blair almost won the nomination because of a deal that he and others had negotiated at the convention. In an effort to defeat Griffin, they agreed to throw all their votes to the candidate who received the most votes on the first ballot. After Griffin was nominated, Blair addressed the convention and made a "capital" speech endorsing the general's candidacy and pledging his support.[78]

Blair demonstrated his commitment by throwing himself into the canvass. As he explained to Chandler: "I have agreed to give my time to Genl Griffin until the election—The District is in a bad way—but I hope we may save it."[79] Blair spoke extensively throughout the district. For example, one announcement advertised him making five speeches in a four-day period.[80] Considering the difficulties associated with travel in a rural area, Blair was particularly active during this canvass. One reason was that the party badly needed him. The Democrats had renominated incumbent congressman Hosea Parker, who was able to attract many dissatisfied Republicans. Griffin also had to deal with the Republican demoralization over the Credit Mobelier scandals. Few national leaders found it possible to generate any enthusiasm among the voters. Blair's strong campaign was in sharp contrast to other party leaders' efforts, and again he was recognized as someone who put party needs above personal ambition.

Blair had strong personal reasons for working so hard for Griffin. Under the rotation system, the next two nominations in the Third District were scheduled to go to Grafton County.[81] As the man who had coordinated campaigns for half the county since 1868 and the county's favorite son during the 1873 convention, Blair was the logical Republican candidate for Congress in 1875. Thus, he worked for Griffin in a difficult campaign to ensure that no one could claim that he had let down the party. He also was placing his name before the voters in preparation for the next campaign. Despite his efforts to generate public support, Griffin lost.[82] The weight of Republican liabilities was too much for him to carry.

The 1874 election was an unmitigated disaster for New Hampshire Republicans. Economic difficulties compounded the weaknesses produced by the Credit Mobelier publicity. Further demoralizing the party organization, the Grangers seized control of the state convention. The Grange was an organization of independent farmers attempting to secure favorable state legislation through membership in the Republican Party. When the Grangers nominated Luther McCutchins for governor, not only did the Republicans find themselves with an "honest farmer" for a candidate, but they also had to defend a platform that had a strong agrarian plank in it.[83] In a letter to the state chairman, Rollins, Blair commented on the Grangers' active hostility to lawyers in politics and speculated that his career might be at an end.[84]

By renominating Congressman Hosea Parker after a challenge from Hiram R. "Farmer" Roberts, the Democratic leadership managed to maintain control of the organization. Suddenly, the traditional roles of the two major parties were reversed. Republicans now spoke for farmers, while Democrats represented business interests. All this was too much for the middle- and working-class Republicans of Manchester, who refused to vote for the "hayseed" McCutchins.[85] The result was a crushing defeat for the Republicans. The Democrats won complete control of the state government for the first time in two decades.[86] In addition, they won many township elections, ensuring that they would decide whom to add or remove from official voter checklists in 1875. At this point, all Blair's hard work of the past ten years appeared to have been wasted.

Another setback for Blair was the destruction of his house by fire in September 1870. As noted earlier, the blaze destroyed all the family's personal effects, including Blair's military records. After suffering these losses, the Blairs never rebuilt the house. At first, a lazy or incompetent architect caused the delay in replacing the home.[87] But, soon thereafter, Blair and his wife began a lifetime of boarding at hotels, at boardinghouses, and with relatives. Eliza apparently felt too weak to maintain a house and was probably the chief advocate for these housing arrangements. Blair had become accustomed to this style of living while involved in political campaigns and did not seem to mind. For the next fifteen years, the Blairs either stayed with Eliza's family or at the Pemigewasset House when they were in Plymouth.

Blair's legal practice expanded enough to allow the family to afford more expensive living arrangements. He was forced to assume more of the firm's business as Leverett became increasingly incapacitated and after Leverett's death in September 1874.[88] Blair then quickly formed another partnership with Alvin Burleigh, a former law student in the office and an active Republican. As part of the firm's business, Blair represented a number of insurance companies, selling policies and serving as a claims adjuster. There is a certain irony in this fact because part of his reason for not rebuilding the family house was the absence of adequate insurance.[89]

After the passage of a century, it is difficult to assess Blair's performance as an attorney. One observer described him as an excellent courtroom advocate.[90] His election to the executive committee of the New Hampshire Bar Association in 1873 and 1874 provides further evidence of his legal prowess.[91] However, this recognition was probably due more to his political prominence than to his legal skills. Just as his legal business proved to be politically advantageous, his politics may have proved to be good business.

During the first forty years of his life, Henry Blair did little to distinguish himself from thousands of other rural political figures across the United States. He survived a difficult childhood with a strong sense of self, and he entered his chosen profession without any problems. Although he was keenly disappointed by his failure to attend college, the lack of a college education had no impact on his professional or political career. He was a moderately successful attorney who quickly recognized politics as his true interest. His service during the Civil War was heroic but ineffective. He used his war record and organizing abilities to create a small power base for himself in Grafton County. His three terms in the state legislature resulted in some solid accomplishments and an ongoing interest in women's rights, education, and reform in general. All this provided a solid base to build on, but none of it ensured that Blair would play a role on the national stage. Yet, in ensuing years, his name became a nationally recognized symbol of reform in the Gilded Age. This development revealed a significant, but often overlooked, element in the politics of the period.

*Chapter 4*

# Congressman

For New Hampshire politicians, election to the House of Representatives was an honor often barren of accomplishment or power. The rotation system ensured that, except in the most unusual cases, a person could serve no more than two terms. That meant that New Hampshire congressmen never had the opportunity to chair committees or form the type of personal alliances necessary to influence the flow of legislation. Instead, House membership was usually viewed as an intermediate step toward securing a Senate seat. Although Henry Blair's congressional career followed this general pattern, he demonstrated an unwavering commitment to reform issues. In addition, he was forced to confront several national problems that broadened his perspective. The almost constant demands made by political campaigns limited what he could accomplish. As a result, some of his contemporaries judged his four years in the House of Representatives as undistinguished. Nevertheless, many New Hampshire Republicans were sufficiently pleased by his record to support his battle for a U.S. Senate seat.

In the summer and fall of 1874, New Hampshire Republicans faced the problem of how to revitalize their party. At the national level, the party faced widespread dissatisfaction caused by the Panic of 1873 and resulting hard times. The party's voters were further concerned about the obviously failing southern Reconstruction policy. Despite southern Democrats' continuing and undisguised efforts to discourage blacks from voting, President Ulysses Grant refused to deploy federal troops to enforce the Fourteenth and Fifteenth Amendments. Congressional Republicans sought to improve this situation by passing a civil rights bill in 1875. Signed by President Grant on March 1, 1875, the Civil Rights Act guaranteed that everyone, regardless of race, color, or previous condition of servitude, was entitled to serve on juries and to receive the same treatment in public accommodations. The act's provisions were highly controversial and offended many conservative and moderate party members. Republicans also sought to rescue the advances brought about by Reconstruction by supporting federal aid to public education. Discouraged by these policies, many previously loyal Republicans withdrew their support from party candidates.[1]

The New Hampshire party leadership was convinced that problems caused by unpopular nominations had led to their 1874 defeat. The *Portsmouth Daily Chronicle* maintained that the older leadership was responsible for the mess in which the party found itself, asserting: "The day of trading is past and new men must come to the front."[2] Sweeping Democratic victories throughout the northern states in the fall 1874 elections emphasized the need for new faces and unity on the part of the Republicans. These perceptions greatly aided Blair in his quest for the Republican congressional nomination. As noted earlier, he was the leading Republican in Grafton County and the logical candidate under the rotation system. He was quite confident about his own position, ordering campaign material from William E. Chandler six weeks before the convention. Significantly, he wrote: "Among others I should like some data showing the present condition of the cause of education in the south and means of showing the work accomplished there by the Republican Party both among whites & blacks."[3] This request indicated that Blair intended to follow the general course he had marked out for himself in the New Hampshire legislature. His interest in public education also placed him in the national Republican mainstream, suggesting that he probably endorsed the Hoar bill and other initiatives. The Third District convention held on January 13, 1875, resembled a ratification session more than a contest. The local paper reported: "Personal and sectional feelings, if there were any, were smothered by the demands of the people that the Third District must unite."[4] Former congressman Jacob Benton roused enthusiasm among the delegates by defending Republican Reconstruction policies in a stirring speech. The harmony of the meeting was confirmed when Blair's friend Chester Pike withdrew his token candidacy, leaving Blair the only major candidate left in the running.[5] Events outside the nominating convention also portended well for Blair. The Democratic state convention nominated Hiram Roberts for governor. Roberts was the Granger—the Republicans called him the "flour barrel"—candidate for the nomination, and his nomination split and weakened the party in the state canvass.[6] The Republicans, in contrast, nominated Person

C. Cheney, the mayor of Manchester, as their gubernatorial candidate. Party members easily united around this popular businessman, attacking what they viewed as the incompetent Democratic administration of state government.[7]

Blair's ability to win the race for Congress depended on the strength of his opponent. The success of the Democrats in the Third District in the last two elections prompted three strong candidates to seek the nomination. George F. Putnam was the chairman of the Democratic state committee, bringing the full weight of the state organization behind his candidacy. Horatio Colony was the twice-elected mayor of the city of Keene, where Republicans often won 70 percent of the vote. Henry O. Kent, the leader of the Liberal Republicans in New Hampshire, expressed willingness to completely ally with the Democrats. All three men came to the convention with substantial support, but the nomination went to Kent when the Putnam delegates swung to him on the third ballot.[8] There is some indication that state Democratic leaders reached an agreement with Kent to give him the nomination in exchange for his past services to the Democrats and his agreement to affiliate with the party in the future.[9] Blair was fortunate that the Democratic nominating process took this turn. Resenting the means by which Kent received the nomination, Colony and his followers did little to help him in the subsequent canvass.[10]

The 1875 Blair-Kent contest was a classic example of Gilded Age campaigns. Neither candidate nor his party attempted to persuade the opposition with arguments but, instead, sought to arouse the party faithful. While some issues were interjected into the canvass, the two men endured vigorous personal attacks as the opposition attempted to discover a weak link that would destroy the confidence of the other party in its own candidate. As was true with previous campaigns, the Republicans spent large sums of money to bring voters retaining legal residence in New Hampshire while working out of state back for the election. Blair explicitly asked for $12,000 from the Republican stalwart Chandler to defray the cost of bringing twelve hundred voters back to the Third District.[11] In addition, the two parties provided large amounts of campaign literature and outside speakers to support their candidates.[12] The Republicans, for example, closed the canvass in the Third District by bringing the black leader Frederick Douglass to Cheshire County to assist Blair.[13] This electoral battle was typical of New Hampshire politics during this period, with unique features supplied only by the personalities of the men themselves.

    The personal campaigns of Blair and Kent were quite different from the bitter partisanship of the rest of the canvass. Blair did not start his public appearances until a month before the 1875 election with a February 10 speech in the small town of Milan.[14] Kent started his canvass several days later, visiting towns after Blair's appearances to encourage voters to compare the two men. Both candidates ignored the personal attacks made by the newspapers and conducted themselves with becoming dignity. They discussed issues—Kent attacking Republican corruption in Washington and Blair attacking Democratic mismanagement in New Hampshire.[15] Both men enjoyed considerable success, with Kent drawing a large and enthusiastic crowd in Blair's hometown of Plymouth.[16] The role played by political parties in the electoral process made this leisurely campaign possible. Just as Blair had directed other candidates' campaigns in part of Grafton County after 1868, local leaders were looking out after his interests. Running as part of party teams, Blair and Kent had specific roles to play. They were to be the statesmen who spoke to the great issues, arousing the party loyalists to defend their parties against the enemy.

    As a campaigner, Blair relied on a mixture of the personal touch and public relations propaganda. Because of his diligent work in previous canvasses, he knew many Republicans on sight. He would address them by name, inquire about their families, and play with any children present.[17] In an era before the modernization of campaign practices, Blair's ability to relate to the individual voter was a great advantage. Surviving reports indicate that he was optimistic and pleasant under almost all circumstances.[18] People returned his warmth and good humor and respected him for his obvious integrity in matters involving personal morals.

    The only portion of a Blair speech recorded during the 1875 canvass reveals him as a fluent and bombastic campaign speaker. After attacking the Democrats for packing the state courts, he concluded the speech with the following: "Let us all who are bound together in unalterable devotion to the great work of progress and reform, regardless of all of the differences as to methods and measures and men, reunite in one mighty host, renew the ties of the past, the touch of the elbow and the glance of the line, and with a shout as of the sound of mighty waters descending from our everlasting hills, unfurl the starry banner of the free, and with faith rekindled and hope exalted and reassured, march irresistible to victory and through victory to peace."[19] Well aware of the excess of his speaking style, Blair wrote to Eliza from the town of Fitzwilliam with the following mocking appraisal: "Spoke at Rindge Monday night—very good meeting of about 200—at this place last night—400—band & delegation from Troy 6 miles distant of 50—Best meeting at which the distinguished orator held the spell bound audience for a spell of over 2 hours."[20]

In a tight contest, Blair defeated Kent by a vote of 12,389–12,180, with 164 scattering votes. An analysis of the voting returns reveals a number of significant points. First, the number of voters casting ballots greatly increased from 1873 to 1875. Clearly, the Blair-Kent election aroused great public interest and encouraged many who had been dissatisfied with previous candidates to return to the political process. That was particularly the case with Republicans, among whom Blair polled nearly twenty-one hundred more votes than Griffin had won two years before. Perhaps the most important change from 1873 was the Prohibition Party's loss of approximately two hundred votes. Prohibition advocates supported Blair in large numbers and may well have provided the new congressman with his margin of victory. Most of all, Blair owed his triumph to the discipline of the Republican Party. In the gubernatorial race of 1875, the Republican candidate, Cheney, carried the townships in the Third District by a 12,391–12,198 vote.[21] Out of nearly twenty-five thousand votes cast, only twenty men did not follow the party lines on the congressional vote.

Like most freshmen, Blair moved slowly into his new role. He was appointed to the Committee on the Pacific Railroad, which was of relatively little interest to him.[22] He immediately allied himself with the radical wing of the Republican Party by voting for a resolution endorsing the possibility of a third term for President Grant.[23] During the two sessions of the Forty-fourth Congress, Blair introduced fifty bills for consideration. Virtually all of them were of a routine nature, including twenty-six requests for relief for individual constituents. He also introduced sixteen petitions from constituents on a variety of subjects and four bills to help veterans gain pension benefits.[24]

Blair's earliest speeches were prosaic in content. His maiden effort was a eulogy of the recently deceased Vice President Henry Wilson. Since Wilson had been born in New Hampshire and had endured great poverty as a youth, Blair found it easy to praise this Republican leader's political course. He particularly noted Wilson's concern for the rights of labor—both black and white, slave and free.[25] His next speaking performance was far more mundane. He complained that he was seated in a draft and wanted some changes made so that he would not catch a cold.[26]

Henry W. Blair in the 1870s. Courtesy New Hampshire Historical Society, Giles Low II Collection, F2186.

Despite an unexceptional start to his congressional career, Blair made a major contribution with three speeches. In each case, the talks were important for what they portended as well as their actual content. On May 18, 1875, Blair obtained the floor to speak on the controversial question of whether the federal government should withdraw paper money from circulation and resume currency payment in specie—gold coin. His speech covered parts of ten pages of double-columned fine print in the *Congressional Record*. He first endorsed the labor theory of value, maintaining that the quality and quantity of human labor needed to produce a commodity determined its value.[27] He went on to claim that legal tender other than gold and silver amounted to "repudiation and confiscation."[28] In equally passionate terms, he asserted that nonspecie money "utterly destroys that inalienable right of property which all just government is organized to protect, and becomes the robber of every creditor in the nation."[29] He prophesied: "Under such a system of finance this country would require nothing further than a mule-skin for a winding-sheet and room enough on the back door of a mad-house to write its appropriate epitaph."[30] This speech marked Blair as a spokesman for the nation's business interests and for the conservative currency policies that many New England business leaders favored. In addition, the clear, if overwrought, language of his presentation stamped him as an able congressional speaker.

The next item on Blair's agenda was to procure federal assistance for public education. This had been a Republican priority ever since the introduction of the Hoar bill in 1871. After Hoar's proposal to mandate a national system of education was defeated, the Republicans supported legislation introduced by Congressman Legrand Winfield Perce of Mississippi. The Perce bill proposed to apply the proceeds from the sale of public lands to public education. In contrast to the Hoar bill, this new legislation allowed the funds to be distributed to the states for administration. Republicans quickly amended the Perce bill to disperse the funds on the basis of school-age population—a change favorable to the southern states. Two further amendments broadened the bill's support. The first amendment assured states with segregated schools that they would be eligible for full funding. The other amendment proposed distributing funds on the basis of state illiteracy rates. Because southern states had higher illiteracy rates than the national average, this amendment was even more advantageous to the South.

The reshaped legislation passed the House in February 1872 with overwhelming Republican support. However, two developments doomed the measure in the Senate. The first was the Panic of 1873 and the following depression, which created a government deficit and made senators unwilling to fund new programs. In addition, Senator Charles Sumner's introduction of a civil rights bill mandating racially integrated classrooms greatly diminished support among southern legislators.[31] There were sporadic attempts to revive the legislation during the next two sessions of Congress, but nothing of substance emerged from them.

Virginia congressman Gilbert C. Walker introduced one of the two bills in that congressional session designed to grant federal aid to public schools. Deeply concerned about the enormous amount of illiteracy among blacks and whites in the South, Walker proposed using the monies raised from the sale of public lands to aid the public schools.[32] Blair's comments on this bill will be examined in greater detail in chapter 5. However, it is important to note several points about his speech in the context of 1876. First, Blair explained the significance of the issue in terms that revealed his deep personal commitment: "I believe, sir, that we are approaching another crisis which involves the existence of the Republic. . . . I believe that we are rapidly nearing the time when the American people will vote directly upon the question, Shall the common-school system, which is under God the source and defense of American liberty, continue to exist?"[33] This theme, taken directly from the tradition of Horace Mann, demonstrates how deeply the ideas learned in Blair's youth influenced his career. Blair identified the Catholic Church and the Democratic Party—both North and South—as the enemies of the measure. His private correspondence confirms that he included the Democratic Party for political effect during a presidential election year.[34] He continued to research the speech after it was delivered with the idea of making changes before it was printed.[35] His care was rewarded when the Republican congressional executive committee agreed to reprint the speech as a campaign document.[36]

Blair's third major address was delivered during the second congressional session and was related to a resolution that Blair himself introduced. On December 12, 1876, he introduced a constitutional amendment to prohibit by the year 1900 "the manufacture and sale of distilled alcoholic intoxicating liquors" as well as the import or export of these substances.[37] Fifteen days later, he addressed the House to explain and defend his proposal. He was careful to explicate the precise terms of the amendment.

Naturally fermented alcoholic beverages, like beer and wine, would still
be allowed to be sold, but fortified liquors would be excluded.[38] Next, he
pointed out the tremendous losses, in terms of crime and loss of production, that the United States sustained because of the presence of 600,000
alcoholics.[39] Noting that all local and state attempts to deal with the problem had failed, he argued that only national legislation would be truly effective. Anticipating that impatient reformers would criticize the limits
of the amendment, he asked: "How can they object until they have tried
to see whether they can obtain even this? Consider the past. Be admon-
ished by history. Do not lose everything by attempting the impracticable.
Remember that this is an effort to procure the enactment of a *law*, which
must carry the heads and hearts of conservative jurists, of dignified and
unconvinced legislators, and the *popular vote*."[40]

This closing passage and the contents of the amendment are an excellent example of Blair's approach to reform. While Blair was committed to eradicating many of the evils that beset American society, his belief
that these changes could be brought about within the traditional political
context distinguished him from most reformers. He was willing to accept
a partial reform that could be enacted into law immediately rather than
wait for a more complete measure that might never be approved. He had
demonstrated this same trait in 1868 when he accepted the teachers' institutes instead of pressing exclusively for a normal school. Equally significant was his willingness to introduce this measure without party backing.
Unlike his speech on the education bill, this one specifically stated that
the prohibition amendment was not a party measure and that it should be
supported by congressmen from both parties.[41] Despite that disclaimer,
Blair knew that the amendment would be popular among New Hampshire Republicans, probably benefiting him personally.

During 1876, Blair, along with most New Hampshire Republicans,
supported the presidential candidacy of James G. Blaine from the neigh-
boring state of Maine. Blair even attended the Republican national convention in Cincinnati to work for Blaine.[42] While he was upset that Blaine
lost, he supported the nomination of Governor Rutherford B. Hayes of
Ohio. During the fall 1876 campaign, he was one of the most active organizers of the Republican canvass in New Hampshire. A major part of
his impact came through the distribution of print copies of his education
and prohibition speeches. Beginning in August, the state and national
committees sent these materials out to carefully selected voters, including

clergymen and educators.[43] Republican newspapers also published parts of the speeches, ensuring that most of the party's voters were familiar with Blair's ideas.

Blair's personal contribution to the 1876 presidential election consisted of much more than speeches. He established a statewide paramilitary organization, known as the "Boys in Blue," that sought to organize all former Union soldiers in New Hampshire into a unit that would work for the Republican Party.[44] One local leader reported: "Every soldier of the late war . . . always have voted the straight Republican ticket with me, and I have no doubt but they will do the same this fall."[45] Both the veterans and the party leadership accepted Blair's role as the leading veteran in New Hampshire politics. The prestige derived from this recognition, along with his local power base, made Blair an independent power within the New Hampshire Republican Party.

After the presidential election of 1876, both Hayes and the Democratic candidate, Samuel Tilden, claimed to have won. Disputed election returns in Florida, Louisiana, and South Carolina left the final determination of the results to Congress. When the Republican-controlled Senate declared Hayes to be the winner, the national Democratic Party and the Democratic House threatened to use all means available to void the decision. The congressional leadership of both parties agreed to break the impasse by forming an electoral commission composed of members of both houses of Congress and the Supreme Court. Many observers in New Hampshire, including most Democrats, expected that the Democrats would gain more from the commission than the Republicans.[46] Blair, who was totally convinced of Hayes's right to the office, voted against the creation of the commission and was the only New Hampshire congressman or senator to do so. His surviving correspondence indicates that his fellow Republicans fully agreed with his vote and appreciated his stand on what was perceived to be principle.[47] When the commission gave Hayes the disputed electoral votes, Blair quickly accepted the findings and voted to seat Hayes in early March.

In the midst of this national drama, Blair was forced to run for reelection to Congress. The battle for the nomination evaporated under the pressure of national events. Republican leaders were loath to weaken Blair's position in Washington by denying him renomination. In addition, he was entitled to a second nomination under the principle of rotation. Soon after the November election, the party leadership in the Third

District assured him of its continued support.[48] So universal was this feeling that the regular congressional convention was dispensed with and the Third District delegates attending the state convention at Concord on January 10, 1877, unanimously nominated Blair.[49] Blair rushed from Washington to address this group in his only campaign speech until after Hayes's inauguration. Vowing not to compromise the Republican's claim to the presidency, he noted that a Republican victory in New Hampshire might be decisive in settling the national crisis.[50]

Fortunately for Blair, the Democratic campaign against him failed completely. First, the party made two nominations that almost ensured Blair's victory. It renominated Daniel Marcy for the governorship and Henry O. Kent for Congress.[51] Marcy had been defeated only one year earlier. His Civil War record was considered suspect, and, in the heightened sectional tensions created by the contest for the presidency, he weakened the entire ticket. The nomination of Kent was almost as shortsighted. He had proved to be a weaker candidate than Blair two years before when the Democrats controlled the state government. There was little chance that his challenge would be more successful with the Republicans in ascendancy at the state and local levels.

One major problem threatened the incumbent's 1877 campaign. Blair had run out of money and could not finance the last-minute activities that were thought necessary in that era. For example, a Republican leader in Colebrook reported that he needed money to bring men living in a nearby logging camp into town to vote.[52] In addition, Blair helped sustain at least two party newspapers in the Third District.[53] Two frank letters from Edward H. Rollins at the beginning of the campaign revealed Blair's acutely embarrassing financial position. While trying to conclude the financial part of the presidential canvass in New Hampshire, Rollins found to his chagrin that he was personally liable for nearly $7,000 because party leaders had not followed through on funds they had obligated. Rollins wrote: "It affords me but little satisfaction, having advanced money on the strength of your promises—to have you come in and plead 'inability to pay' when the elections are over."[54] Under unrelenting pressure from Rollins, Blair finally paid the assessment.[55] Just before the election, Blair was forced to write to William Chandler begging for $500 to pay expenses that he could not cover. Noting that Kent had received at least $10,000 for the district campaign while he had received only a few hundred dollars, he once again indicated that he was being placed in debt because of the cost of the canvass.[56] The election returns on the evening of March 13, 1877, demonstrated that the money available to Democrats in the Third District was insufficient to overcome Blair's other advantages. The final totals were Blair 12,638, Kent 11,828, Weston 71, and others 14.[57]

After almost seven months of continuous political activity, Blair's life moved at a much slower pace until Congress met again in the fall of 1877. The break between sessions gave Blair an opportunity to pursue issues that he had introduced during the Forty-fourth Congress. As a result of his prohibition amendment, he had the opportunity to address large public meetings on the subject. In May 1877, he spoke in Lowell, Massachusetts. As a major speaker at the September 1877 meeting of the State Temperance Camp Meeting Association, he emphasized the practical nature of his specific proposals and the necessity of national action.[58] Between the two speeches, he traveled to California, reportedly in an effort to learn more about his work on the Pacific Railroad Committee.[59] While Blair was in California, President Hayes visited Plymouth, New Hampshire, staying in the same hotel where Blair usually resided.[60] Since the new president's policies were becoming increasingly controversial, there is a strong possibility that Blair planned the trip to California to avoid being too closely identified with Hayes.

The reasons for Blair's reluctance to be publicly linked to the Hayes administration became clear when Congress opened the first session of the Forty-fifth Congress. Hayes was determined to pursue a uniform civil service policy and other new policy initiatives that antagonized many Republicans. The new civil service policy did not require use of the competency entrance examinations adopted in the Pendleton Act of 1883. However, by making all patronage appointments subject to this policy, Hayes tried to eliminate some of the most flagrant abuses by officeholders. Specifically, the new policy stated: "No officer should be required or permitted to take part in the management of political organizations, caucuses, conventions, or election campaigns. . . . No assessment for political purposes on officers or subordinates should be allowed."[61] Since most Republican and Democratic political leaders used these methods to influence nominations and to raise money, the reaction was quick and largely negative among party professionals.

Much more significant in determining the political future of the country was Hayes's southern policy. The president shared with other Republicans the desire for a strong wing of the party in the South, but he offered a completely new approach to accomplishing this goal. Convinced that congressional Reconstruction had failed, he sought to create a party composed of former Whigs and other conservative whites. He recognized that Republican economic policies had a great appeal among southern businessmen dissatisfied with the antitariff orientation of the national Democratic leadership. For many Republicans—black and white, North and South—Hayes's new policy represented a desertion of blacks in their time of need and a betrayal of the historic mission of the Republican Party. Further dismayed by Hayes's announced policy of appointing white southern Democrats to important patronage positions, black leaders, stalwart senators, and members of the party rank and file wrote numerous columns in Republican newspapers voicing their opposition.[62]

In this atmosphere of recrimination and intraparty hostility and competition, Blair moved with considerable caution. On October 25, 1877, he attended an informal meeting of Republican congressmen who were trying to find some means to unite the party behind Hayes.[63] While many participants probably were concerned about how the attacks on the president might affect the distribution of patronage in their states, this does not seem to have been Blair's major concern. There is no mention in his surviving correspondence about any major problems with Hayes in this area. In fact, Blair was on the winning side in a major battle over which New Hampshire man would be appointed collector of the Port of Boston.[64]

On December 6, 1877, Blair sent a letter to the friendly editor of the *New Hampshire Sentinel* that placed him in the middle of the growing controversy.[65] He tried to both criticize and defend the administration. While endorsing the civil service plan, he maintained that patronage workers should not be prevented from exercising their constitutional right to take part in political campaigns. The Democratic *Manchester Union* gleefully exposed the inconsistency of his position and ridiculed his efforts to achieve some compromise on the civil service issue.[66]

Blair's December 1877 critique of the president's southern policy was much more decisive. As an acknowledged candidate for the U.S. Senate, Blair could not afford to allow the debate on Hayes's southern policy to become so bitter that the party would lose control of the legislature and no Republican could be elected. Action on his part seemed imperative to prevent a split among New Hampshire Republicans. However, he could not alienate either faction if he expected to receive the votes of both in the Senate race. He charged: "The lie has been given by these acts of the administration, to our whole theory and practice of reconstruction at the South. . . . There can be no good ultimately resulting from a neglect to obey or an evasion of the fundamental law."[67] He maintained that the president was not guilty of trying to destroy the country or the party but simply chargeable with poor policy decisions. He then continued with his major point—New Hampshire Republicans should not let this controversy destroy their party and organization.

A year later, Blair returned to the question of the proper Republican policy toward the South. Since he was still campaigning for the Senate, his speech was not entirely free from political considerations, but he spoke out much more forcefully. The 1878 fall elections in the South had demonstrated the failure of Hayes's policy to create a conservative and white Republican Party in the region. Speaking in favor of the Edmunds electoral bill, which had previously passed the Senate, Blair called for national control over presidential elections. He declared: "No State is sovereign in that sense and to that extent that it can impose a fraud upon the nation. And the nation has of necessity, the right and power to ascertain whether that duty has or has not been performed."[68] By asserting the right of the federal government to continue its activist role in protecting southern black Republicans, Blair openly challenged Hayes's policy of conciliating southern white conservatives. Believing in the concept of positive government powers, he argued that the national government derived certain implied powers from the Constitution that allowed it to fulfill its most basic functions.[69]

Blair did not restrict his work during the Forty-fifth Congress to the southern policy controversy. Once again, he strongly supported federal initiatives to make education available to all citizens. As with the prohibition amendment, he sought politically acceptable methods to promote these reforms. He sponsored a bill "to establish a polytechnic school for the United States, or a school for instruction in science and the useful arts, to be supported by the surplus income of the Patent Office."[70] He emphasized that this institution would not require any congressional appropriations. Drawing on the ideas of a Patent Office employee, he proposed a very specific curriculum for the polytechnic school. It would contain eight schools of instruction including mathematics, civil engineering, mining engineering, machinery, architecture, chemistry, forestry, and agriculture. Like military academy applicants, the students would be appointed by members of Congress and would have to meet specific entrance requirements.[71] In addition, students would be required to take nine history courses, including American and European surveys and the history of art and of science.[72]

Most of Blair's attention during the Forty-fifth Congress focused on financial matters. By 1878, the rapid advance of industrialization in the United States had raised a number of questions that Congress had to confront. The proper relation between the federal government and business was being explored under the heat of increased pressure from competing interests. Like most Republicans, Blair believed that the country benefited from the growth of industry and that growth should be fostered in carefully delineated ways. He also believed that the federal government should play a role in economic infrastructure development, within carefully prescribed limits. His proposal for a national technical school offered a way to expand educational opportunities while building the cadre of trained engineers increasingly needed by American industry.

Blair viewed the protective tariff as one example of proper government action. In February 1879, he defended this practice in a long speech to the House. He not only wanted industry protected; he also issued a strong attack against the "Chinese slave-trade" on the West Coast as a threat to American labor.[73] While viewing a balanced tariff policy as the best way to protect all societal interests, he also recognized that the economic vitality of his congressional district depended on his constituents' ability to sell goods abroad.[74] When the prosperity of his own constituents was threatened, he could be as overprotective as any other congressman. For example, when a new tariff proposed by Democrats in 1878 threatened to end the potato and potato starch tariff, he defended the necessity for this specific rate. Pointing out that one-sixth of the potato starch produced in the United States was manufactured in Coos County in his district, he claimed that Canadian competition would unfairly destroy the prosperity of northern New Hampshire.[75]

Blair strongly believed that competitive market forces should be allowed to operate within the country, with the federal government providing protection only against international competition. Determined not to fund corporate endeavors without regard to fiscal restraints, he voted against a bloated rivers and harbors special interest appropriation.[76] Two examples involving the nation's railroads illustrate his ideas more completely. He introduced legislation encouraging the rapid settlement of federally granted land along the Pacific railroads.[77] His idea was to use

this revenue to decrease the railroad debt to the government, thereby enabling the termination of that relation. He was particularly vehement in
his protests against government grants to aid the construction of the Texas
and Pacific Railroad.[78] Part of the reason for this was his continued distrust
of southern leaders. However, his main objection was the following: "No
member of the company proposes to invest anything in the enterprise personally, but simply to run in debt on the credit of the government to the
full cost of the road."[79]

In 1878, Blair made a distinctive contribution in an area of great political controversy. The passage of the Bland-Allison Silver Purchase Act
over President Hayes's veto, along with the imminent resumption of specie payments and the retirement of paper money, made currency policy
an area of great contention. At the beginning of the first session, Blair became involved in a lengthy debate with several Democratic members, including S. S. "Sunset" Cox, over the advisability of specie resumption in
stages.[80] Noting that paper was usually discounted several cents in relation
to gold coins, Blair characterized the government's use of paper money
as immoral because it would, in effect, be only partially paying its debts.

The ensuing debate over the Bland-Allison bill revealed that Blair felt
much the same way about the remonetization of silver. He believed that
the existence of paper money and the increased amounts of silver coins
being issued would lead to inflation, robbing investors of their capital
through government action.[81] Again he saw this political and economic question in ethical terms. Indulging in the typical rhetorical excess
of the time, he asserted: "It is useless to restore the confidence of all the
lunatics in creation."[82] Viewing his opponents as irrational, he refused
to compromise with them. Despite the overwhelming victory achieved
by the silver forces, his well-researched stands on currency questions
earned him considerable respect both in New Hampshire and outside the
state. One veteran newsman claimed that only future president James A.
Garfield was better prepared to discuss these issues in the House of the
Representatives.[83]

For a junior member of the minority party, Blair saw four successful
years in Congress. Even without a major piece of legislation to claim as
a legacy, he still made a significant impact. He demonstrated the necessary skills in performing the routine duties of his office. He pleaded
his constituents' cases before the bureaucracy in Washington, handed
out patronage, and defended local economic interests in a manner that

satisfied his district. In fact, many Republican leaders and voters were so pleased with his performance that they wanted to break the rotation tradition and run him for a third term.[84] Equally important for his political future, Blair created a firm and positive public image. Already accepted as a war hero, he established himself as a strong partisan Republican who supported continued federal assistance for southern blacks. More important, his willingness to actively embrace reforms based on personal experiences distinguished him from other congressmen. By the end of his second term, he was clearly identified with the movement to use federal funds to improve American education. He was, perhaps, the best-recognized political leader of national prohibition in the United States. Finally, he achieved a strong reputation as a defender of "sound" currency and conservative financial practices.

In the late winter of 1877, Blair began actively seeking a seat in the U.S. Senate. When invited to run for a third term in the House, he quickly rejected the offer. The Senate was the final goal of all ambitious politicians in the Gilded Age. During the troubled administrations of Andrew Johnson and Ulysses Grant, the upper chamber of the national legislature had assumed greater and greater power. Senators dictated national policies in certain areas, dominated state party organizations, and controlled many of the most important patronage positions in the country. In addition, their six-year terms provided vast resources with which to seek re-election. Even the presidency seemed to be a poor prize in comparison.

The intricacies of the political system complicated Blair's efforts to win a Senate seat. During this time period, state legislatures elected members of the U.S. Senate. This meant that the actual election was decided by the members of the majority party in the legislature. In New Hampshire, as in most other states, a party caucus of legislators held a nominating convention with all the members of the caucus being bound by the results of this meeting. Therefore, individual candidates for the Senate had to try to persuade a majority of caucus participants to support them.

New Hampshire's rotation system ensured that there would always be a surplus of Senate candidates. Since both governors and congressmen were restricted to two terms in office, all of them attempted to win Senate election at some time during their careers. That usually meant that there would be ten to fifteen candidates splitting the votes of any caucus. Legislators often cast votes for favorite sons on the first ballot, a fact that further complicated the situation. The result was that, if the top candidate or candidates did not have a commanding lead, a dark horse—one who had not campaigned actively—would be selected on the third or fourth ballot. Since most legislators wanted the patronage advantage of supporting the winning candidate, the person gaining momentum after the first ballot usually won.

Blair's campaign to win the support of state legislators began one month after the November 1878 election. In what constituted a large mail campaign for that time period, he sent every Republican state legislator some appropriate government documents, discreetly inquiring how they thought the Senate race would develop. One of Blair's chief competitors, Aaron F. Stevens, graciously thanked Blair for the material but understandably made no comment on the electoral contest.[85] An attorney from the city of Concord thanked him for the Agriculture Department report, "although a half acre of land constitutes my only claim as an agriculturist."[86] Despite problems like the above, Blair's efforts to reach state legislators were successful, and a number proved willing to commit themselves to support him.[87] The majority of his correspondents refused to compromise their independence, and one proclaimed: "As a free man I shall duly consider the question and be governed by what I believe to be for the best interest of our State and Country."[88]

The responses to Blair's mail campaign suggest that many Republican legislators viewed the Senate contest as an opportunity for personal gain. Typical of the letters to Blair is the following excerpt: "As I told you *I am not going to ask* you for any money whatever I do in this matter, but I will ask you this; if you are elected Senator I would like to have you get me a situation in Washington."[89] Others pleaded poverty and asked for government positions for themselves or their relatives.[90] There is no record that Blair made any promises of this type to secure votes, but his major opponent, Bainbridge Wadleigh, apparently did. He promised to secure a patronage position for the representative from the town of Salem.[91] In addition, he formed an alliance with the *Manchester Mirror*. The paper agreed to support Wadleigh in its editorial columns, and he agreed to have his supporters vote to make the *Mirror* the state printer.[92] The amount of this petty influence peddling is difficult to estimate, but it does not seem to have been decisive in determining the campaign outcome.

By February 1879, veteran political observers identified Blair, Wadleigh, and Stevens as the leading contenders.[93] Each candidate followed a distinctive strategy. As the incumbent, Wadleigh had to win on the first or second ballot or be perceived as a loser. In addition to using his position to offer patronage to some legislators, he warned wavering voters that he was going to win and would remember how individuals cast their ballots.[94] Stevens's plan was shrewdly based on recent political history in New Hampshire. When early favorites in previous caucuses failed to win on the first two ballots, the legislators searched for another candidate who could gather widespread backing. Stevens carefully collected promises of second-choice support from legislators planning to initially back other candidates.[95] He soon had enough commitments to believe that he would be the nominee.[96] Stevens would lose if either Wadleigh or Blair did particularly well, but in case of a deadlock he was in a perfect position to gain the nomination.

Blair's plan for winning votes relied on the large number of personal contacts he had made during past campaigns. Knowing most of the leading Republicans at all levels of the party on a first-name basis, Blair was able to appeal directly to them. Equally important was the fact that many party workers were loyal to him to the extent that they openly canvassed for him with legislators across the state. Perhaps the most important of these individuals was Ruel Durkee—the reputed "King of the lobby."[97] While Durkee's aid could easily be overestimated, Blair was pleased to have this pragmatic politician on his side. Numerous Blair allies contacted legislators who would be voting in the caucus, extracting information from some and promises of support for Blair from others.[98]

Wadleigh was unable to secure overwhelming support because of his Senate record. First, he had sponsored legislation that favored corporations over inventors in the area of patent law. Republicans and Democrats attacked him for not protecting the rights of individual citizens and abusing his office for the benefit of friends.[99] In addition, he was universally censured for his inaction in the controversy between President Hayes and New York senator Roscoe Conkling. Conkling attempted to prevent political enemies from being appointed to key patronage positions in New York City by calling on other senators to defend the right of senatorial courtesy—the provision that no person could be appointed from a state without the consent of that state's senators.[100] Rather than offend either the president or Conkling, Wadleigh avoided voting on the issue. Supporters of both Hayes and Conkling in New Hampshire immediately branded him a traitor to their cause.[101]

As Wadleigh's political fortunes declined, Blair's campaign received an unexpected boost from the New Hampshire Republican leader William Chandler. There is no surviving evidence that the two men worked together at any time during this senatorial contest. It is clear, however, that Chandler was opposed to several candidates—particularly Wadleigh.[102] His efforts to weaken other candidates encouraged Blair's supporters, but whether his motive was a desire to advance Blair's prospects or to defeat the other candidates cannot be ascertained.[103] Resenting Chandler's interference in the contest, Blair had no contact with him.[104] At the same time, he made no effort to disassociate himself in the public mind from Chandler's activities. It appears as if the two men followed strategies that were mutually beneficial without reaching any understanding.

Chandler's involvement in the campaign came to an explosive climax on June 7, 1879—five days before the caucus vote. He issued the thirty-two-page broadside *Reply . . . to the Slanders of . . . Bainbridge Wadleigh.* The title was extremely ironic because the pamphlet focused on Wadleigh's poor Senate record rather than defending Chandler's reputation. Chandler charged that a businessman who benefited from Wadleigh's patent legislation was spending a great deal of money trying to obtain Wadleigh's reelection.[105] Chandler further asserted that Wadleigh misrepresented the facts in his speech on the patent bill to secure passage of the act.[106] Perhaps the most damaging claim was that Wadleigh refused to vote on controversial matters. Not only did Chandler mention the Hayes-Conkling controversy, but he also charged that Wadleigh had "dodged" votes on the Electoral Commission of 1877, the reelection of Senator Aaron Cragin, and other emotionally charged issues.[107] He concluded this indictment with the following blast: "Stepping into the Senate upon the prostrate form of one of New Hampshire's most brilliant public men, you thought enforced self restraint, hypocracy [*sic*], and self-righteousness would be the most politic course; but on the first serious temptation you fell."[108]

The impact of this massive and pointedly personal attack was enormous. The surviving letters to Chandler indicate that any hope Wadleigh had to be elected had disappeared.[109] While Chandler's correspondents may have overstated the result for his benefit, Wadleigh's candidacy had been seriously weakened. On short notice, Wadleigh produced a weak reply that may have been more damaging to him than Chandler's original attack.[110] It also served as a pretext for a sharp rejoinder from Chandler just hours before the caucus. Wadleigh had charged Chandler with supporting a corrupt subsidy for a mail contract between the United States and Brazil that benefited the New Hampshire native and shipper John Roach. Since Blair also had supported the Roach subsidy, Wadleigh was striking at him through Chandler. As a master of personal infighting, Chandler easily brushed aside Wadleigh's criticism.[111] Here was another instance where Chandler's and Blair's interests coincided, and they appeared to be working in concert. However, there is no evidence that Blair played any role in the attack on Wadleigh or Chandler's defense of the Roach contract. Blair, in fact, probably would have been greatly harmed if a large number of legislators believed him to be partially responsible for Chandler's attack.

When the Republican caucus met at 8:15 P.M. on June 12, 1879, the tension and excitement of the Chandler-Wadleigh controversy promised that the evening would bring dramatic events. All but 2 of the 189 Republican legislators took part in the caucus, with the winning candidate needing 94 votes to secure the nomination. The first ballot resulted in the following tally: Blair 68, Wadleigh 45, Moore 23, Marston 22, Stevens 20, and all others 19.[112] Wadleigh's total was unexpectedly small and meant that he did not stand a chance for reelection. While Blair was undoubtedly pleased to be leading, he was disappointed at the same time. He was keeping a running record of the vote himself and was immediately aware that two members of the caucus who had promised to support him had failed to do so.

The next four ballots revealed that Stevens's carefully planned strategy was bearing fruit. Wadleigh's supporters quickly deserted him when his cause became hopeless and generally went to Stevens. Blair seemed to be stalled and unable to make any gain. Despite the appearance of his coming defeat, his backers continued to vote for him.[113] Although Stevens probably was convinced that he would be the winning candidate, his predicted victory did not materialize in the next three ballots.

The last ballot was conducted with "intense pressure on each legislator."[114] The final tally announced at 12:36 A.M. on Friday, June 13, was as follows: Blair 94, Stevens 92.[115] There was considerable exultation among Blair's exhausted supporters, and Blair was escorted into the hall, where he delivered some extemporaneous remarks. One recorded phrase directed to his recent opponents may explain part of his success: "I have every reason to express to the distinguished competitors in this contest my thanks for their urbanity and kindness of treatment I have received at their hands."[116] The press was astounded by the manner in which Blair maintained support through the long contest. The reporter for the *New York Times* summarized this perplexity: "The fight has been principally noteworthy in the surprises the successive ballots afforded, which showed the best calculations of able political managers to be entirely out of the way."[117]

Several factors help explain Blair's hold on his followers, but two deserve special mention. Blair attributed his victory to the faithfulness of the temperance Republicans, who refused to desert him under any circumstances. There is no question that the reform Republicans' refusal to be swayed by vote changes on each succeeding ballot gave stability to the Blair forces unknown in past caucuses. This episode also revealed sufficient support for reform programs among the rank-and-file leadership of the Republican Party to allow politicians to build careers on that tradition. In addition, Blair's temperance stand enlisted the support of the president of the state Senate, Jacob H. Gallinger. Already active in prohibition organizations, Gallinger was showing the political acumen that would soon make him the boss of New Hampshire Republicans.[118] In fact, Gallinger appeared to be the floor manager of the Blair forces during the voting. James O. Lyford, an active politician in this period, observed: "Blair developed a remarkable personal following, which he successfully held for many years. All of his campaigns were directed by himself and he was without equal in New Hampshire politics in the art of attaching men to his political fortunes."[119] Displaying both good humor and modesty, Blair attracted supporters easily and maintained their loyalty through his loyalty to them.

Although the caucus should have settled the question, Blair's Democratic opposition attempted to turn Republicans against him before the actual election by the legislature. The Democrats attacked Blair as incompetent. The *Boston Globe* asserted that he was "weak, willful, opinionated and hypocritical" and maintained that his election would be a "calamity if not disgrace to New Hampshire."[120] Since no one had thought to make Blair's nomination unanimous after the five-hour caucus, there was the potential for a revolt against him. But there was no major defection when, on June 17, 1879, the legislature voted to officially select him as New Hampshire's newest senator. Only three Republicans in the House of Representatives voted for other candidates, and they clearly did so to recognize some of those who lost in the caucus vote.[121] That night, the

Third Regiment band serenaded Blair at his room in the Eagle Hotel, and he replied with a short speech about his continued commitment to implementing the Republicans' southern policy and temperance reform.[122]

No one, probably including Blair, was sure how he would handle his new responsibilities. Eugene Hale of Maine, a future colleague of Blair's in the Senate, summarized the reaction outside the state: "Blair will do, but New Hampshire ought to furnish United States Senators with a little more gumption."[123] Many political observers assumed that Blair was a protégé of the better-known Chandler who would exercise little independent judgment. A quick inspection of Blair's House record, however, would have revealed his commitment to a number of programs and reforms that did not interest Chandler. In addition, the caucus voting indicated that Blair had a secure political base—a campaign advantage that Chandler lacked. Blair's freedom to be his own man in the Senate allowed him to grow in perspective in that body, ultimately transcending the parochial limits of the political world of New Hampshire. Yet, throughout Blair's political career, his northern New Hampshire heritage remained a central influence, serving as the basis for his most enduring contributions.

*Chapter 5*

# Origin of the Education Bill

Blair returned to Washington after four years in Congress ready to assume his new senatorial duties. He quickly replaced Charles Bell and took his seat after being sworn in on June 20, 1879.[1] Before he could become directly involved in the session, he was prostrated by the physical and emotional fatigue created by the caucus battle. His inability to withstand the summer heat in Washington aggravated his condition.[2] As a result, he made no substantial contribution to the debates of the first session of the Forty-sixth Congress. Like many other freshmen senators, he may also have been somewhat intimidated by his surroundings, further explaining his silence. Despite physical weakness and the demands of his new position, Blair was forced to look for housing for the family. As a veteran of the Washington housing market, he was able to find a large and inexpensive house near the capitol. The building was involved in litigation at the time, and the rent was less than $100 a month.[3] Blair was particularly pleased with this arrangement because he had spent most of his financial reserves while campaigning for the Senate.

As Blair came to know his fellow senators, he discovered that he shared a common background and training with many of them. Despite the hardships of his early years and his limited formal education, he found himself at no distinctive disadvantage. David Rothman's statistical portrait of Senate members during the Gilded Age confirms this point. Rothman found that 40 percent began life in a subsistence economic situation where the families could make no real financial contribution to their children's careers. Fortunately, the openness of the U.S. legal profession at that time minimized economic and educational barriers to entering the profession. Seventy-three percent of senators in the 1870s were lawyers, many of whom started life in difficult circumstances with educational opportunities similar to or fewer than those Blair experienced.[4] Thus, Blair had no reason to feel socially inferior or more poorly prepared than his associates. Equally important, when Blair appealed to his fellow senators to assist people lacking the resources to take advantage of the opportunities of American life, he had sympathetic auditors.

Blair's legal training and political prowess allowed him to fit into the Senate with little need for extensive orientation. During the nineteenth century, approximately three of four lawyers began their political apprenticeships as prosecuting attorneys or state legislators. Sixty-four percent of eastern lawyers, including Blair, sacrificed their legal businesses to pursue their political inclinations. Sixty-two percent of all senators in the 1870s and 1880s were professional politicians who had considerable experience in government before entering the Senate. Many of them had served in the House of Representatives before coming to the upper house and were familiar with national issues and legislative procedures.[5] Blair, therefore, entered an institution that was becoming increasingly professional with solid credentials of his own.

Blair's first major task came with his appointment to the Committee to Inquire into Alleged Election Frauds, popularly called the Wallace Committee. The Senate Democratic leadership formed this committee to expose what it considered to be unfair Republican election practices in urban areas of the Northeast. It expected this committee to produce examples of Republican misuse of election machinery that could be used to counteract stories about southern Democrats' treatment of blacks during the 1876 campaign. Republicans were reluctant to serve on this committee, so, when Blair entered the Senate, he promptly replaced Senator Angus Cameron of Wisconsin, who gladly gave up his position.[6] Blair spent most of July and August 1879 investigating election practices in New York City, Providence, and Boston with committee chairman William A. Wallace of Pennsylvania, J. J. MacDonald of Indiana, and Oliver R. Platt of Connecticut.[7]

Blair had few illusions about his work on the Wallace Committee. He wrote to Eliza: "The work may prove to be very important & it may not."[8] The latter description proved to be more accurate, and one Republican paper called the investigation a "farce."[9] Despite the absence of constructive accomplishments, Blair enjoyed the experience. Trips to Coney Island and Martha's Vineyard provided a welcome break from the routine of committee work and gave him relief from the heat.[10] The highlight of the trip for Blair was the committee's visit to the home of Rhode Island senator Ambrose Burnside. Blair was openly impressed by the former Union

general, confiding to Eliza: "Many distinguished persons were there."[11]
The committee issued final reports in May 1880 just before the presidential nominating conventions. Blair signed the Republican minority
report, which he sent to the Republican presidential candidate, James A.
Garfield, on July 5 for the nominee's use during the impending canvass.[12]
Although the Wallace Committee accomplished little of substance, committee membership helped introduce Blair to his new colleagues and the
traditions of the Senate, giving him the confidence to take part in the debates in the second session.

The political nature of the Wallace Committee's work demonstrated
that, despite his six-year term, Blair was still deeply involved in partisan
activities. Shortly after returning home from his work with the committee, Blair once again went to Maine to help the Republicans battle the
Greenback threat. By presenting his views on the currency question in a
variety of forums, he helped the Republicans win a narrow victory in state
contests.[13]

Blair's work in Maine was part of his effort to support the presidential
candidacy of James G. Blaine. Most New Hampshire Republicans en-
thusiastically backed Blaine. Blair had committed himself to the Maine
politician before the 1880 campaign began in earnest and apparently became an important part of Blaine's staff.[14] As the national convention
approached, he contacted Blaine supporters from the South and the Midwest.[15] Although disappointed when his favorite lost, he quickly adapted
and worked hard for the election of Garfield. Having participated with
Garfield in the currency debates when both men were members of the
House, Blair undoubtedly felt a shared bond with the compromise candidate. His active support of the national convention candidate sent a clear
message to New Hampshire Republicans that they should remain loyal
to the party.

Blair's sure grasp of the patronage opportunities provided by his Senate seat was not matched by his legislative initiatives. He had minimal interest in the committees to which he had been appointed and contributed
little to the floor debates. When he did make comments, they added little
to the substance of the discussion. He introduced a resolution sponsored
by the Women's Christian Temperance Union (WCTU) to raise women's
age of consent to twenty but never took further action on it.[16] The same
was true of his prohibition activities. He met with WCTU leader Frances
Willard and other temperance leaders in New York, but he introduced no

Henry W. Blair in the 1870s. Courtesy New Hampshire Historical Society, Giles Low II Collection, F2189.

legislation in this area.[17] Instead, his only resolution was to supply federal equipment on loan to the New Hampshire militia. Complaining that many Senate committees served no useful purpose and should be abolished, he sought to define positive roles for these committees over the next decade.[18]

Blair's appointment to the Education and Labor Committee in early December 1880 served as the springboard for most of his constructive work as a senator.[19] The timing of this appointment was particularly important because the Senate was considering a bill introduced by Ambrose Burnside to grant limited federal aid to public education. Burnside's bill, introduced on March 24, 1879, was admittedly modest in its provisions. The revenues from the sale of public lands were to be placed in a fund with only the interest being distributed to the states. This small sum was to be distributed to land grant colleges until their annual income reached $30,000.[20] During the December 1880 debate on the bill, the Colorado Republican Henry M. Teller offered an amendment to make the revenue from the land sales, rather than the interest, available for distribution.[21] Although this amendment failed in a tie vote, the Burnside bill passed with an overwhelming majority of northern Republicans and southern Democrats voting in its favor.[22]

Blair's strong support for federal aid to education elicited his first significant remarks in the Senate. In a short speech delivered on December 18, 1880, he reaffirmed his commitment to strengthening public schools and enunciated some principles and specific proposals that made him a national figure for the next decade. Acknowledging that neither the Burnside bill nor the amendment provided enough money to do any practical good, he maintained that the legislation was still important "because it necessarily draws attention to the subject-matter of education." He then confronted a major objection to this type of legislation—the constitutionality of direct federal aid to states for public education. He asserted: "I believe it is simply in accordance with the principles of the Constitution itself, that if the State fails to educate the child who is to be the citizen of the nation as well as the State, the nation may interfere and by compulsion if necessary provide within the geographical limits of the State means of education."[23] He never wavered from this belief that the government must be an agent for change in American society, protecting the nation and individual citizens by providing financial support for universal education.

During further debate on the Burnside bill, Blair claimed that his goals were to improve schools while, at the same time, preserving local control of public education. He expressed confidence that local officials—particularly those in the South—would willingly carry out the proper policies if the Burnside bill and the Teller amendment provided sufficient funding support. In an emotional outburst, he stated: "If the Senator will make a motion to amend the bill, or if he or anybody will appear here with a proposition to distribute fifty millions of money immediately throughout the United States and give forty millions of it to the South, I will vote for that proposition. I will vote for it every year as long as I am in Congress, and will advocate it as long as I live, if it is wanted."[24] This was not political bombast on Blair's part. He had devised what he considered to be a practical plan for strengthening public education. From this point on, he chose to subordinate all other interests to the fulfillment of this one vision of reform.

Blair's ideas about federal aid to public education were not simply the product of his personal experiences. In the aftermath of slavery, other individuals and developments contributed to the national debate on the role of the federal government in advancing public education. The education provided by the Freedmen's Bureau was one of the most widely accepted parts of the program for integrating former slaves into American life. When congressional Reconstruction returned the responsibility for educating illiterate blacks back to the states, many states found their tax bases too small and their debts too great to allow them to fund education for all needing assistance. Recognizing this problem as a national rather than a regional crisis, several members of Congress introduced legislation to remedy the situation.

On February 15, 1870, Massachusetts congressman George F. Hoar introduced the first comprehensive plan for federal aid to public education. Hoar, who was Blair's Senate colleague throughout the 1880s, proposed a truly national system of education. His bill authorized the Interior Department to appoint federal school inspectors for every congressional and school district. These inspectors would assess the quality of education in their districts and report their findings to a federal superintendent of schools appointed by the president. Whenever a state failed to meet certain minimum standards of education, the president would decide whether the federal government should step in to run the school system. Hoar proposed financing this program through a direct tax of fifty cents per year

on each resident of a delinquent state and interest from a fund created by
the revenue from certain public land sales.[25] The Hoar bill was such a
radical departure from previous practices that it failed to gain enough support to even force a vote on its provisions. The recently formed National
Education Association (NEA), while endorsing the idea of federal aid, refused to back the Hoar bill.

Despite the Hoar bill's lack of success, this measure elicited a most
significant response from one quarter. Two spokesmen for the American
Catholic population felt compelled to explain their position with respect
to both federal aid and public education. Orestes Brownson, the editor of
*Catholic World*, attacked both the Hoar bill and an article favoring federal aid to education by future Republican vice president Henry J. Wilson.
Brownson charged that the Republicans were trying to centralize power
in their own hands and to create a homogeneous and Protestant nation.[26]
At the same time, the archbishop of Rochester, New York, warned that
government control of education would deprive American children of an
adequate religious education.[27] The only acceptable option, in his view,
was to make government financial assistance available to both parochial
and public schools. With the church's position clearly stated, these and
other Catholic spokesmen chose not to continue the debate at this time.

The failure of the Hoar bill did not end attempts to extend federal aid
to public education. In January 1872, Legrand W. Perce, a Republican
carpetbagger from Mississippi who chaired the House Education Committee, introduced another piece of legislation. The Perce bill proposed
that revenues from the sale of public lands be used to fund public education—half to go into a national education fund to be used in the future
and half to be distributed immediately. In contrast to the Hoar bill, this
proposal carried no threats of federal intervention. The provisions of this
act were modified by two amendments that Blair later integrated into his
own bill. Congressman Milo Goodrich of New York offered an amendment to distribute the money according to the percentage of illiterate
adults in the various states. Designed to attract southern Democratic votes,
this system of allocation would have directed 80 percent of the funding
to southern states. The Goodrich allocation plan remained an important
provision in all four of Blair's efforts to secure federal aid for public education. The Democrat Frank Hereford of West Virginia offered an amendment, which passed, to ensure that racially segregated schools would not
be penalized. Hereford's provision, demanded by southern Democrats,

was retained in some of Blair's proposals. The amended Perce bill drew support from Republicans and southern Democrats, passing the House on a crucial test vote by a 112–99 margin.[28] This unusual coalition, which surfaced again during the Hayes-Tilden election controversy, played a key role when Blair tried to pass his own bills.

House members continued to introduce education bills throughout the 1870s. Bills offered by successive chairmen of the Education and Labor Committee, Gilbert C. Walker and John Goode, were similar to the Perce bill.[29] As already noted, Blair commented extensively on the need for federal aid to public education during the discussion of the Walker bill. Each house of Congress passed one act providing for federal aid to public education over the decade.

To offer his own version of the education bill, Blair needed to be appointed to a committee where he could appropriately introduce it. The crucial person involved in that determination was perhaps the most colorful member of the Senate, William Mahone of Virginia. Standing only a few inches above five feet tall and weighing only one hundred pounds, Mahone added a foot-long beard and a large western hat to complete his striking presence. Despite his outlandish appearance, the little Virginian had proved himself to be a talented organizer as a Confederate general and railroad president. Blocked from the regular channels of advancement in the Virginia Democratic Party by his humble birth, he rose to power as one of the leaders of the Readjuster revolt. This movement sought to reduce Virginia's debt liability and to allow the state government to provide services for its poorer citizens. The Readjusters—initially the agrarian wing of the Democratic Party—joined with blacks and mountain white Republicans to sweep the 1879 state elections in Virginia. The legislature promptly elected Mahone to the Senate, where he found himself in a most advantageous position.[30]

The partisan complexion of the Forty-seventh Congress—thirty-seven Democrats, thirty-seven Republicans, and two independents—was ideal for Mahone's purposes. Although Mahone and David Davis of Illinois were classified as independents, Davis was expected to vote with the Democrats. With Vice President Chester Arthur, a Republican, casting the deciding vote on which party would organize the Senate, Republicans desperately needed Mahone's vote to ensure their party's control of committee chairmanships. Malone's price to vote with the Republicans was to be given control of all federal patronage in Virginia and to be appointed

The Honorable William Mahone of Virginia, general in the Confederate army.
Courtesy Library of Congress Prints and Photographs Division.

chairman of the Senate Agriculture Committee. Despite their failure to meet all his demands until the fall of 1881, Mahone supported the Republicans and allowed them to organize the Senate.

For many Republicans, Mahone's ascendance to power presented both a problem and an opportunity. The Virginia politician's open refusal to fund the full debt obligations of his state violated all Republican financial principles. At the same time, Mahone and the Readjusters promised and followed up with specific actions to help black Republicans vote and access state services.[31] Blair welcomed Mahone into the party and ignored the unorthodox fiscal policies of the Virginia leader.[32] Mahone's faults were undoubtedly fully redeemed in Blair's eyes when Blair was named chairman of the Senate Committee on Education and Labor in March 1881.[33]

More than just political opportunism, Blair's alliance with Mahone revealed the policy priorities that would govern his actions for the remainder of his career. While Blair continued to defend the protective tariff and to vote for conservative financial policies, he devoted his greatest efforts to preserving the gains of Reconstruction and pursuing more advanced social reform. He viewed the Readjuster movement as the best means of securing full rights and privileges for southern blacks.[34] For example, he constantly pointed out that the Readjusters had reopened the public schools for the benefit of blacks as well as whites. Recognizing that northern Republicans could no longer intervene directly in the South to protect blacks, he determined that a new strategy was necessary.[35] As he wrote to Chandler: "Mahone's success completes the work of the war."[36] He demonstrated his commitment to this new approach by journeying to Virginia and campaigning for the Readjuster ticket in the late summer of 1881.[37]

Blair's appointment as chairman of the Senate Committee on Education and Labor in only his second year in the Senate requires further explanation. Because seniority and party caucus systems were still poorly formed in the early 1880s, junior members often assumed significant organizational positions.[38] The committee's relatively low profile provides an additional explanation. During this time period, most Americans expected little or no federal action in the fields of education and labor. In comparison to the committees dealing with appropriations, defense, tariffs, and railroads, the Education and Labor Committee seemed to have little jurisdiction and therefore little power. Most senators were more than willing to allow someone with a strong interest in education and labor, including a first-term colleague, to chair this committee. Blair eagerly sought the chair appointment and was granted it without controversy.

By the time Blair assumed the chairmanship of the Education and Labor Committee, a number of individuals and organizations inside and outside Congress had created a receptive atmosphere for his legislative initiatives. As early as 1879, the trustees of the Peabody Fund, which provided substantial private assistance to southern education systems, advocated federal aid to public education.[39] J. L. M. Curry, the director of the Peabody office and an antebellum Alabama politician, was an active lobbyist for direct national aid to southern schools during 1881 and 1882.[40] The Peabody Fund's reputation for educational and political conservatism made Curry's efforts particularly effective. From a much more liberal perspective, the former North Carolina carpetbag Republican leader Albion Tourgee made the same appeal. In both his novels about his Reconstruction experiences, A Fool's Errand (1879) and Bricks without Straw (1880), Tourgee asserted that federal aid to education was essential if blacks were to have any chance for advancement in the South. He did not confine himself to indirect methods of persuasion. He wrote directly to Garfield, strongly urging the new president to support federal funding for public education.[41]

Professionals directly involved in education provided additional support for national aid to public education. U.S. commissioner of education John B. Eaton claimed that the most pressing problem facing the country was the widespread illiteracy found in most of the South.[42] The 1880 census substantiated Eaton's point, showing that the absolute number of illiterate adults had increased since 1870, although the percentage of adults unable to read and write had declined slightly.[43] Later, the NEA made that same point at a public hearing. The House and Senate Education and Labor Committees, with Blair playing a prominent role, met in joint session to hear the NEA testimony. State school superintendents from the South vividly described how the high taxes levied on relatively poor populations produced so little revenue that their education systems could not be sustained.[44] Thus, several sources in American political life were pressing for federal government action in this area.

In the early 1880s, members of Congress introduced a number of education improvement proposals with a variety of funding plans. Although Burnside had died since the last Congress had met, Senator Justin S.

Morrill reintroduced the amended Burnside bill. Most observers regarded this measure as a possible long-range solution to the problem but as
totally inadequate to meet the present crisis.[45] Two members of Congress
offered legislation that provided for large federal expenditures immediately. Congressman John C. Sherwin of Illinois introduced a bill to allot $50
million to the states in equal shares over the next five years. Sherwin's bill
accepted the prosouthern amendments to the Burnside bill, proposing to
distribute the money to states on the basis of illiteracy and without regard
to racial segregation policies. The most significant innovation of Sherwin's plan was his willingness to use general revenues to finance public
education rather than relying on a single tax source.[46] This bill was not reported to the House floor for debate because the House leadership judged
other legislation to be more important.

In an even bolder move, Senator John A. Logan of Illinois proposed
that all internal revenue derived from the "manufacture and sale" of liquor be set aside for education. Logan's plan would have revolutionized
the American public school system. At that time, revenues from alcoholic
beverages amounted to more than $65 million a year, representing about
one-quarter of all direct tax revenue raised by the federal government. Under Logan's plan, the federal government would have provided more than
half of all funding for public education, with the remainder coming from
state and local governments. Given the size of the federal commitment,
Logan maintained that any concessions to the South would be unfair to
the rest of the country.[47] Blair, who considered federal domination of public education undesirable, refused to report the Logan bill.

On December 6, 1881, Blair introduced Senate Bill 151 "to aid in
the establishment and temporary support of common schools."[48] Drawing
on previous proposals, he selected those elements that he thought would
provide the best possible solution to the contemporary situation. Like
Goodrich and Sherwin, he considered illiteracy to be the primary problem that Congress should address. While fully aware that distributing
funds on the basis of illiteracy would bring little money to his constituents
and send more than 70 percent of the funds to the southern states, he was
determined to complete the tasks of the Civil War and Reconstruction.
He wanted blacks to be able to assume full citizenship privileges and believed that improved education was the only practical means to produce
that result. In contrast to Logan's plan, he proposed limiting federal aid
from the general revenues to a ten-year period so that local governments

would have an incentive to continue funding and control at their level. Hopeful that substantial federal aid would produce relatively quick results, he proposed that $15 million be expended the first year and that appropriations be reduced by $1 million each year until reaching $6 million in the final year.[49] Despite uncertain Republican control of Congress, the education bill appeared to have a reasonable chance of passage.

At this critical juncture, a personal political crisis forced Blair to turn his attention elsewhere, disrupting the momentum generated in favor of his education legislation. While this episode will be discussed in detail in chapter 9, a general review of developments will explain why his reform standing was briefly dimmed. Facing increasing financial difficulties in 1881, Blair accepted a large legal fee from Jacob R. Shipherd. Shipherd was the director of a company that had a large claim on the government of Peru and was seeking the support of the U.S. government to recover a substantial sum of money. If Blair had been a private citizen, the arrangement would have been entirely proper. Because he was a member of the Senate, he was perceived to have a conflict of interest. Although a congressional investigation later cleared him of all charges, he had little time for other matters during this controversy.

The adverse publicity surrounding Blair's relationship with Shipherd made it impossible to pass any education legislation. None of the bills introduced between 1879 and 1881 were ever seriously debated in either house of Congress or brought to a vote of any kind. Despite the absence of a sustained debate on the topic, Blair gained the floor on June 13, 1882, to make the first of his massive speeches on the state of education in the United States and the need for federal aid.[50] In 1882, members of Congress did not have paid professional staffs to research speeches and to handle routine constituent services. Senators' schedules were so demanding that Senator Joseph E. Brown was prompted to suggest that each senator be allowed to hire one clerk for his office at government expense.[51] Blair had to literally run from department to department gathering information for the speech while he also secured pensions, arranged for postmaster appointments, and mailed seeds to farmers. His willingness to conduct in-depth research in the midst of the Shipherd investigation underscores his devotion to the principle of access to quality public education for all Americans.

Blair began his June 1882 speech by directly addressing the troublesome problem of the constitutionality of federal aid to states for public

education. His major contention was that the republican form of government guaranteed to each state and the nation by the Constitution could
not be achieved without an educated electorate. Like Horace Mann before him, he asserted that four million illiterate voters in northern cities and the South would destroy the American political experiment. In
addition, he assured his listeners that federal aid to education could be
justified under the general welfare clause of the Constitution.[52] One contemporary critic maintains that Blair was attempting to justify the exclusion of some groups from the electorate on the basis of literacy.[53] That
appears to be a misreading of his purpose. Blair had spent his entire political career at the national level defending the right of southern blacks to
vote and expected this bill to help them continue to do so. Although, like
many New England Republicans, he was concerned about the impact
of immigrant votes on his political future, he was not willing to return to
the anti-immigrant proposals made by the nativist movement during the
1850s.

In this same speech, Blair described what several European countries
were doing to educate their citizens. He made two significant points: Eu-
ropeans were more successful in educating their citizens than Americans,
and European central governments funded their school systems. Then,
using a series of detailed tables prepared by the Bureau of Education, he
highlighted the precise failings of the contemporary American education
system. He took great pains to point out that the failure of southern schools
was not due to the unwillingness of states and localities to tax themselves.
The South was already doing as much, in proportion to its wealth, as the
rest of the country, but these efforts were not enough. Commending the
legislation that had been introduced into Congress, Blair urged consideration of the Burnside-Morrill approach as a good long-range solution. He
described his own plan in some detail, noting that both federal and state
governments would supervise expenditures, and showing where the first
$15 million would be distributed.[54] He concluded by stressing the gravity
of the situation: "We may postpone the remedy but the evil will increase.
The issue cannot be evaded. Common-school education must become
universal or the form of our government must be changed. I believe that
the next ten years will decide the question."[55]

A series of labor hearings occupied Blair for several months before the
1884 session, but he continued to press his education proposal. Unlike
many of his other reform efforts, this proposal enjoyed extensive support

within the political establishment, and a large number of powerful lobby-ists and pressure groups were willing to assist. Blair was a featured speaker at the August 1882 inaugural meeting of the National Education Assem-bly in New Jersey.[56] The proposed legislation gained further momentum in December 1882 when Chester A. Arthur became the third president to endorse the idea of federal aid to public education.[57] That same month, the American Social Science Association endorsed the principle of the Blair bill, and the NEA actively lobbied in favor of the bill itself.[58] All these organizations had a vested interest in the welfare of professional ed-ucators, but other interests were preparing to make themselves heard in the growing debate.

For Blair and many others, the primary objective of the legislation was to complete the promises made to educate blacks during Recon-struction. Northern-based philanthropic agencies like the Slater and the Peabody Funds and their directors, Atticus Haygood and J. L. M. Curry, made strong pleas for greater expenditures to help eradicate black illitera-cy in the South.[59] As a former congressman and Confederate leader, Cur-ry gave the cause great respectability among conservative whites in the South.[60] Black Americans from all social stations and occupations were almost completely united behind the Blair proposal, believing that feder-al aid was their only chance to secure adequate funding for black schools. The Colored National Convention's decision to endorse federal aid by an overwhelming vote in September 1883 reflected this belief.[61] Black news-papers and other community spokesmen were enthusiastic in their sup-port of the education bill.[62] When the Interstate Educational Conference and southern white groups also backed the principles of the bill, southern Democratic politicians found themselves under tremendous pressure to do the same.[63]

The second session of the Forty-seventh Congress convened in De-cember 1882. Because the Peru investigation of Blair during the first ses-sion had delayed discussion of the education bill, this bill got caught in the rush to complete work on the Pendleton Civil Service Act and the ex-tended debate on the tariff. Blair himself was forced to become involved in the tariff discussions to defend the interests of the potato farmers in Coos County and the timber companies in the northern part of New Hampshire.[64] In addition, a number of other education bills were await-ing their own hearing during the short session.

The large number of competing bills and issues ended any possibility that federal aid to education would be considered during this Congress. On January 9, 1883, Senator John Logan of Illinois, who had introduced a bill to use internal revenue monies for public education, and Vermont senator Justin Morrill, who had introduced a proposal for federal aid to provide college training for public school teachers, prevented the Blair bill from being discussed.[65] After an attempt to rush an education bill through the House of Representatives failed by two votes in late February, all further efforts were abandoned for the session.[66]

Undiscouraged, Blair and his allies tried new strategies to influence public opinion. Speeches by Hayes and Blair in Connecticut in July 1883 launched another big push. In late August, Blair offered to make a major concession to southern Democrats when he reintroduced his bill. At the National Education Assembly meeting in New Jersey, he said he would agree to local rather than federal administration of the funds allocated in the education bill.[67] Southern educators at the Louisville Exposition endorsed this approach during a September meeting.[68] Later that fall, Blair's positive experience conducting a labor investigation in the South left him with no doubt that the southern leadership would handle the federal monies as the legislation required. Working with his labor panel colleague James Pugh of Alabama, Blair rewrote several phrases to make the bill more acceptable to southern senators and congressmen.[69]

When the Forty-eighth Congress convened in December 1883, the battle for passage of the education bill began in earnest. On December 5, Blair introduced revised legislation that was quickly referred to his committee.[70] Massive public interest and special lobbying efforts continued throughout the session. J. L. M. Curry seemed to be everywhere assuring southern senators and congressmen that this legislation was absolutely necessary for the advancement of their constituents.[71] A tremendous number of petitions, largely from the South, flooded into Congress demanding passage of the bill.[72] Blair also arranged for representatives from the national meeting of state school superintendents to appear before a joint meeting of the House and Senate Education Committees.[73] As support swelled, Blair conducted a massive research project to prepare for the speech introducing the bill. Although each senator now had a clerk and Blair also could request help from a clerk assigned to the Education and Labor Committee, he did most of the work himself. In late January, he was able to report the legislation out of committee and have it placed on the calendar for full Senate action.[74]

Despite having to deliver a major speech on pensions on March 17, 1884, Blair was prepared to make his supreme effort explaining the education bill the next day. For the next ten days, he was constantly on his feet explaining, defending, and persuading. The major provisions of the bill were as follows: (1) funds would be appropriated to states on the basis of the illiteracy rate among residents over the age of ten; (2) black schools were to receive a fair share of the money, but segregated schools were allowed; (3) states were required to match one-third of the federal appropriation for the first five years and match dollar for dollar in the last five years; (4) 10 percent of the money could be used for teacher training but not for school construction; (5) states were allowed to distribute the funds, but they were to document all allocations in an extensive report to the federal government.[75] Blair opened his speech with the assertion that the bill "is, in fact, the logical consequence and the conclusion of the war."[76] The Civil War had freed slaves from physical bondage. Now, Blair was determined to free them from the fetters of ignorance. He emphasized that the bill was necessary for the creation of an enlightened electorate and the continuation of a republican form of government.[77]

The remainder of his speech was a closely argued case for federal aid to public education. With the assistance of John Eaton, the commissioner of education, Blair had carefully extracted data from the 1880 census returns to demonstrate the overwhelming need for this legislation. He noted that more than seven million Americans over the age of ten were illiterate and that 70 percent of the black population could not read and write. One of every seven voters was illiterate. Southern states accounted for three-quarters of illiterate voters.

To further justify the need for federal action, Blair pointed out that 4,955,602 young people of school age were not attending either private or public education institutions.[78] He supplemented this information with testimony from state school superintendents, claiming that they needed more money than their states could provide. He included appeals from the Peabody Fund director, Curry, the American Social Science Association, and the Union League Club of New York along with fifty-eight petitions from citizen groups.[79] The twenty-seven detailed statistical tables presented with his testimony filled seventeen large pages in the *Congressional Record*.[80] Blair closed his speech by noting that, in light of the South's small tax base, the appropriations requested were just a minimum and should actually be increased.[81] This three-hour performance may

have been one of the most impressive one-man presentations of new legislation in the U.S. Senate's history.

Over the next week, Blair answered questions about his proposal and
defended its provisions. His bill created a major dilemma for Senator John
Sherman, a Republican and constant presidential candidate. If Sherman
voted for the Blair bill, he would have to defend spending vast sums of
money in the South. Having based most of his career on a "bloody shirt"
platform, he feared losing credibility among Ohio Republicans and perhaps his Senate seat. On the other hand, by voting against the legislation, he risked alienating both black and white Republicans in the South,
thereby forfeiting any opportunity to become president. To avoid taking
a stance, he tried a parliamentary maneuver to get rid of the legislation
before any further discussion took place.[82] Blair refused to back away and
counterattacked: "Whenever we approach this bill some infinitesimal,
unimportant maneuvering . . . in which I am not especially adept, seems
to be summoned . . . to postpone the bill." In a sharp rebuke to Sherman,
he continued: "I assure the Senator that there are occasionally new ideas
in this country and that people are coming to consider new questions and
new issues, and it is necessary to learn something in regard to them as we
go along."[83] Sherman quickly withdrew from the fray, but he remained an
implacable enemy of the measure and its author.

In the debate that followed, Blair further justified the constitutionality of the bill. He cited the 1836 distribution of the federal surplus to aid
education as a precedent for his measure.[84] He countered the contention
that the bill proposed an unequal, and thereby unconstitutional, distribution of funds by comparing the education bill to the notorious rivers and
harbors bill. He asserted that both bills were based on the same principle—need. The appropriation in the rivers and harbors bill went to areas
with waterways, and the education money would go to states with high
rates of illiteracy.[85] He pointed out that the education bill required only
temporary assistance from the federal treasury. He maintained that he opposed any permanent program and that he was simply trying to deal with
a unique crisis.[86] By this time, only a few senators continued to question
the constitutionality of the bill. Southern Democrats, who could have
challenged this expansion of the federal government, were reconciled by
the concessions in the bill and Blair's willingness to trust state officials to
administer the program.

To his surprise, Blair discovered that his fellow Republicans were some of the most outspoken critics of the measure. Many of them felt that the Democratic leadership in the South could not be trusted to administer the program fairly. Senator Sherman bluntly stated that he would not vote to give federal aid to the southern states. He was joined in that sentiment by Kansas senator John J. Ingalls, who argued that there was no "obligation to educate the blacks of the south."[87] These criticisms seemed to threaten the bill with immediate defeat. However, three Republican senators—George Hoar of Massachusetts, Shelby Cullom of Illinois, and Benjamin Harrison of Indiana—offered amendments that, with some concessions from Blair, might salvage the legislation. These amendments proposed the following changes: (1) distributing less money in a shorter length of time; (2) forcing the states to match the federal appropriations; (3) directing that all aid be sent to the South; and (4) requiring that black and white schools receive an equal share of the federal funds.[88]

When extended debate did not resolve these issues, the Republican senators attempted to reach consensus through the party caucus. A meeting held on March 31, 1884, was inconclusive, and a committee was appointed to reach a solution. Three days later, the committee recommended a compromise plan. The caucus agreed to support the Blair bill with the following amendments: (1) reduce the appropriation to $77 million spread over eight years on a 7–9–11–13–11–9–7–5 basis; (2) mandate that no state could receive more from the federal government than the amount appropriated in state and local education budgets; (3) require that black and white schools receive equal amounts of money; (4) require states to submit extensive annual reports on the expenditure of federal funds; and (5) allow segregated schools to receive federal funds.[89] Although Democratic senators from the South did not like the idea of following the dictates of the Republican caucus, Blair convinced them to accept the compromise version of the legislation.

After beating back Sherman's attempt to cripple the bill, Blair secured Senate approval of it on April 7, 1884. The overwhelming vote of 42–22 was a personal victory for him. He had held together a most unusual team of northern Republicans and southern and border state Democrats in a time of great partisan and sectional animosities. The Republican support for the bill was 23–7, and southern and border state Democrats voted in favor 18–7. The major source of opposition came from northern Democrats, among whom only 1 of 9 voted for the bill.[90] Unable to prevent the

John Sherman. Courtesy Library of Congress Prints and Photographs Division.

voting, Sherman took the politically expedient step of failing to vote on the measure. Although Blair recognized that his own role was just part of a much larger movement, the bill's passage represented a sweet moment of triumph. Curry accurately assessed the importance of Blair's contributions when he observed: "Senator Blair deserves much credit for his earnestness, persistency, and full arguments."[91]

The education bill's success in the Senate was not matched in the House of Representatives. Blair lobbied for passage and public support, noting: "The Lord passed the Bill through [the] Senate—I do not dare risk it without great effort on our part in the House."[92] He had an important ally in House Education Committee chairman Albert S. Willis of Kentucky. Willis secured a majority report from his committee for his own education bill—similar in many respects to Blair's.[93] A few Republican committee members, led by Congressman Joseph D. Taylor of Ohio, proposed a politically impossible alternative plan. Taylor's plan would have assigned specific sums to counties on the basis of illiteracy with the program still being administered by the states. Since this allocation plan favored the black majority counties in the South, it would have greatly reduced southern support for the bill. While Taylor's motivation remains obscure, the effect of his measure would have been to doom federal aid to education in the House.[94] Faced with opposition from House Democratic leaders, particularly Speaker John C. Carlisle, neither bill made it to the floor.[95] In the rush to adjourn the first session before the start of the 1884 presidential campaign, Carlisle had little difficulty postponing votes on these education bills.

The 1884 election of the Democratic candidate, Grover Cleveland, as president significantly affected debate on the education legislation during the second session that met in early December. Many Republicans who felt comfortable with a Republican president overseeing the southern Democrats' administration of the program were much less enthusiastic about having a Democratic administration in charge. Faced with declining Republican support, proponents of the education bill became even more dependent on Democratic votes. Writing to Cleveland three weeks after the election, Blair pleaded with the new president to help pass the legislation during this session. He assured Cleveland that his administration could "become illustrious in the annals of America and mankind" if he were the president to administer the program.[96] This flattery brought no tangible result, and Blair and Willis had to continue their battle alone.

Willis tried to unite the House proponents of federal aid to education by agreeing to accept the Blair version of the bill instead of his own and by helping organize a conference of southern Democrats who pledged to pass the Blair bill.[97] Blair continued to work behind the scenes trying to generate public pressure and additional Republican support for the measure.[98] Threatened by renewed efforts to pass the measure, House speaker Carlisle and the Democratic leadership tried to defeat it by introducing a constitutional question. This ruse failed, and the test vote indicated that there was a safe majority in the House favoring the legislation.[99] Recognizing their weak position, the Democrats on the Rules Committee refused to allow the measure to reach the House floor for a vote.[100] This failure did not daunt Blair and his allies, who thought this would be just a temporary setback.

The intensity of the debates created several powerful enemies to the bill, and these individuals and groups grew more powerful over the remainder of the decade. With the backing of northern and border state Democrats, Senator James B. Beck of Kentucky proposed a plan for reducing federal expenditures and lowering taxes. Beck charged that the Blair bill was a scheme to spend the federal surplus and thereby save the protective tariff.[101] His reform program, endorsed by the House Democratic leadership and later strengthened by Cleveland's support for tariff reduction, was probably most directly responsible for the ultimate defeat of the Blair bill. Catholic writers and speakers further weakened its chances of passage by criticizing its sole emphasis on strengthening public schools.[102] However, the church never took any official stand on the legislation—a distinction that would escape Blair.

Just as there were critics who felt that Blair had gone too far, others were equally convinced that he had not gone far enough. Most of these spokesmen supported the black cause and attacked him for the political compromises he had made to secure passage of the measure. Other than political expediency, Blair had no real defense against charges that his bill gave legal sanction for segregation under federal law.[103] His response was that this legislation was the only means available to provide adequate funding for black schooling and that it would not pass without white southern votes. It appears that most black leaders accepted this explanation, and they overwhelmingly supported the Blair bill.[104] However, northern Republicans, such as Sherman and Taylor, continued to question whether the southern states could be fair to blacks when distributing funds. They presented strong evidence based on past performance to justify their concerns.

To many deeply concerned reformers, Blair's flexibility marked him as a political opportunist. In reform circles, Albion Tourgee was the bill's most important critic. Tourgee, the former carpetbagger turned author, called for a virtually national system of schools that would have protected black rights.[105] While his proposal directly addressed the problems of discrimination and education system improvement, the plan never could have passed in Congress. Blair had compromised at several points to secure a measure that he felt could be passed in the political climate of that time. Although the Democratic press characterized Blair as an impractical visionary, he was committed to achieving immediate results. If this meant modifying part of the program to retain its essence, he was willing to do so.

By the end of the March 1885 congressional session, Blair's name and his education bill were well recognized by the public. His identification with the reform movement was secure despite the investigation into his financial dealings with the Peruvian company. Blair demonstrated a continuing commitment to the political battleground as the proper place to secure needed changes in American life. As a result, he carefully adjusted his proposed policies to the political realities of the time. He accepted amendments to the education bill to ensure passage. He supported the Mahone movement in Virginia despite his fiscal conservatism. His startling emergence from relative obscurity diverted attention from his failing efforts to secure reform. His political embarrassment in 1882 and the return of the Democrats to control of the House in 1883 thwarted his plans. Like the reformers of the 1840s and 1850s, Blair believed that he was morally right and would ultimately succeed.

*Chapter 6*

# A Sense of Place

As Blair sought to remedy the imperfections of American society, he became more conscious of the heritage shared by the mountain sections of the eastern United States. His reform work led to the discovery of a mountain region in the upland South quite similar to the mountains of New England. Keenly aware of the significant role played by sectional rivalries during the Civil War era, he and many of his compatriots came to appreciate the strong influence of region on patterns of behavior.

Blair's recognition of desirable features in the land and people of the White Mountains and New Hampshire lakes region began during his youth. Americans in this time period were looking for a unique identity to distinguish their "New World" from other nations. Not having ancient institutions and long pedigrees to call on, they were forced to define themselves in terms of recent history and natural settings. Among the characteristics selected were the War for Independence, political freedom and constitutional government, Andrew Jackson's victory over the British army at the Battle of New Orleans, the rugged Atlantic Coast, the Hudson River valley, Niagara Falls, and the mountainous wilderness of northern New England.

John Ward and other scholars have described Americans' efforts to create a national identity as the process of inventing tradition.[1] In particular, Americans began to assign significance to specific geographic areas. Many states claimed exalted qualities and self-promoting characteristics. At first, the area covered by the Appalachian Mountains did not fit easily into the new American identity. Part of the range was in the South, part in the early West—in Pennsylvania and Ohio—and part in New England. For European pioneers, the mountains initially posed a barrier—a perception reinforced by the British Proclamation Line of 1763, which forbade migration beyond the crests of these mountains. Following the War for Independence, settlers surged into and through the Appalachians.

From the beginning, these pioneers challenged established authority, as evidenced by the "State" of Franklin, the Whiskey Rebellion, the "Republic" of Vermont, and the Indian Stream Republic.[2] This tradition continued in the southern mountains during the Civil War when inhabitants resisted both Union and Confederate governments.[3]

Initial settlement patterns in the New England Appalachians revealed nothing distinctive about the region. Virtually all the early settlers were from southern New England. Rather than moving as individuals or families, dozens—sometimes hundreds of people—moved from the same neighborhood or community. People from Massachusetts traveled to northern New England overland and along lakes and river bottoms. Large numbers of Connecticut pioneers paddled up the Connecticut River to find land in New Hampshire and Vermont.

Several significant features of these migrants helped shape a regional identity. First, the settlers were ethnically and culturally homogeneous. They shared religious training, a belief system, and a commitment to public education. They came from a township form of government that relied on politically active community members and annual public meetings to approve budgets and policies. Most of them were farmers, but they expected to sell their surpluses commercially and to have access to craftsmen and local businesses.[4]

The land on which these pioneers struggled to survive was not hospitable. For many thousands of years, this territory had been covered by a glacier. When the ice finally melted, it left behind a scarred land. The tops of mountains had been rubbed and pressed down, and great ravines had been gouged into their sides. Moreover, the topsoil had been scraped away from much of the lowlands, leaving unproductive deposits of gravel, sand, rocks, and clay.[5] Residents also had to contend with harsh weather. On April 19, 1862, a Vermont farm girl living close to Blair's home reported: "Father got up in the morning . . . [to go] out the back door[.] *Lo and behold* he could not get out[,] the snow was completely over the top of the door but one corner next [to] the well[.] [H]e dug a little hole through just enough to creep out."[6] In 1816—the year of no summer—the region experienced snow in eleven months and frost in every month.[7]

Despite these challenges, northern New Englanders made considerable progress because of the strength of their community institutions. For example, northern New Hampshire residents built schools in virtually every village and spent most of their tax dollars supporting this enterprise.

As important as public education was to the early settlers, they pursued knowledge in other ways as well. Newspapers and periodicals were circulated widely, keeping them generally well informed about events outside their immediate communities. The towns also established a variety of public libraries, including the first free public libraries in the United States.[8] The existence of libraries seemed to encourage individual ownership of books. For example, a bookstore in the township of Walpole, New Hampshire—with a population less than two thousand—had more than thirty-one thousand volumes for sale in the 1840s.[9] Blair's personal library contained four hundred books in the 1870s.[10]

New England state governments supported community efforts to improve and expand public education. In 1846, the New Hampshire legislature authorized the creation of a state agency to assist towns and cities with public schools. The first state school commissioner compiled extensive statistics demonstrating the need for additional teacher training institutes, improved teacher pay, and better-constructed schoolhouses.[11] The results of this sustained effort were dramatic. In his seminal study of the upper Connecticut valley in Vermont and New Hampshire, William Gilmore notes that, by the 1840s, 97 percent of adult males and 82 percent of adult females were literate. Only Sweden had achieved a higher level of literacy among its rural population.[12]

Northern New England's educational success can be partly attributed to the important role played by organized religion. Ministers in the small New Hampshire towns of Conway, Stoddard, Canaan, Keene, Tilton, Claremont, Thornton, and Hanover had doctor of divinity degrees.[13] Of the sixty Congregational ministers in Vermont in 1800, "twenty-five graduated from Yale, thirteen from Dartmouth, eight from Harvard, three from Princeton . . . and two from Brown."[14] These clergymen were expected to be the intellectual as well as the spiritual leaders of their communities.

The arrival of the railroads in the 1840s challenged up-country farmers, who soon discovered that they could not compete with farmers from the rich farmlands of the Midwest. To stabilize local economies, northern New Englanders began to diversify.[15] Tourism became the fastest-growing sector. Seeking to dramatize the region, entrepreneurs persuaded officials in the White Mountains to name their highest and most prominent peaks after the founders of the country. This innovation quickly attracted summer visitors who were members of the southern New England elite. Among those hosted by one major hotel were Nathaniel Hawthorne,

Henry David Thoreau, the historian Francis Parkman, and the painter Thomas Cole.[16] The infant railroad industry sensed an opportunity, and rails were extended to the base of the Presidential Range by 1851.[17]

With more tourists able to reach the region, the leading hotels made a collective decision to target and cater to upper-class clientele exclusively. Seizing on the early success of Thomas Cole's paintings of Crawford and Franconia Notches, the hotels began to hire artists for the entire summer season to further attract their socially conscious guests. To ensure that they would have talented artists for the entire season, they offered free lodging for the painters and their families. The artists were expected to portray their host hotels and the region favorably and to sell their products to the guests as souvenirs of their stay in the "wilderness." This arrangement proved to be beneficial for all concerned. The guests were entertained, the artists made valuable contacts and sales, and the paintings displayed in the homes of socially prominent families provided free advertising for the hotels among the population they wished to attract.[18]

Writers quickly joined the ranks of the regional publicists. Nathaniel Hawthorne's short stories about the White Mountains introduced northern Appalachia to a large audience who had not yet visited the mountains.[19] Two other writers reached an even broader public through more popular venues. Thomas Starr King wrote a series of very favorable articles about the mountain region for the *Boston Transcript*. In 1859, his collected articles were published as the best-selling *The White Hills: Their Legends, Landscape and Poetry*.[20] Sarah Josepha Hale of Newport, New Hampshire, wrote articles for female readers of Boston and New York newspapers. She frequently referred to northern New England as the measure of the nation's domestic and educational attainments. Her columns were quite popular, and she was able to parlay this work into editorships of *Ladies Magazine* and *Godey's Lady Book*. By 1860, the latter magazine boasted a readership of 150,000.[21]

The combined efforts of hotel owners, railroad companies, painters, and writers created a clear and positive image of northern Appalachia. Portrayed as living in a glorious place where the virtues of the unhurried past remained, northern New Englanders and the region came to be viewed as special. They sought to overcome the challenges of an unforgiving soil and frigid winters by leading active lives aimed at improving their communities and national society. As an important way in which to accomplish these aims, they committed themselves to providing everyone with access to a good education.

Blair's education bill was a perfect expression of this commitment. Blair fully accepted the regional image and used it to explain and justify his own reform efforts. He affirmed the strengths of his home state in an address to the New Hampshire State Fair in 1885: "As I come into contact with the representatives of other states I grow more and more proud of New Hampshire. The people of no other state in the Union have had more to do with molding the destinies of this great nation. Go where you will you will find concerned in the management of every great enterprise, men who were born on the hills or by the waterfalls of our own little state." He continued: "Here is everything that goes to make up the highest type of civilization. We have newspapers, common schools, and churches which are accessible to all. The natural beauties of our state are worth more in a material sense than as though the state possessed the most productive soil in the world."[22] In this one speech, Blair touched on virtually every element of the northern New England stereotype, showing his great pride in the state and its accomplishments.

While passionate about his native state, Blair also acknowledged the challenges of living there. He told one audience that he knew from personal experience how working the rocky New Hampshire soil "made a boy's back ache." He declared that the "people of this state are intelligent, for a person has got to know as much as any human being to get a living from a farm in New Hampshire."[23] Noting the harshness of the winter weather faced by these same husbandmen, he described these experiences as forging independent spirits and self-sufficiency.

His firsthand knowledge of New Hampshire farmers' struggle for economic survival made Blair a strong advocate for their interests. The Democrats' effort to reduce the tariff on potato starch brought a strong protest from the New Hampshire senator. He pointed out: "One-sixth of the starch manufactured in this country is made in a single county in my state, the county of Coos." He went on to say that Canadian farmers enjoyed such a price advantage that any reduction in the tariff "must be the utter destruction of the industry." When a colleague asked whether Coos County farmers made a comfortable living, Blair replied: "Fairly comfortable livings, as we get our livings in New Hampshire."[24]

Blair sometimes used the interests of his agricultural constituents to defend the broader economic interests of industrialists and the Republican

Party. For example, in 1890, the Democrats challenged the general principle of the protective tariff—a policy that Republicans and many businessmen supported. The Democrats proposed that lumber be included
on a "free list," that is, a list of goods that could be imported without any
taxes. Although large American lumber companies had the most to lose
from this proposal, Blair concentrated on how devastating the changed
tax laws would be to small farmers in New Hampshire. Drawing on his
personal experience with the Bartletts, he asserted: "The farmer depends
on [sales of his lumber] for money with which he pays his taxes, with
which he educates his child."[25]

During debates on the education bill, Blair relied on his memories
of New Hampshire public schools to demonstrate why all states needed
some federal support for public education. At one point, a Senate colleague from Connecticut challenged the education bill's proposal to distribute funds on the basis of states' illiteracy rates, claiming that New
England had the will and means to educate its own children without federal assistance. Blair agreed that New England's "masses are much better educated already." However, he maintained that New Hampshire still
had inadequate school buildings, pockets of poverty and illiteracy, and too
few teacher training institutes—problems that could be addressed with
federal assistance.[26] He further noted that the heavy taxes on real estate
used to finance local schools threatened the economic health of New
England communities. The only way to maintain high literacy rates while
relieving some of this economic pressure was through a broad-based national assistance program.[27]

The declining tax bases in small towns prompted Blair to analyze
rural depopulation in his old congressional district. In a discussion with
Rhode Island senator Nelson Aldrich, he acknowledged that many farms
were being abandoned. However, on the basis of data from his own analysis, he asserted: "It is well understood that many of these abandoned
farms in New Hampshire, in high picturesque locations, which are being
sought for by the millionaires of New York and other portions of the country, are getting to be the summer residences of those men who go there
and . . . invest their capital . . . and [are] gradually building up the villages
around themselves."[28] What appeared to be a decline in fortune for rural
New Hampshire was, to his way of thinking, a way in which to increase
property values, improve the rate of tax collection, and add more contrib-
utors to local economies.

Although Blair was not a particularly introspective person, his references to his native state had a mystical side. In a February 1881 U.S. Senate speech, he contrasted the seemingly constant interactions in urban areas with the more isolated existence in northern New Hampshire. He observed: "I have never felt so utterly alone as when absorbed in my duties here. The tender woods, vast, dark, and silent, are full of companionship, and the spirit of nature speaks with many-voiced and varied tones to him who seeks her wild and secret home."[29] This strong identification with the natural world remained an important part of Blair's worldview throughout his public career.

While seeking support for the education bill, Blair began to see some parallels between his native mountain region and mountain areas of the Upper South. At first, he spoke about this other section of the eastern mountains in general terms. However, the enthusiastic response of white educational and political leaders from the southern mountains convinced him that the people of southern Appalachia could benefit from the education bill as much as black Americans. He felt an even closer affinity with the mountain South after learning that this region had provided many soldiers for the Union army during the Civil War.

Two individuals further influenced Blair's impressions of southern Appalachia. Before Blair introduced his bill, the eastern Kentucky congressman John White sought federal aid for public education. Bills introduced by White in 1881 and 1882 proposed to allocate federal funds on the basis of illiteracy rates.[30] Although this legislation was never reported out of committee, Blair recognized White as a valued ally. Several years later, Professor W. E. C. Wright of Berea College, an institution devoted to the educational uplift of students from southern Appalachia, alerted Blair to the growing perception of the southern mountain region as a distinct cultural entity.[31]

The newly identified southern mountain region captured the interest of many middle-class Americans. But, unlike their northern counterparts, the southern mountain people never gained control over their own iconography. Their image was largely created by the events of the Civil War era, when the southern Appalachian population emerged into public view as seemingly staunch defenders of the Union. Northern observers, including Blair, recalled that conflicting loyalties within southern Appalachia had incited regular army and guerrilla warfare. The intense suffering of the civilian population received wide publicity, and the mountain South entered the national consciousness as a benighted region.[32]

Witnessing the rapid growth of urban America, many people came to believe that all parts of the nation were experiencing the same progress. When tourists and writers visited the southern mountain region, much as they had done in the northern mountains, they assessed the land and the people and found them wanting. The land, ravaged by the Civil War, was unproductive, and transportation was inadequate. Memories of the Civil War were fresh, and the people were dazed and bitter. Public institutions were highly partisan and ineffective.[33] The low level of literacy meant that the region contrasted unfavorably with northern New England. Shocked by the backwardness of the region, many observers concluded that this unusual convergence of developments was the normal condition of southern Appalachian society.

Southern Appalachia's public image was further tarnished by outside groups that benefited from negative portrayals of the region. Facing a voting coalition of lowland blacks and highland white Republicans, Upper South Democrats chose to demonize both groups. The "Lost Cause" literary and intellectual movement to glorify the Confederate war effort demeaned both populations, and Democratic spokesmen eagerly reported unflattering news items about both groups.[34] Businessmen seeking to make great fortunes through the extraction of mountain natural resources justified their often exploitative policies as a means to improve the lives of these "unfortunate" people.[35]

Local color writers like Mary Noailles Murfree and John Fox Jr. presented unflattering images of southern mountaineers in their popular novels. These writers helped create an identity that emphasized poverty, ignorance, and a penchant for violence.[36] The rise of mass-circulation newspapers in the late nineteenth century spread negative images of the highlanders nationwide. Desperate for sensational stories that would attract advertisers, subscribers, and daily readers, these newspapers portrayed the southern mountains as a region of seemingly endless violence. The Hatfield-McCoy episode and other confrontations reinforced the emerging stereotype of the southern mountain people. It was no accident that a New York reporter first coined the term *hillbilly* during these years.[37]

Reformers and missionaries further contributed to the region's negative image. For example, to build support for education reform, Berea

College president William G. Frost blamed the "backwardness" of the southern mountain region on the inadequacies of the public education system.[38] Christian home missionaries made the same assessment about the spiritual life of the mountain people and sought to "improve" the training of the clergy and the social life of the laity.[39] Many female reformers and their associated organizations worked to bring "middle-class order" to the lives of southern Appalachian residents. They organized settlement schools, nursing services, and self-help agencies designed to mold the southern mountaineers into "real" highlanders like their northern counterparts.[40] When they sought funding to carry out these reforms, their national giving campaigns used the emerging hillbilly stereotype to generate sympathy and support among middle-class and elite Americans.[41]

Unlike northern New England, the mountain South had few local spokespersons to contest this insidious image. Political leaders were often capitalists who profited from the stereotype and were not longtime residents of the region. At one point, West Virginia's two U.S. senators owned coal mines in the state but lived in Maryland.[42] Local color writers were usually outsiders as well. Most southern Appalachian tourism entrepreneurs limited their publicity to a few select locations, such as western North Carolina, where their efforts to create a positive counterimage of the "Land of the Sky" were only partially successful.[43]

Blair's perceptions of the region were based on more than an unexamined acceptance of the southern mountain stereotype. His sponsorship of the education bill prompted people from throughout southern Appalachia to contact him with striking examples of the inadequacy of the region's educational facilities and programs. Winston County, Alabama, according to one observer had a literacy rate of 30 percent. Perry, Leslie, Clay, and Clark Counties in eastern Kentucky reportedly had short school terms, inadequate buildings, and virtually no tax base. The Alleghany County, Virginia, superintendent reported: "Our school system is in very bad condition and very unpopular." County superintendents pointed out the terrible conditions in the East Tennessee counties of Johnson, Grainger, Morgan, Hancock, and Cumberland. The report on Cumberland County read in part: "Little money means short terms, poor teachers, and poor schools."[44] Blair also received and had printed in the *Congressional Record* a published description of the region that confirmed the stereotype in every detail.[45]

Blair did not depend solely on correspondence for his assessment of southern Appalachia because he made extensive visits on at least two occasions. In the late 1880s, he campaigned for the Republican-Readjuster coalition in western and southwestern Virginia. A Virginia Republican leader assured him: "Nothing contributed more to our great gains than your education bill."[46]

Public and political leaders in the region supported everything that Blair had heard. B. L. Butcher of Beverly, West Virginia, wrote: "I am convinced that four-fifths of our people would sign a petition for national aid."[47] His assertion was largely confirmed when Blair received fourteen West Virginia petitions during one congressional session.[48] Appalachian Republicans in Kentucky, North Carolina, and Tennessee made the education bill a major part of their campaigns in the 1880s and claimed that its popularity was responsible for their growing number of victories.[49] The North Georgia Democrat Joseph E. Brown also endorsed the legislation as necessary for his fellow mountaineers.[50]

Through his Senate work, Blair became familiar with labor issues in the mountain South. In 1883, he and Senator Henry L. Pugh of Alabama were appointed as a subcommittee of the Senate Education and Labor Committee to investigate labor-management relations in the upland South. A Senate resolution passed on August 7, 1882, authorized the Education and Labor Committee to study relations between labor and capital, wages and hours, workers' living conditions, and the causes of strikes and report any legislation necessary to promote labor peace.[51] Not content with bringing witnesses to Washington, Blair and Pugh held hearings in Birmingham, Alabama, and other southern cities. Blair sought to hear all sides of the situation, inviting many workers to give candid testimony before the subcommittee.

The two senators quickly discovered that the mountain South was experiencing rapid industrialization. Many mountain streams provided power for textile mills. Drawing on abundant local sources of raw materials, Birmingham and Chattanooga were producing a great deal of iron for the national market. Despite the growth in manufacturing, many businessmen complained that they were at competitive disadvantages compared to their northern counterparts. Most of them were severely undercapitalized in businesses that favored large and well-integrated companies. In addition, these businessmen were located far from their primary markets and had to bear heavy transportation costs.[52]

In their testimonies, businessmen said that they had to reduce labor costs as much as possible to overcome financial challenges. One way to do this was to offer jobs to populations with few options, such as convict labor. Unable to afford the construction of modern prisons or the upkeep that such facilities demanded, Alabama, Georgia, Tennessee, and North Carolina placed their convicts at railroad construction and coal mine sites in Appalachia. Lease agreements with private companies ensured that the states would be paid for this convict labor and that the companies would house, feed, and clothe the prisoners. Convict workers provided the companies with a steady and cost-effective workforce that could be used to weaken the organizing activities of unions or to substitute for workers demanding better wages and working conditions.[53]

Free laborers testifying before the subcommittee vociferously objected to the convict labor system. As an alternative, a labor leader from Birmingham proposed that the federal government provide construction loans to workers to allow them to build and equip their own factories.[54] Blair and Pugh also interviewed twelve convicts at the hearings, some of whom said they had benefited from the system by learning trades.[55] While uncovering a great deal of information, the Blair investigation did not recommend legislation to reform or end convict labor.

Skilled black craftsmen appeared before the committee to state their grievances with the labor system in the upland South. One of these men pointed out that black southern artisans had learned their skills as slaves. However, nearly two decades after the Civil War, skilled ex-slaves were receiving 20–40 percent less compensation than whites for the same quantity and quality of work. In addition, white laborers, especially those in labor unions, strongly resisted efforts to place black workers in skilled jobs. In another session, a white labor leader testified that there was no prohibition against black membership in his organization, but he was unable to verify this claim.[56]

Textile mill owners speaking at the hearings were openly exuberant about the opportunities for exploiting the labor of women and children. One manufacturer asserted: "I can find enough women and children within 50 miles of where I am now sitting to run factories enough to increase the value of our exports $100,000,000." Another textile magnate claimed: "You put a boy or girl into a manufacturing establishment, and it is just about as good as a school; it awakens the intellect and makes the individual bright."[57]

Blair's self-education about the mountain South convinced him of the region's potential to emulate the northern New Hampshire experience. Addressing the U.S. Senate in the late 1880s, he declared that southern Appalachia "is of the utmost importance and in regard to which there is comparatively little information."[58] In another speech, he asserted that the southern mountain people and their leadership "deserve sympathy and assistance rather than derision."[59] Describing southern Appalachia as a "poor and sparsely settled" region, he noted that both black and white southerners were "growing up in absolute ignorance."[60]

Blair's recognition that mountain people throughout the eastern part of the United States faced difficult challenges broadened his perception of what his reform agenda could accomplish and strengthened his efforts to work with southern political leaders. Blair was able to demonstrate that his legislative initiatives were not sectional or racial in purpose or impact. He also established that the northern mountain people were an identifiable group in need of assistance. Thus, fortified both personally and politically, he returned to the Senate determined to work for passage of his education bill.

*Chapter 7*

# Debate and Defeat of the Education Bill

After winning reelection to the Senate in 1885, Blair eagerly sought passage of his education legislation. More and more reform groups sought his assistance with their crusades, making him one of the national symbols of political reform. His strategy continued to be one of educating the public through enormous outpourings of information. Once again, he described his reform proposals as a way of preserving republican government in the American Protestant middle-class tradition.

Although Blair expected that public pressure would be sufficient to allow his politically acceptable measures to pass through the reluctant Congress, he was operating in an increasingly hostile political climate. The Cleveland administration's decision to emphasize tariff reduction as its major reform threatened to limit the revenues needed for some of Blair's bills. This policy, combined with an increasingly hostile racial environment in the South, made working with the Democrats much more difficult. Also, Blair's Republican colleagues were slowly backing away from reform issues arising from the Civil War and were embracing programs favored by the nation's business interests.

In the summer of 1885, Blair continued to press for several reforms, seemingly unaware of the changed conditions. All his efforts to secure Cleveland's public support for the education bill had failed, and Curry's appointment as the American minister to Spain had greatly weakened the lobby for this measure.[1] Undaunted by this turn of events, Blair acted quickly to bring his reform program before the Congress when the new session opened in December 1885. In January 1886, he reintroduced the federal aid to education bill.[2] The next day, he introduced resolutions to authorize state votes on constitutional amendments for prohibition and women's suffrage.[3] After being named to the select committee on the

113

women's suffrage resolution, he immediately began in-depth research on that issue.[4] But all other activities were subordinated when his Senate Education Committee reported the education bill.

The education bill that was reported to the full Senate on January 6, 1886, was essentially the same bill that had been passed two years before. While not encouraging changes, Blair indicated his willingness to restore money for school construction that had been deleted from the bill in 1884.[5] Buoyed by continued public support, he waited out the delaying tactics of his Senate opponents.[6] Finally, on February 9, he introduced the legislation for formal debate with an extended speech repeating his arguments of the previous year and demanding expeditious action. Although he presented some statistics in a slightly different form, he sought to limit debate by portraying the bill as essentially the same measure. He pointed out that those who had previously voted for the bill would appear to be inconsistent if they did not do so this time.[7]

Blair's efforts to smooth the way for the education bill provoked Edward P. Clark, the most consistent opponent of the measure, to launch a vigorous protest. As a writer for both the *New York Evening Post* and the *Nation*, Clark crusaded against federal aid to public education for the next few years. He maintained: "The worst thing which could befall the cause of education in the South would be a series of liberal appropriations from the national Treasury for a series of years."[8] Determined to stop federal involvement in education, he asserted that "the work of public education in the South is now in a most hopeful condition," without offering any evidence.[9] Not content with simply being a publicist, Clark directly contacted senators to suggest strategies for defeating the legislation.[10] Unfortunately for Blair, Clark had the contacts, the national forum, and the persistence to make him a formidable adversary.

While unable to debate directly with Clark, Blair had the considerable advantage of presenting essentially the same proposal as the year before. That tactic left those who had supported the measure in the previous Congress with no opportunity to speak against the legislation without appearing to be opportunistic. When defending his bill, Blair often abandoned traditional senatorial courtesy. Like the antebellum reformers, he assumed that anyone disagreeing with him was morally wrong and opposed to basic American principles. When Senator John T. Morgan of Alabama questioned the constitutionality of the bill, Blair struck back without offering any quarter: "It is because the Senator from Alabama

Senator Henry W. Blair. Courtesy New Hampshire Historical Society,
Giles Low II Collection, F2197.

who taunted me and spoke of the disgraceful report which I have placed before the Senate is a relic of the ante-war period; it is because he is not republican in sentiment; it is because he does not represent the existing order of things, does not represent the American people or republicanism in its true and large and real sense. . . . [H]e represents a state of things that is passing away. He represents ideas that received their death-blow with the final battle of the war."[11] This sharp debating style did not endear Blair to his colleagues, but it ensured that his opponents would attack with care.

Most often, Blair used expressions of public support to promote his bill. When responding to Morgan, for example, he offered considerable evidence that the Alabama senator did not speak for his own constituents.[12] Turning to his Republican compatriots, he reminded them that the party's southern candidates had enjoyed success in recent elections by using the Blair bill as an important part of their appeal. In addition, the principle of the legislation had been incorporated into the party platform.[13] To bolster his case, he cited statements by John Adams, Thomas Jefferson, Horace Mann, Ulysses S. Grant, and other notables as well as contemporary authorities.[14] All these tactics kept the debate moving and ensured that any attempt to defeat the measure would be vigorously rebuked.

As had been the case two years earlier, the most direct attacks on the bill came from Blair's fellow Republicans. Kansas senator John J. Ingalls attempted to defeat the bill by obtaining a quick vote on a politically inexpedient amendment when many Senate members were absent. The Ingalls amendment proposed to end favoritism toward the South by distributing funds on the basis of school-age population. Since his scheme would have removed all incentives for southern Democratic support, it would have effectively destroyed the bipartisan coalition necessary for Senate passage. Despite this element of surprise, Ingalls lost his bid to bury the measure by a 24–19 vote. An ominous portent for the future was the fact that a majority of voting Republicans supported Ingalls.[15]

An amendment offered by William B. Allison of Iowa posed a greater threat to the education bill. Borrowing heavily from Albion Tourgee's ideas, Allison proposed to allocate funds in states with segregated schools "in proportion that the illiteracy of the white and colored persons . . . bears to each other."[16] Blair and his allies instantly recognized that, while it was theoretically desirable, this allocation plan would upset the delicate political balance that allowed southern Democrats to support the bill. By limiting the discretion of the states, this amendment would have direct-ed most of the southern allocations away from white school districts and into black schools. The Virginia Republican Harrison H. Riddleberger charged that Allison was raising the race issue.[17] On March 2, 1886, Blair presented a statistical table demonstrating that in one year under the Al-lison plan southern blacks would receive $3,422,025 while whites would get only $1,889,679.[18] He concluded: "Now, sir, this amendment destroys this bill and we have to select today whether we will defeat this bill or de-feat this amendment."[19]

Two days of intense debate followed Blair's remarks. Republicans who opposed the Blair bill used the Allison plan—ostensibly more favorable to blacks—to mask their opposition to the entire bill. Most Republicans who had supported the Ingalls amendment to offer no special assistance to blacks now backed Allison's proposal. Allison's true motive for proposing the allocation plan was patent as well since he had voted for the Ingalls amendment.[20] Fortunately for Blair, a number of Republican senators, in-cluding Hoar of Massachusetts, Harrison of Indiana, and Warren Miller of New York, helped him respond to Allison's arguments. Hoar and Har-rison agreed that the Allison amendment was designed to defeat the en-tire bill.[21] Referring to his own bill in a letter to former president Hayes, Blair observed: "This bill is just as well as a bill can be & in the only form which has the slightest chance to become law."[22] He was later forced to admit that, under his bill, black children would receive a fair share of the money only if southern whites agreed to this distribution. This issue was finally resolved in Blair's favor when an innocuous substitute for Allison's amendment was passed in an unrecorded vote.[23]

After some frantic maneuvering to shape the final version of the Blair bill, the Senate passed this legislation by a substantial majority on March 5, 1886. Blair led the effort to amend the bill by adding $2 million for school construction.[24] Despite the fact that he was making the unusual re-quest to amend his own legislation, this change was made without major opposition. The original Allison amendment was voted down 40–17, with all the Democrats voting against it.[25] Then, by a vote of 45–21, the Sen-ate passed the amended bill. Although the unusual coalition of southern Democrats and northern Republicans held together, several Republican senators found it expedient not to be recorded as voting on the final bal-loting.[26] Blair received credit for his persistence and skill in guiding the legislation through the Senate against determined opposition.

The next hurdle was to secure a vote on the bill in the House. Again, the major obstacle was the Democratic leadership's strong support for tariff reforms that would have reduced the federal monies available for social programs. Rather than accept full responsibility for blocking the bill and the associated political risks, Democratic leaders decided to try a less obvious strategy. Blair explained the situation in a letter to Frederick Douglass: "In the last congress power to prevent consideration was vested under the rules of the House in one man unless there was a two-thirds majority. Now that power is placed in committees & what Morrison Randall or Carlisle could do alone, they now accomplish by constituting an *Education* Committee adverse to this bill by a two-thirds vote. There has never been so wicked a case of political packing as this performance—at least to my knowledge."[27] He urged Douglass and other interested Republicans to bring public pressure on the House to remedy the problem. A week after the first letter to Douglass, Blair wrote a second note to the black leader thanking him for his efforts and assuring him: "The chances are today in favor of [the bill's] passage."[28]

A strategic maneuver planned by Blair's chief ally in the House, Albert Willis of Kentucky, and forty other House members gave Blair cause for optimism. Willis discovered that the majority of Labor Committee members favored the education measure.[29] To the consternation of the Democratic leadership, Willis was able to get another version of the Blair bill assigned to the Labor Committee on March 29, 1886, by a vote of 138–112. While the margin of victory was smaller in the House than in the Senate, the basic alliance between southern Democrats and northern Republicans held up well. By a vote of 54–29, southern and border state Democrats supported the bill's assignment to the Labor Committee.[30] Believing that the legislation would pass if it reached the House floor, Blair continued to contact outside sources to maintain public pressure. He wrote to former president Hayes: "Really it is a great & hopeful opportunity—We *must* succeed now. Please help now with everybody in every way right off."[31]

Developments outside Washington sidetracked this golden opportunity to report the education bill. A bitter confrontation between the increasingly powerful Knights of Labor and part of Jay Gould's railroad empire spurred demands by businessmen and middle-class professionals for federal legislation that would provide a mechanism for arbitrating labor disputes. The conservative Democratic leadership in the House opposed this initiative. Apparently recognizing that they could not halt all the legislation that they opposed, Speaker Carlisle and his allies reached an unacknowledged compromise with the Labor Committee that the arbitration bill would be passed if the education proposal was not reported out of committee.[32] An attempt to introduce the education bill through a committee minority report failed when the committee chairman refused to include it in a May 17 omnibus package of committee actions.[33] Thus, for the second consecutive Congress, the House leadership seemed to have successfully thwarted attempts to introduce and pass the education bill.

Blair refused to despair, continuing his efforts to form alliances and arouse public opinion. He convinced the Women's Christian Temperance Union to supply clerks and cash for a direct mail campaign that would include "eight thousand petitions . . . printed & circulated, five thousand copies of the bill, circulars &c & thousands upon thousands of letters written."[34] The Knights of Labor endorsed the Blair bill and tried to intervene on its behalf with members of Congress.[35] But, for Republicans, the most powerful evidence of support came in the fall elections of 1886. Republican congressional candidates in the Upper South used the Blair bill as their major appeal to voters and gained ten seats in the balloting. As a result, a January 1887 party caucus made the legislation a party measure and required Republican House members to support it.[36] Suffering from these political reverses, southern Democrats also resolved to pass the legislation to remove the issue from future elections.

All this boded well for the short session of Congress that met after the 1886 elections. Under increasing pressure, the Labor Committee agreed to report a substitute education bill to the floor. This was fine with Blair and his allies because they could amend it to their satisfaction once debate started. Determined to lower taxes and reduce social programs, the Democratic leadership fought the substitute bill by using every device at its command to prevent consideration. Contrived filibusters twice prevented introduction of the bill. These tactics could not be used indefinitely, and finally Speaker Carlisle was forced to the extremity of bringing the work of the House to a complete standstill. He refused to recognize anyone whom he thought might introduce the proposal. Since a large majority of congressmen supported the bill, the regular business of the House could not be transacted. Finally, the Rules Committee, under direct control of the leadership, refused to allow any legislation to be introduced.[37]

Even if the bill had passed, it probably would not have become law. Earlier that year, President Cleveland had vetoed a somewhat similar spending bill in the name of government economy and probably would have vetoed the vastly more expensive education bill.[38]

The events of the lame-duck session spurred a continuing debate about the Blair bill. Both proponents and opponents perceived that the battle was reaching its climax and that a major effort had to be made to influence public opinion and members of Congress. Opponents of the bill who had not publicly voiced their objections realized that they could no longer ignore the issue and took to the offensive. Following Blair's example, the journalist Edward Clark sent materials to newspapers and congressmen sharply criticizing the measure. Although Clark had long attacked the bill, he adopted a new laissez-faire philosophy, maintaining that the federal government should not fund services that individuals or communities could provide themselves.[39] This argument persuaded former backers of the education bill, such as General S. C. Armstrong of the Hampton Institute and the *New York Times*, that federal aid would be detrimental to the very people it was supposed to help. For many northern Republicans who had used this same reasoning to limit government regulation of business, Clark's appeal had particular force.

Facing opponents who had been energized by the debates of early 1887, Blair continued his crusade with increased vigor. Immigrants to northern cities were among those least impressed by his reasoning. Up to this point, Blair had believed that educating Americans about the objectives of his bill would build public support for moral reform that political leaders would be forced to follow. He now realized that certain groups could not be persuaded by his statistics and that politicians dependent on these voters often ignored national public opinion.

Ross B. Paulson's insightful study of the women's suffrage and prohibition movements suggests that, in the 1880s, this same realization spread throughout the reform community. Reform advocates could not adjust to the presence of immigrants and other changes brought by industrialization, eventually deciding that the exclusion of these new Americans from the electorate was preferable to the defeat of reform initiatives.[40] Blair's participation in this reactionary movement included a bill to promote Sunday as a day of worship, a measure to require English literacy for citizenship, and a proposed constitutional amendment to prohibit the use of public funds in parochial schools.[41] Unlike most of his previous proposals, which showed a basic trust in people and a desire to promote individual growth, this new legislation imposed restraints on individual activities. Although Blair had initially viewed prohibition as a public health measure to free people from a type of bondage, his efforts to legislate it increasingly reflected this new attitude.

By proposing a constitutional amendment to prohibit the use of public funds in Catholic institutions, Blair singled out the Catholic Church for particular attention. Ever since his political beginnings in the 1850s, he had harbored strong suspicions of Catholic motives. Although the New Hampshire constitution prohibited Catholics from holding state elective offices, they remained politically active. When the state's rapidly expanding French-speaking population supported Republicans, Blair accepted them as a legitimate part of the political system despite their Catholicism. But, as Catholic political leaders with strong support from their constituents expressed opposition to prohibition, and as some lay and clerical church spokesmen opposed the education bill, his public attitude changed dramatically. The first manifestations of his new attitude came during the 1886 congressional sessions. At that time, Blair appealed to Catholic leaders to publicly support the movement to have the education bill reported to the House floor.[42] When they declined to make public statements, he attacked the church in a published article.[43]

When Blair reintroduced his education bill in the Fiftieth Congress amid growing opposition, he lashed out at Catholics again. On February 15, 1888, he attacked the Jesuits as leading opponents of the measure and accused the *Washington Post* and the *New York Evening Post* of being "organs of Jesuitism." He charged: "I tell you, sir, that upon this floor . . . a Senator showed me, and I read with my own eyes, the original letter of a Jesuit priest, in which he begged a member of Congress to oppose this bill, and to kill it, saying that they had organized all over the country for its destruction, that they succeeded in the Committee of the House, and they would destroy the bill inevitably, and if they had only known it early enough they could have prevented its passage through the Senate." He continued: "They have begun in season this time, but they will not destroy this bill."[44] Although Blair assured his fellow senators that he was not speaking against the entire Catholic Church, his argument was unconvincing. At this point, his excesses in defense of the education bill began to cast him out of the mainstream of American politics.

Catholic leaders' responses to Blair's outburst were relatively restrained. The institutional leadership made no official statement, depending on individual Catholics to refute his charges. The most direct reply came in an article published a month after Blair's Senate speech by John G. Shea, who had attended the Senate session. The article dealt with the question of the constitutionality of the bill. Deeply angered, Shea attacked the education bill as "madness," "un-American," and "sectarian."[45] He went on to characterize Blair as a "mouthpiece" for militant Protestants who were trying to suppress Catholic parochial education.[46] A more balanced article appeared in the *Catholic World* five months later. The author, August D. Small, never mentioned Blair or the education bill. Instead, he called for a universal education system in which local government funds would support specific religious traditions. Small's major argument was that the absence of religious instruction subtracted from the completeness of a young person's education.[47] Despite this limited Catholic response, Blair's vitriolic remarks presaged more active opposition from Catholic spokesmen in the future.

Leading college and university presidents, including F. A. P. Barnard of Columbia, were outspoken critics of Blair's plan.[48] An incredulous Blair asked a supportive southern educational leader: "How can colleges expect to flourish unless there be common schools from which to fuel them?"[49] Even in the South, there were increasing signs of open revolt. In Arkansas, Texas, and Kentucky, Democratic conventions and legislatures opposed the Blair bill.[50] Blair was further embarrassed when a New Hampshire legislative committee controlled by his fellow Republicans refused to report a resolution in favor of the education bill.[51] As always, Carlisle and the Democratic leadership in the House of Representatives presented the most significant roadblock. The fact that 1888 was a presidential election year strengthened the resolve of Cleveland and other party leaders to make tariff reform their chief issue and to oppose any measure requiring increased federal expenditures.

Despite the growing opposition, Blair reintroduced the education bill into the Fiftieth Congress and prepared to push for passage as soon as possible. Less than two weeks into the session, the Education and Labor Committee unanimously reported the same bill that the Senate had passed in 1886.[52] On January 17, 1888, Blair was finally able to open debate on the measure. Impressed by the growing volume of northern criticism, he spent a great deal of time discussing the education problems of urban and rural areas in the northeastern states and how federal funding could be used there.[53] He then launched into an unexpectedly analytic description of the relation between education and economic well-being. In almost Marxist terms, he contrasted the industrial North with the agricultural South. He went on to point out that the absence of education depressed southern wages—and therefore all wages—and prevented the South from becoming an economically potent consumer market for northern products.[54] Ironically, his realistic depiction of the economic situation offended some of his fellow Republicans, resulting in little additional support.

In succeeding months, Blair tried few new strategies to secure Senate passage of his bill. Generally, the debate was listless, with most participants repeating sentiments expressed at some time during the previous four years. Despite the lack of enthusiasm displayed by the senators, the bill's opponents made every effort to delay a vote. Senator Preston B. Plumb of Kansas revived the idea of distributing funds on the basis of states' populations rather than illiteracy rates. However, his attempt to defeat the measure by weakening southern support was decisively voted down 50–24. Senator James E. Berry of Arkansas then proposed that states be freed from the requirement of making reports to the federal government. His proposal was rejected by the Republican majority and a few Democrats in a 45–26 vote. At this point, Blair attacked Jesuits as leading opponents of the education bill and secured a 39–29-vote victory.[55] Southern and border state Democrats voted 16–12 in favor of the bill. The political significance of the legislation can be gauged by the fact that all senators felt compelled to commit themselves. Those who did not vote announced their position by pairing their intended vote with that of another absent senator of the opposite point of view. Even the reluctant John Sherman, making another run for the Republican presidential nomination, was paired in favor of the Blair bill.[56]

As had been true during the previous two sessions, the major challenge was to get the education bill reported to the House floor. Once again, the Republican caucus adopted the Blair plan as a party measure, ensuring implacable Democratic leadership opposition. By stacking the Education Committee with members hostile to the bill, the House Democratic leadership effectively blocked the bill.[57] The Republican minority on the committee could not find enough sympathetic Democrats to form a quorum to demand action.[58] In addition, the House Rules Committee blocked every attempt by the bill's backers to force a debate and vote. The final attempt to bring the bill to the floor nearly resulted in a riot when the Rules Committee chair ruled the motion out of order.[59] While Blair was upset by this turn of events, forces outside Congress seemed to promise a break in the deadlock.

The presidential campaign of 1888 provided Blair with an opportunity to go directly to the people to secure backing for the education bill. The Republican national convention nominated Benjamin Harrison, a supporter of the Blair bill, for president. In a further attempt to win southern votes, the party endorsed federal aid to public education in its platform.[60] In succeeding months, Blair campaigned throughout the Upper South for Harrison and the education bill. The violent confrontation organized by conservative Democrats at his Staunton, Virginia, speech attests to his effectiveness.[61] The sweeping Republican victory in the fall of 1888 seemed to vindicate Blair's hard work. Not only was Harrison elected, but the Republicans also gained control of both houses of Congress. Carlisle and his supporters were no longer in a position to block federal aid to education legislation. During the lame-duck session that followed, Blair largely ignored congressional debates and worked to ensure the support of the new president. He sent Harrison correspondence from southern Republicans and lobbied him directly at the traditional New Year's Day reception at the White House.[62]

Determined to educate the public about key reform issues, Blair agreed to perform a task that was unusual for a major political figure of that time. He accepted an invitation to write a personal column on political matters for the *New York Mail and Express*. It is not clear from surviving manuscripts whether he received compensation for his articles, but it seems probable that his primary motivation was to use this avenue to influence public opinion. The extant columns—not all issues of the newspaper have been preserved—are typical Blair productions and leave no doubt that he wrote his own material. Beginning in February 1889, he produced more than fifty articles over twenty months.[63] Most of his essays dealt with topics under consideration in the Senate, but several of them were light and telling satires on the peculiar political customs of Americans. He showed a real ability, also reflected in congressional debate, to poke fun at himself and his Senate colleagues.[64] When one considers all the other responsibilities that he had at this time, his willingness to turn out consistently high-quality columns attests to both his ability and his commitment to keep the public informed.

Despite these new demands on his time, Blair never lost sight of the legislative opportunities offered by the Republican victories of 1888. Throughout 1889, he continued to pressure Harrison to openly announce his support of the education bill before Congress met.[65] In all his speaking engagements, he sought to keep federal aid to education before the public. In July 1889, for example, he was a major speaker at the national convention of the American Institute of Instruction.[66] The Democratic *Manchester Union* praised his analysis of the education bill as "entitled to respectful and thoughtful consideration."[67] However, one member of the audience voiced a criticism increasingly heard about Blair's speeches on education when she observed: "Did not like it because it was so filled with statistics."[68] Blair continued his attacks on the Jesuits in a *Mail and Express* article that appeared soon after the new Congress convened.[69]

In the fall of 1889, Blair campaigned in Virginia for William Mahone and the Readjusters.[70] Mahone had been a friend of the Blair bill on the Senate Education and Labor Committee, and Blair had made many political speeches in the South before. What had changed was the political atmosphere in which his addresses took place. With the Republican Party now controlling Congress, some partisans viewed the coming session as an excellent opportunity to break the Democrats' hold on the South. Both the tariff bill and the education bill had proved to be popular issues, but Democratic machines using a combination of intimidation and fraud had successfully prevented Republican victories. Frustrated Republicans decided that the only way their party could succeed in the South was to use the power of the federal government to ensure that blacks could vote and that their votes were counted accurately.

Blair's New Hampshire colleague William E. Chandler led the movement to uphold black voting rights. As early as 1887, he had introduced a bill requiring national supervision of elections in selected southern states.[71] Long before Congress met in 1889, he and Congressman Henry C. Lodge of Massachusetts indicated that they would reintroduce this legislation.[72] Harrison also voiced his support for policing southern elections.[73] According to the historian Thomas A. Upchurch, most Republicans were willing to sacrifice other legislation, including the education bill, to pass this election bill.[74]

Southern Democrats were outraged by Republicans' proposed oversight of their region's election practices. Before Congress convened, a group of southern political leaders began to research and write a state-by-state analysis of Reconstruction. The correspondence of one of the authors reveals a purely political motive aimed at defeating the Chandler and Lodge bills.[75] At the same time, race relations in the South were becoming more violent. Brutal lynchings increased the outrage of northern Republicans and the defensiveness of southern Democrats. The most basic condition necessary for the continued cohesiveness of the Blair bill coalition—relative peace and trust—was disappearing. Not all this was obvious as Congress opened. The election bill was scheduled to be debated after the vote on the education bill, but Blair quickly detected the changed atmosphere when he sought votes for his measure.

Emerging economic issues also made the education bill a lesser priority for most congressmen and their constituents. Both parties now perceived the tariff question as the major question dividing them, and the Democrats became increasingly unwilling to jeopardize tariff reform by voting for any bill that would increase federal spending. In addition, southern and midwestern farmers were demanding relief from economic pressures. Many of their representatives embraced the expanded silver coinage issue as a solution to the farmers' problems and placed this item at the top of their legislative agenda. Finally, despite any clear evidence that the two parties were becoming more disciplined during this period, there was growing aversion in Congress to bipartisan measures like the education bill.[76] All these forces provided opponents of the Blair education bill with opportunities to persuade supporters to reconsider their position.

Blair's opening remarks on February 5, 1890, consisted of a long list of endorsements from education organizations, black groups, and party platforms.[77] He was careful to include past statements by Harrison indicating the president's willingness to support the legislation.

Blair made no effort to explain the provisions of the essentially unchanged bill. The next day he reintroduced much of the statistical information he had previously used to demonstrate the need for federal aid to southern schools.[78] He expected that this perfunctory performance would be followed by quick passage of the measure. Much to his surprise, he learned that most of his colleagues planned to vote against the bill.[79] In a panic, he took two immediate steps to reverse the votes of his increasingly skeptical Republican colleagues. In a February 10, 1890, article in the *Mail and Express*, he warned his fellow Republicans that black voters would desert the party in the South and the North if the education bill failed.[80] On the same day the article appeared, he wrote to Harrison warning him: "There is a strong & very dangerous effort among Republican Senators including some who have hitherto given their support to the measure to secure its defeat."[81]

When Republican senators failed to recommit to his education plan, Blair pressed even harder. Beginning on February 10, he assumed the role of a one-man filibuster on many afternoons over the next six weeks. Once again, he sought to demonstrate the extent of illiteracy and how federal aid could be used to solve what had become a national problem.[82] To persuade southern senators to remain in the coalition, he presented evidence of the tremendous support that the bill enjoyed in their region.[83] He also requested a personal interview with Harrison to discuss the fate of the education bill but was rebuffed.[84]

Blair now began to lobby all day and well into the evening. These personal appeals gradually bore fruit as individual senators agreed to reconsider their positions.[85] Blair also continued his efforts to build a groundswell of public pressure for the bill's passage. Revealing his siege mentality in a *Mail and Express* column, he attacked Catholicism while denying opposition to any particular religious denomination: "The public school system is the republic and creates a free citizenship. The other gives a religious training primarily, and inculcates the idea of church authority as that which must guide the individual whenever the church asserts it, and it is for the church to decide, not the individual, when its jurisdiction attaches as the guide for action."[86]

Between February 17 and February 20, 1890, Blair spoke almost continuously—both to educate the public and to prevent defeat of the measure. Increasingly, he focused on the role of the South's "old aristocracy" in opposing the bill. Although he presented numerous letters and documents supporting his plan, his speeches shed little new light on the subject.[87] His talks became so predictable "that when Mr. Blair began his speech there was a general exodus of senators on both sides of the chambers, and of the eighty-two senators, only five remained while Blair was talking."[88] The press gallery also vacated. Convinced that publicity was essential to the success of his campaign, Blair lashed out: "I do not suppose that will get into any newspapers in this country. I should be surprised if it did. I have not noticed in the press of this country the report of a single fact that has been put in here during the three or four days that I have laid this most startling matter before the Senate. One would think that the press of this country was under bonds to keep silent or to spread falsehood."[89] Believing that there was a newspaper conspiracy against the education bill, Blair proposed that 500,000 extra copies of the *Congressional Record* be printed and delivered to subscribers so that the information could reach the public.[90] Still, he continued to prepare long speeches "with a pile of manuscripts and papers on his desk about eighteen inches high."[91]

Although Blair succeeded in preventing the immediate defeat of the education bill, his performance was becoming the object of ridicule. Both friends and foes increasingly viewed his reform program as futile. When he complained that none of the newspapers would report the content of his speeches, one editor informed him that the public was not interested in "last year's birds' nests."[92] With his education bill obviously in trouble and the rest of his reform program standing little chance of immediate enactment, Blair seemed to be an impractical Don Quixote. Even Republican newspapers in New Hampshire joined the chorus, spreading stories of how the Senate Republican leadership scheduled its meetings during Blair's speeches.[93]

The fact that Blair had tried to shape many of his reform proposals to take into account the political realities of the 1880s made the newspaper indictments of him particularly ironic. Just as the positive image of him as a reformer gave him political power, the reverse perception weakened the position of both him and his proposals. Several members of the original coalition continued to support his education plan, attacking the opposition's claims that the return of economic prosperity in the South rendered the measure unnecessary. Virginia Democratic senator John S. Barbour declared that the southern economy was not improving and that wealth was concentrated in the hands of a few individuals. Republican senator Anthony Higgins of Delaware reported that only three areas—Florida, Texas, and the Appalachian highlands—were experiencing economic growth. Characterizing the remainder of the southern region as underdeveloped, he pointed out that agricultural and rural areas most needed to strengthen their public schools but had the fewest resources available to them.[94] While opponents of the Blair bill could not refute these arguments, they remained unpersuaded.

Growing weary of his tactics, the Senate forced Blair to accept a vote on the education bill on March 20, 1890. Despite two last-minute pleas from Blair, Harrison remained silent, allowing Republicans to argue that the bill was not a party measure. The day before the crucial ballot, Blair thought he had won enough senatorial support to achieve a one-vote victory. To his surprise, the bill was defeated. He explained the final result: "The vote of both Senators from Ohio had been confidently relied upon up to two hours of the close of the debate, and that of Mr. Sherman hoped for until he gave it against the bill. Which proved to be correct in every particular, with the exception of Ohio, which could have made the Senate a tie—34 votes for and 34 votes against the bill—which would have then as I believe have passed with the casting vote of the Vice-President."[95] Blair was extremely bitter about this turn of events, blaming "Jesuitical opposition" and the "Southern unreconstructed aristocracy" for the measure's defeat. The vote was recorded as 37–31, with Blair voting against the bill so that he could move for reconsideration. For the first time, a majority of southern and border state Democrats voted against the bill, and 40 percent of the Republicans voted against the bill.[96]

In desperation, Blair and his allies turned to the Republican-controlled House to revive the legislation. Several measures were submitted to the House Education Committee for consideration. A bill sponsored by the North Carolina black Republican Henry P. Cheatham and closely resembling Blair's proposal was the only one reported. The Republican leadership saw little reason to pursue the issue after the adverse Senate vote despite a second endorsement of the bill by Blair's Senate committee. At the same time, the explosive debate on the southern elections bill made maintenance of the old northern Republican and southern Democrat coalition virtually impossible. Early in 1891, Cheatham moved to have his bill made a special order of business and failed.[97] Blair recognized, as did virtually everyone else, that the legislation was politically dead for that session and probably for all time.

Blair and his supporters turned their wrath on the Republican Party. Black leaders, in particular, were upset by what they perceived to be Sherman's treason. Having loyally backed the Ohio senator for president every four years, they now viewed him as personally sabotaging their hopes for a better education system. Sherman's argument that improvements in the southern economy would provide adequate revenue for improving public education was dismissed as a political evasion.[98] What Blair and the black leadership did not want to admit was that the political situation making the education bill a model compromise proposal from 1881 to 1888 had disappeared. The relative racial calm of the 1880s was about to be replaced by a wave of racial hatred that would sweep through the South during the 1890s. In addition, a variety of partisan and economic issues were weakening the tradition of reform that had guided Republican initiatives through Reconstruction.

Blair never fully accepted the defeat of the education bill. In a speech delivered two years later, he asserted: "The defeat of the education bill was not only a calamity; it was a crime—a crime against humanity."[99] Although he continued his other reform work, he exhibited little of his usual enthusiasm. Quite often when discussing an unrelated topic, he returned to the education bill. The following excerpt from a *Mail and Express* article is typical: "Mr. Hale also wants to build a $349,000,000 navy. As much more is wanted for the army for coast defense and various new-fangled ways to kill folks. I wish we were not too poor to squeeze out ten millions a year to educate the children who cannot go to school at all, and who are growing up to be bad citizens and to slaughter themselves in future wars just because they will be too ignorant to know any better. But we are too poor for that."[100] In addition to being intellectually outraged by Congress's refusal to invest in public education to improve American society, Blair felt deep personal disappointment. This was not simply the end of a piece of legislation. The education bill was Blair's final effort to ensure that others would have access to educational opportunities that had not been available to him. He believed strongly in the other reforms that he supported, but he had lived this one. When the education bill failed, something of great importance to Blair was removed from his life.

*Chapter 8*

# General Reformer

Although the education bill was his major reform effort, Blair supported numerous social improvement and environmental programs. His reputation for leading reform movements prompted many activists to enlist his support. Some of these movements contributed to the impression that he was a visionary crackpot. For example, he reportedly sponsored legislation to melt the polar ice cap as a project to divert the Gulf Stream.[1]

Blair can best be described as a pragmatic reformer. Throughout his twelve years in the Senate, he sought ways to bring peace between capital and labor, improve the lot of southern blacks, end the abuse of alcohol, and provide women with greater rights. Because his views were shaped by the world preceding the Civil War, his rhetoric and solutions often did not correspond to current social and economic realities. Still, he was willing to work for changes that he thought would improve American life and to give the disadvantaged a fair hearing.

Perhaps the most successful of Blair's campaigns, from his perspective, was his effort to secure greater recognition of the rights of American workers. He accepted the Republican doctrine of the 1850s that there was no inherent conflict between capital and labor. At the same time, he recognized that the quality of life of American workers seemed to be declining as the United States became more industrialized. Unwilling to blame the economic system, he sought ways to restore harmony to the American workplace. Not unexpectedly, he concluded that most problems could be solved by educating laborers, discouraging alcohol use, and reducing race and gender disparities in pay and working conditions. While many contemporary and later observers dismissed these solutions as treating symptoms rather than problems, many labor union leaders in the Gilded Age regarded Blair as a special friend. He lent the prestige of the federal government to their efforts to reach the public, often using the same techniques that he did with the education bill.

A Senate resolution passed on August 7, 1882, authorized Blair, as chairman of the Senate Education and Labor Committee, to conduct a comprehensive investigation into the growing labor unrest in the United States. As already noted, these hearings educated Blair about southern Appalachia and its political and economic leaders while also providing insights into the state of the industrial economy. The Senate resolution called for an Education and Labor Committee study of relations between labor and capital, wage and hour provisions, workers' living conditions, and causes of strikes. This resolution also authorized the committee to report any legislation necessary to promote labor peace. Probably the most important item from Blair's perspective was the part of the resolution that allowed the committee to break up into subcommittees to take testimony anywhere in the country.[2]

Because Congress was in session during the fall of 1882 and the winter and spring of 1883, the hearings got off to a slow start. Growing criticism of the committee's lack of activity forced Blair to schedule four days of hearings in Washington in February 1883.[3] A telegraphers' strike against Jay Gould's Western Union Company changed his original plan to hold committee meetings in August 1883. Working with Samuel Gompers and other union leaders, he arranged to spend most of August and September in New York City interviewing the principals in this dispute.[4] In October, he and other members of the committee took testimony in Manchester, New Hampshire, and Boston. After these sessions, they visited factory and housing sites in Massachusetts, Connecticut, and Rhode Island. In November, the investigation concluded with testimonies in Birmingham and Opelika, Alabama, and Atlanta, Columbus, and Augusta, Georgia. The Senate Education and Labor Committee secured more than four thousand pages of testimony on a wide variety of subjects, including materials that were not part of its original charge. In a remarkable display of stamina, Blair was present at every session and took an active role at all times.

The February 1883 meetings in Washington reflected Blair's lack of preparation and the labor movement's low expectations of the potential of the hearings. Hobart D. Layton, grand secretary of the Knights of Labor, appeared as the major witness. The Knights leader, Terence Powderly, declined an invitation to participate, apparently viewing the hearings as insignificant. Layton emphasized his organization's opposition to strikes.[5] He attacked management practices, such as company towns, child labor, blacklisting, and "pluck me" company stores. After affirming the conservative nature of his organization, he concluded: "I find that the mere idea of organization on the part of the laboring men is repugnant to the manufacturers and employers as a class."[6] When questioned by Blair, he agreed that most workers had an inadequate education and were not prepared for alternative employment. Blair used similar tactics to extract information related to his reform or political concerns in other contexts.

Political problems sometimes arose from the unstructured testimony. Remarks by Frank K. Foster of Cambridge, Massachusetts, a spokesman for the Trades and Labor Union of Boston and other organizations, provides a particularly graphic example. In the midst of otherwise undistinguished testimony, Foster referred to French Canadian workers in New England as the "Chinese of the East."[7] For Blair, Foster's assertion represented a political crisis. Many French residents of Canada had been working in New Hampshire mills since the Civil War. During the 1870s, this transient population began to settle in the United States and to seek citizenship. These new voters represented a group that could be the balance of power in a closely contested state like New Hampshire. Fortunately for the Republicans and Blair, there was considerable hostility between New Hampshire's largely Democratic Irish population and the French-speaking immigrants. Thus, the Republicans often fared quite well among French voters despite the general anti-Catholic tone of Republican rhetoric. Nonetheless, for Republicans like Blair with statewide political ambitions, Foster's insult had to be countered by positive testimony about French Canadian workers.

Before the hearings resumed in August 1883, a change in Blair's personal life gave added meaning to his exploration of the impact of industrialization. Although Plymouth served as his official residence, his connection with this town had grown increasingly tenuous over the course of his congressional career. Unable to rebuild his house after the fire, and having to sell much of his village land to settle debts, Blair had no roots there. He had been forced to end his legal partnership and now recognized that the contacts he had made in Concord and Washington offered him far greater opportunities than he could find in Plymouth. He also had arranged for young Henry to attend Phillips Exeter Academy in the southern part of the state.[8] Prompted by these factors and political considerations, Blair and his wife changed their official address to Manchester—the state's largest and most industrialized city. Because Eliza was still too weak to run a house alone and Blair could not afford a full-time maid, they resided in a hotel. Living in Manchester exposed Blair to a wide range of urban and labor problems in a population that was 20 percent French.

Blair's education in the new urban and industrial realities continued when the hearings resumed in New York City on August 6, 1883. For two days, Blair along with Florida senator Wilkinson Call, Alabama senator James L. Pugh, and Senator James Z. George of Mississippi toured sites throughout the city. They inspected tenement apartments and talked with workers' families, toured a cigar factory and interviewed workers on an informal basis, and stopped briefly in a black ghetto to examine how living conditions compared with those in the South.[9] These firsthand accounts of adverse social and economic conditions, along with the unresolved issues emanating from the telegraphers strike, underscored the importance of the hearings. The combined efforts of Samuel Gompers and Blair ensured a steady supply of important witnesses. Gompers and Adolph Strasser of the Cigarmakers International Union of America spoke for labor, Henry George explained his reform ideas, and Jay Gould defended his industrial and financial policies.

At the time of the hearings, Gompers chaired the Federation of Organized Trades and Labor Unions, but he had not yet achieved national prominence. Despite his relative obscurity, his testimony proved to be quite impressive to the committee. He was well organized, and his answers appeared to be logical and comprehensive. He called for a national eight-hour workday law, weekly payment of wages, national charters for labor unions, and a national bureau of labor statistics.[10] Although an English immigrant himself, Gompers opposed the active importation of workers under contract and called for the permanent exclusion of the Chinese workers.[11]

Strasser reinforced Gompers's testimony by calling for federal regulation of child and female labor and for an end to Chinese and convict laborers as competitors in the job market.[12] Both men asserted the right of laborers to strike, crediting unions with the organization of peaceful strikes and the elimination of wildcat walkouts. Eager to dispel public concerns that unions might endorse radical ideologies like socialism or communism, Strasser explained: "We have no ultimate ends. We are going on from day to day. We are fighting only for immediate objects—objects that can be realized in a few years."[13] This philosophy, which continued to guide the renamed American Federation of Labor (AFL), was a point of view that Blair could heartily endorse. Never an unquestioning supporter of American industry, Blair sought to alleviate some of the problems that American workers faced without harming the existing economic system.

The testimony of Henry George was significantly more theoretical than that of the two trade union leaders. He immediately sought to downgrade the importance of American unions, claiming that they were too weak to bring about needed changes in the national economy. He maintained that monopolies—particularly those controlling valuable land—dominated the relation between labor and capital. Claiming that businesses had a natural tendency toward monopoly, he insisted that government action was the only antidote. To achieve needed changes in the economy, he proposed federal government nationalization of the telegraph and other basic services, the elimination of tariffs, and an added value assessment on land.[14] He also asserted that the basic problem in the industrial system was not overproduction but underconsumption caused by low wages. George's testimony, while of considerable interest to Blair, seemed to have little direct impact on the New Hampshire senator's thinking. Blair saw little reason to challenge the capitalist system that most Americans thought was transforming the United States into an urban and industrial giant.

Gould's comments at the hearing stood in stark contrast to George's economic philosophy. Displaying a total lack of concern for the social consequences of his actions, Gould reminisced: "Railroads had then got to be sort of a hobby with me—I didn't care about the money I made, I took the road more as a plaything to see what I could do with it."[15] Despite his reputation as a robber baron, Gould proved to be a candid and almost appealing figure. At first, he was so diffident that Blair had to request that he speak louder. In a rather lengthy explanation of his start in business, he related his almost comic ineptitude as a young farmhand and the tremendous relief he felt when his father allowed him to seek his own fortune. However, the more human side of this feared and hated business leader quickly disappeared when he began to analyze the American economic system. Maintaining that both prices and wages were governed by the law of supply and demand, he blamed a surplus of labor for low wages and claimed that wages could not be raised under these conditions.[16]

Throughout his remarks, Gould attacked the committee's mandate, insisting that the government should not interfere with natural economic forces or become involved in the relation between capital and labor.[17] While expressing willingness to sell the Western Union Company to the government, as Henry George had suggested, he predicted that patronage appointments of political workers would quickly undermine service efficiency. He went on to suggest that the post office would be much improved if it were to become a private corporation.[18] From his perspective, the most impractical program of all was one like unemployment insurance, which removed basic economic motivations from the workers.[19] Although Gould probably won no converts to his point of view, the committee did not criticize his position.

As committee chairman, Blair used his power to ensure that witnesses provided the information needed to fulfill the committee's mandate and to gather evidence on items of interest to him. When hearing testimony on the conditions faced by female workers, he used this opportunity to raise questions about women's rights in other areas. He considerably elevated women's stature by calling them to testify before a Senate committee. Women had not testified on any subject before the early 1870s, and no female workers had ever made an appearance of this type.[20] Most of those testifying were middle-class and professional, and their concerns often had to do with discrimination based on gender. Female clerks seeking federal government employment reported forming a union—the Women's National Industrial League—to protest their exclusion from certain job levels.[21] Referring to another common problem, Mrs. M. W. Farrar, the superintendent of the Working Women's Protective Association, decried the lack of equal pay for the same work.[22]

Fully aware that they were challenging traditional roles and mores, most of the women appearing before the committee took a militant position about what was necessary to achieve desired changes. Helen Potter, a public health professional from New York, probably spoke for all of them when she declared: "I have not seen the man who has the right to command me and therefore I do not obey."[23] Several witnesses were careful to point out that most women worked out of financial necessity and often did not have the luxury of a male provider. All agreed that improved educational opportunities and women's suffrage offered the most promise for addressing women's economic and social needs.[24] They maintained that educational opportunities, particularly vocational training, would help women build the skills necessary to enter the job market. Giving women the right to vote would help lessen or end the discrimination against women. The exact impact of this testimony on Blair is difficult to assess. From this point forward, he pushed hard for legislation to improve the lot of American women. However, his support for women's suffrage gave him the political advantage of increased support for prohibition.

The exhaustive New York hearings were followed by much shorter sessions in New England. Although many millworkers appeared at these hearings, they introduced little new information. The most telling observation came from James Nutting, a worker at the Manchester Mills: "I think if you will find a skilled operative, you will find a person who has no complaint to make. If you find a poor mechanic or poor operative, you will have an element for complaint."[25] Further testimonies revealed considerable differences in the wages of skilled and unskilled workers, along with claims that the latter lacked any pride or interest in their work. Wage disparities continued to grow as industrial mass production methods became more sophisticated, but neither union leaders nor Blair addressed this problem.

By holding three days of testimony in Manchester, Blair was able to pay off some political debts. These meetings in his recently adopted home city also provided him with an opportunity to assuage previous criticisms of French Canadian workers. Blair allowed their spokesman, Joseph Augustus Chevalier, a Catholic clergyman, to speak at length about the contributions made by the French. Chevalier described how the community had preserved its cultural heritage, contending that these practices had made the French more reliable and productive workers than other immigrant groups.[26] At Chevalier's request, several leading Republican businessmen, including two former governors of New Hampshire, appeared before the committee to confirm this positive appraisal.

The committee's hearings in Alabama and Georgia introduced Blair to the white political, business, and educational leadership of the South. Blair found them to be much more sympathetic figures than he expected. He recognized this changed perception in his concluding statement at Augusta: "I shall go back to New England. I can hardly say with any more friendly feeling toward the South than which I brought here, but certainly with an enlarged knowledge and appreciation of your great natural resources, and of the courtesy, the intelligence, and the enterprise of your people, to which I shall at all times and on all occasions be ready to bear testimony."[27] As noted earlier, this very positive experience greatly increased Blair's willingness to work with southern Democrats on the education bill.

Despite the hospitality of his hosts, Blair did not hesitate to investigate problems reported by southern workers. Much of the testimony in Alabama centered on the convict labor system used at the Pratt coal mines near Birmingham. Convicts called to the stand, including a confessed murderer, told of the poor working conditions and physical abuse that they had experienced until quite recently.[28] To counter that dismal picture, John H. Bankhead, the incumbent warden of the state penitentiary system, and other officials described how the abuses had been corrected.[29] The convicts agreed that conditions had improved. They pointed out that a skilled miner could often fill his work quota in a short time and then be paid in cash for his production for the remainder of the day. A number of convict miners claimed to be more financially secure than they had been as free men and farmers. They also cited opportunities for released convicts to work in the mines for full wages, regardless of race.[30]

The convicts, businessmen, and state officials appearing before the committee described the convict labor system as a way in which to transform rural workers into productive members of the new industrial society. While this system may have benefited a few men who became skilled miners, its abuses were numerous and horrifying. The committee identified some of these problems, but members never investigated the full extent of the worker exploitation. Blair, for all his sensitivity to racial and other types of injustice, did not make an issue of system abuses.

The 1883 hearings also provided a forum for blacks to voice their dissatisfaction with employment opportunities and conditions. Concerned about the rights of black Americans his entire adult life, Blair sought and received candid answers to questions that must have embarrassed his white hosts. The testimonies revealed a clear split between black accommodationists and more militant spokesmen. However, it is interesting to note that more than a decade before Booker T. Washington attained national prominence black southern leaders were presenting similar ideas. Former Alabama black congressman James K. Green observed: "But if they will give us schools, we will agree to let them keep counting us out, so that we won't have no more confusion and fuss."[31] A black minister from Columbus, Georgia, voiced similar sentiments: "Our people do not care about social equality; they do not ask for it. All they ask is equal rights before the law."[32] B. R. Wright, a black schoolteacher from Augusta, presented an alternative point of view. Proud of his heritage, Wright claimed to be descended from a Muslim member of the Mandingo nation. He demanded equality of treatment and opportunity, asserting: "I think that the differences between races are simply matters of education, training, surroundings."[33]

The one issue that virtually all blacks and whites agreed on was the need for federal aid for public education in the South. In many cases, their endorsement of the principles of the Blair education bill seemed to come as a spontaneous plea for help rather than as a response to directed questions.[34] Those testifying seemed to share with Blair the idea that education was the key to all reform efforts. Like Blair, they believed that universal education would reduce prejudices, poverty, immoral behavior, and social conflict. Blair came away from this southern trip convinced that the people of the region wanted federal aid for education and that their leaders were sincere in their commitment to this legislation.

Although the hearings greatly increased public knowledge of the issues important to America's industrial workers, women, and blacks, they resulted in little legislation of lasting value. Immediately after the February 1883 sessions in Washington, Blair introduced two pieces of legislation ardently desired by labor leaders. The first bill authorized national labor groups to receive a charter of incorporation from the federal government.[35] This bill would have settled the question of the legal status of unions, but there was little support for the idea, and it was never brought to a vote. Blair's proposal to prohibit the use of convict labor on all federally funded projects also was rejected.[36] While the threat of the federal government withholding funds was a relatively mild one, opponents feared that the bill might weaken the practice of substituting convict for free and organized labor. Blair introduced one measure that did pass. In keeping with his belief that an informed public could find solutions to the problems brought by industrialization, he proposed the establishment of a bureau of labor statistics. He spoke several times at length about the need for information about the condition of labor and eventually served on the House-Senate conference committee that agreed on a final version of the legislation.[37]

Increased labor unrest, culminating in the May 1886 Haymarket Square tragedy in Chicago, revealed the limits of Blair's approach to industrial relations problems. For the first time, a national labor union attempted to organize large groups of workers in New Hampshire. In two major strikes at Concord and Manchester in the spring of 1886, workers demanded the right to be represented by the Knights of Labor.[38] A strike of five thousand laborers at Manchester's Amoskeag mills alerted Blair and other New Hampshire politicians to the significance of this new movement. The Manchester city government responded by providing police protection to strikebreakers.[39] Influenced by his experiences with the labor investigation, Blair took a more enlightened approach. Once again, he introduced a bill to allow national labor unions to incorporate.[40] Then he acted as the Senate floor leader for the labor arbitration bill even though it had been used to defeat the education bill in the House.[41] Connecting local interests with the larger national issue, he also introduced a petition from the Manchester Knights of Labor supporting the arbitration bill.[42] While these efforts were appreciated by labor leaders, Blair proved unable to help organized labor in any material way.

Blair advocated for better working conditions and higher pay without ever questioning the economic system itself. In 1891, he demonstrated his commitment to higher worker compensation by supporting efforts of federal workers to win back pay.[43] However, his December 14, 1892, address to the AFL national convention provides a truer picture of his conservative approach to the rights of labor.[44] Invited by Gompers to discuss the education bill, Blair decided that an analysis of the labor market in the South would best illustrate the tangible benefits of federal aid to education. His speech emphasized class conflict: "The old master class still owned the land and made the laws, and therefore really owned all who labored on the land and were subject to the laws."[45] Although this analysis has gained increased support among modern historians, Blair was simply restating the abolitionist position that slave owners dominated the South despite their small numbers. Instead of proposing class solidarity, confrontation, and the threat or use of violence as counterstrategies, he suggested education. He maintained that an educated southern labor force could demand high wages and that higher wages in the South would lead to better pay for all American workers.[46]

The labor investigation may have laid the groundwork for an additional legislative initiative. In March 1884, Blair was one of four senators who signed a report favoring women's suffrage.[47] As previously noted, he had introduced legislation to expand women's rights while serving as a state legislator in 1866. His support helped advance the women's suffrage movement in New Hampshire. As early as 1873, the radical suffragette Lucy Stone was the featured speaker at the New Hampshire Woman's Suffrage Association state meeting.[48] Within five years, the state legislature passed a bill allowing women to vote in school board elections.[49] These changes undoubtedly influenced Blair, but the testimony that he heard at the labor hearings seemed to increase his resolve to press women's issues.

Blair decided that only when women were able to vote would the substance of his reform program be fully enacted. His first challenge was to persuade Congress to adopt a resolution proposing an amendment to the Constitution. On December 8, 1886, he introduced discussion of the resolution for women's suffrage with an emotional plea for equity. Brushing aside all the opposition arguments as insubstantial, he spoke to what he felt to be the central issue: "But it is impossible to conceive of suffrage as a right dependent at all upon such an irrelevant condition as sex. It is an individual's personal right. It may be withheld by force, but if withheld by reason of sex, it is a moral robbery."[50] Blair requested a delay in the debate because another member of the select committee could not be present to take part in the discussion.

On January 25, 1887, Blair submitted his amended resolution for further consideration. To build public awareness of the need for women's suffrage, he had the suffragette testimony from an 1880 committee investigation read into the *Congressional Record*. After a series of short remarks, including some by Blair, the Senate defeated the resolution by a vote of 34–16.[51] Despite this expected defeat, Blair and his allies felt that they had accomplished a major part of their purpose by introducing the question into serious political debate.

Blair's reform program included a number of legislative initiatives that the historian Gaines M. Foster has grouped under the title *Christian*. Foster identified a cohort of "Christian lobbyists" that pushed a consistent agenda throughout the 1870s and 1880s. Coming from small towns in New England and the Midwest, these reformers were struck by the unsettled nature of American society as it made the transition to urban environments. Having experienced the Civil War as young adults, all viewed the federal government as an appropriate vehicle to achieve broad-based national reforms. They proved willing to sacrifice states' rights and individual rights to reach their goals.[52]

These activists started their crusades well before Blair became a member of Congress. In 1873, pressure from Anthony Comstock and the Christian lobby secured legislation that prohibited the sale, possession for sale, or use of the mails to disseminate materials depicting or advocating obscenity, pornography, birth control, and abortion. This statute was revised in 1876 to prohibit the distribution of these same materials in the District of Columbia and the federal territories where Congress had exclusive jurisdiction. Congress also outlawed polygamy, and this statute was upheld by the Supreme Court.[53] As Foster observed: "The Christian lobbyists no longer felt moral suasion sufficient to ensure the moral citizens necessary to the survival of the republic."[54]

In the late 1880s, Blair's attempt to enact a Sabbath law setting aside Sunday as a day devoted to religious duties marked him as the Christian lobbyists' congressional spokesman. At a Senate hearing, Blair announced that Congress had received approximately twenty-one thousand petitions calling for this reform. He then introduced a bill titled "To secure to the people the enjoyment of the first day of the week, commonly known as the Lord's day, as a day of rest, and to promote its observance as a day of religious worship."[55] Because Congress had direct control over the U.S. territories, the bill banned all Sunday work in these territories as well as plays, games, and amusements. On a national scale, the bill banned Sunday activities such as the collection, handling, and transportation of mail, military and naval parades and drills, and interstate commerce.[56] The Christian lobbyists formed the American Sabbath Union to help generate support for this legislation.[57]

Expecting widespread support for the bill, Blair was unsettled by the principled opposition expressed in a Senate committee hearing. The most persistent critics were members of the Seventh-Day Adventist Church. They maintained that observing the Sabbath was a purely religious exercise and therefore beyond the purview of government regulation. Although the proposed law exempted those observing the Sabbath on another day from penalties, Seventh-Day Adventists continued to protest against it.[58] Religious liberals supported their assertion that the federal government had no authority to regulate Sunday practices. When a Seventh-Day Adventist claimed that the church's followers just wanted to be left alone, Blair replied: "There is a good deal of humbug about the so-called dictates of one's own conscience. If a man is to set up his conscience against the obligation to do what is right, an unintelligent, uninformed conscience of that kind might be allowed to destroy all society."[59] In this and other reform work, Blair viewed the sacrifice of some individual rights as necessary to achieve a greater community good.

Despite Blair's best efforts and the pressure brought by Christian lobbyists, the Sabbath bill never became law. In fact, Blair was unable to bring it to a vote.[60] The activists were able to obtain some restrictions on Sunday activities. They convinced Congress to close the Columbian Exposition on Sundays. President Benjamin Harrison ordered the army to move its inspection from Sunday to Saturday. Postmaster General John Wannamaker ordered his department to reduce the amount of work on Sundays and gave local post offices the option to close on Sundays.[61] Thus, a major reform effort ended with just a few symbolic gestures aimed at appeasing the Christian lobbyists.

Blair's work with the Christian lobbyists was a natural extension of his previous efforts to implement moral reform through legislation. While still a congressman, he introduced a resolution for a constitutional amendment mandating national prohibition. This December 1876 proposal was a compromise that he hoped would be moderate enough to pass Congress and gain approval by the states. It "forbade the manufacture, sale, importation, and transportation of 'distilled alcoholic intoxicating liquors,' not beer or wine, and none of its provisions were to take effect before 1900."[62] Even with all these concessions, Blair was unable to win passage for the resolution in the House or, later, in the Senate.

While keeping New Hampshire antiliquor forces strong, Blair continued to advocate for a prohibition initiative that he deemed politically possible to implement. He actively participated in a nationally focused crusade against the abuse of alcohol.[63] In late 1882 and early January 1883, he attached an amendment to the Pendleton civil service bill that forbade federal employment to habitual drunks.[64] He also received tremendous publicity from a public address delivered in Woodstock, Connecticut, on July 4, 1883. He shared the platform that day with former president Rutherford B. Hayes, who expressed support for federal aid to public education. Blair's oration, "National Evils," included a discussion of intemperance.[65] Reports of his remarks reached a wide audience, and his association with Hayes greatly increased his standing among many Republicans.

On December 5, 1883, Blair introduced a joint resolution for a prohibition amendment to the U.S. Constitution that was later defeated.[66] While ardent prohibitionists ridiculed this proposal for allowing the consumption of cider, beer, and unfortified wine, the resolution offered a specific plan for temperance forces to rally around. Blair continued his educational campaign with the publication of his article "Alcohol in Politics" in the January 1884 issue of the *North American Review*. He outlined his views with considerable clarity: only federal controls would be effective, both the manufacturing and the selling of alcoholic beverages should be prohibited, light alcoholic drinks should be permitted for the moment, and any proposal must be capable of being passed in the current political atmosphere.[67] Even if a constitutional amendment was not immediately passed, he contended: "The continual public discussion of a national measure is a national notice to the maker and dealer to quit."[68]

In 1885, Mary H. Hunt, the superintendent of the education department of the Women's Christian Temperance Union (WCTU), sought congressional support for legislation requiring instruction about the destructive impact of alcoholism in all federal schools. Blair introduced this legislation, maneuvering it through Congress until it became law.[69] Then, determined to broaden public support for a prohibition amendment, he presented the rationale for a gradual approach to national prohibition in an April 1886 Senate speech. Responding to attacks from temperance advocates wanting total and immediate prohibition, he proved that he could be as frank with them as with the opponents of the education bill. He reminded them that they had to create a resolution that would be supported by the voters, members of Congress, and enough state legislators to approve the amendment.[70] While praising local and state campaigns to reduce drinking, he pointed out that these steps could not effectively limit access to alcohol over a long period of time.[71] Through this speech, he hoped to convince prohibition advocates to unite behind one piece of legislation to build public pressure for passage.

In September 1886, Blair served as temporary chairman of the Anti-Saloon Republican convention in Chicago.[72] Later, this organization named him to its national committee. As one of the key speakers at the Chicago convention, he emphasized the political significance of prohibition and argued that the Republican Party was the only practical vehicle for securing this reform.[73] In addition to this major address, Blair spoke at many local meetings. He soon recognized that new communication channels would be needed to reach people who would not attend public gatherings.

Continuing frustration over the failed 1876 resolution led Blair to change his strategy. Following the lead of the National Temperance Society and WCTU, he took a more aggressive approach also favored by the Prohibition Party, the Good Templars, the Sons of Temperance, and numerous citizens' petitions. His new resolution modified the proposed language of the amendment to require total and immediate prohibition. Following the introduction of this resolution in December 1887, the Senate Education and Labor Committee held public hearings where many of Blair's allies testified. Although his resolution was reported out of committee in the House of Representatives in 1890, it never passed either house of Congress.[74] This ended his formal ties to prohibition initiatives, but he continued to lobby for national prohibition for the next three decades.

Blair strongly believed that public information and education would bring necessary reforms without extensive government action. His efforts to sway public opinion by providing as much information as possible forced congressional members to confront issues they wanted to avoid and to vote on legislation they thought politically dangerous. They viewed Blair as not playing by the rules in order to gain publicity for himself rather than for his programs. For example, Kentucky senator James B. Beck attacked Blair personally in the summer of 1882. Exasperated by prohibition amendments that Blair had appended to several pieces of legislation, Beck accused him of gaining a "cheap reputation" for virtue with his temperance activities.[75] Ohio senator and perennial presidential candidate John Sherman deeply resented the fact that Blair's education bill forced him to choose between two major interest groups—blacks and antisouthern northern whites—both of which he needed to realize his presidential ambitions.[76]

In the summer of 1887, Blair began writing a detailed study of the prohibition controversy.[77] In December 1887, he completed a massive 562-page volume entitled *The Temperance Movement; or, The Conflict between Man and Alcohol*. Published in January 1888, and profusely illustrated with portraits of temperance leaders, this book was an impressive demonstration of Blair's research skills. He presented considerable medical and scientific information, descriptions of secular and religious organizations opposed to the abuse of alcohol, and political strategies to be followed in persuading lawmakers to vote for the prohibition amendment. Although he had presented most of the ideas and information in other contexts, the publication of a book was a deliberate strategy on his part. Convinced that the public simply needed access to this information, he made no pretense about presenting an original argument. Fully one-third of the text consisted of direct quotations from specialists in a variety of fields. His success as an author undoubtedly exceeded all his expectations. The first edition of twenty thousand copies sold out in four or five

weeks.[78] Perhaps the most important personal benefit for Blair was the extra money that the book royalties supplied to supplement his inadequate
congressional salary.

The success of Blair's book encouraged prohibition advocates to keep
pressing for this reform. In January 1889, a state constitutional convention
met in New Hampshire to address several controversial issues. Convention participants agreed by a 166–131 vote to place a liquor prohibition
referendum on the ballot.[79] In keeping with Blair's practical approach,
the temperance forces made a major concession to rural public opinion
by specifically excluding cider from the provisions of the amendment.[80]
Because new amendments had to secure a two-thirds majority, no one expected prohibition to be added to the constitution. The Republican gubernatorial candidate in 1888 had been a strong temperance advocate,
winning by only a small majority.

Faced with rapid changes in the state's population and economy, prohibition advocates were protesting the passing of an older way of life.[81]
Prohibition had been a traditional part of New Hampshire politics for
more than four decades. Long before the Republican Party made its appearance, astute New Hampshire politicians had respected the predomi-
nantly rural sentiment on this issue. The rapidly growing urban areas now
threatened this older lifestyle and the reformers who drew their strength
from it. Rural towns were losing population rapidly, with literally thousands of farms on mountain and marginal land being abandoned.[82]

The result of the town meeting vote on the amendment was a shock-
ing defeat for the prohibition forces. Not only did their amendment not
win the necessary majority, but it unexpectedly lost in the total vote. The
antiliquor forces were overwhelmed 30,976–25,786. As expected, the cities were particularly hostile, with 63.3 percent of urban voters opposing
the amendment. The "Irish" wards in Dover and Manchester were ada-
mantly opposed, casting more than 90 percent of their ballots against prohibition. What was particularly disturbing to the prohibition forces was
that they carried only 91 of 225 rural townships, winning only 48.7 percent of the vote in those communities.[83] A close inspection of the returns
indicated that a substantial number of rural Republicans—thought to be
the major supporters of the measure—had voted against prohibition. This
development encouraged many Republicans to suggest a reassessment of
the party's stand on this reform.[84]

The waning support for societal reform created both political and philosophical problems for Blair. Republican leaders no longer had to depend on the popularity of reformers like Blair to win elections. These leaders concluded that the forces of urbanization and industrialization would determine political power in the future. The changing perspectives of Republican leaders and the growing political influence of two railroad corporations threatened Blair's efforts to stay in office. More disturbing to Blair at the time, however, was the fact that, without any interference from politicians, voters had rejected prohibition. A defensive Blair declared, despite the amendment's defeat: "No curse can long survive which has already one-third of the numbers of the people and two-thirds of their moral and intellectual convictions, with the almost total amount of their material interests arrayed against it." He then concluded with a classic reaffirmation of his reform strategy: "Besides this, there has been the great debate. The discussion of a good cause is always victory. . . . Discussion will kill [evil], and discussion will continue while there is wrong to be made right."[85]

This same logic encouraged Blair to continue to push measures to help black Americans. Although the education bill was his major effort in this area, he actively supported initiatives to preserve black voting rights. In 1889, he campaigned for William Mahone in Virginia in an effort to block racist policies proposed by the Democratic opposition.[86] He also agreed to support the Lodge election bill requiring national supervision of elections in southern states despite the fact that its introduction had helped defeat the education bill. In a move that everyone recognized as extremely ironic, he argued against the southern filibuster holding up the Lodge bill. In fact, he called for amending Senate rules in a way that would have prevented his previous conduct.[87] While voicing support for the election bill, Blair could not resist asking: "What is the importance of the vote to an ignorant man?"[88] He expanded on that theme in an 1890 article for the National Education Association. He maintained: "The Southern problem, or the race problem of the South . . . [its] solution depends upon the proper use of the same means which have improved the condition of men everywhere, regardless of race or color. . . . Right education of the physical, mental, and spiritual powers of each individual will perfect society, and nothing else will do it."[89] When the Lodge bill failed to come up for a vote, Blair regretted its failure but viewed this outcome as less important than the defeat of the education bill.

Although Blair viewed voting rights as a secondary issue to public education, he never relaxed his vigilance in this area. He believed that all groups in American society should have access to the political process — especially those people who supported his reform program. Despite his alliance with southern Democrats during the education bill debates, he never forgot their oppression of black Republican voters. In an effort to sustain federal election laws, he had his minority report for the 1878 Wallace Committee investigation of northern urban political corruption placed in the *Congressional Record*. Despite ill health, he rose in the House on September 29, 1893, to protest the reappearance of the states' rights doctrine in the arguments of southern spokesmen. He noted: "I listen to this debate, presenting precisely the same old arguments, and observe that the very substance of all this is said here in favor of the repeal of these election laws is precisely what was said before the war."[90] These remarks not only indicated Blair's consistency on the subject but also demonstrated his stubborn unwillingness to give up the fight for black political rights under increasingly adverse circumstances.

During an 1893 debate on Tennessee's recently passed Dortsch law requiring literacy on the part of voters, Blair challenged the right of any government to restrict suffrage. He maintained: "I am one of those who believe that everyone that God has made of mature mental and physical powers, is a man, and, if he lives under a republican form of government, has a right to vote, regardless of race, color, educational qualifications, or pecuniary qualifications. In other words, it is an inherent right, manhood suffrage."[91] This statement highlights an important difference between the older reform tradition coming out of the Civil War and the newer perspectives of the Progressive movement. Blair's ideas came from the Republican ideology of the Civil War and Reconstruction period. Progressives were more likely to push for changes in the makeup of the electorate than to try to educate voters in the manner that Blair proposed. Later Progressive attempts to use literacy tests and poll taxes to prevent poor, black, and illiterate Americans from voting were alien to Blair and the tradition he represented.

Blair did not confine himself to education and politics when he sought to improve the lives of black Americans. He also spoke out on social issues emerging from the increasingly hostile racial climate in the southern states. In January 1890, he opposed legislation to fund the transport of blacks to Africa.[92] Although Bishop Henry Turner, radical black leaders, and many poor blacks in the South favored this legislation, Blair stressed the need for an American solution to discrimination. Increasingly aware of the physical dangers that blacks in the South faced, he introduced the first federal antilynching legislation in 1894. This resolution called for a federal investigation—another example of Blair's concept of the government's role as educator—and publication of the results.[93] In a letter to Fredrick Douglass, Blair explained: "No Legislation is possible until there is an exposition & authentication of the facts as far as possible. ... If we can get some of the facts officially & impartially stated there will be improvement & perhaps in time remedy."[94]

When southern congressmen successfully prevented consideration of the resolution, Blair began his own investigation.[95] He pointed out that he did not want to sponsor the resolution "after what [he had] been through with the education bill and of other measures which [he had] pressed against general opposition."[96] Despite this hesitation, he introduced the resolution when no other congressman dared to be associated with it. This was to be one of his special contributions to Gilded Age reform—his determination to bring legislation before the public for discussion even if it meant public ridicule.

All these reform activities showed a consistency of commitment and strategy that made Blair stand out among politicians of the Gilded Age. No other leading elected official at this time established such a clear record of support for legislation aimed at improving the quality of life of the least fortunate in the United States. For Blair and many of his contemporaries, the freeing of the slaves justified the antebellum reform tradition. Since the federal government had been the vehicle for ending slavery, he believed that other problems also could be solved at this level. While change was desirable, he and other reformers were basically satisfied with America's political, social, and economic structure. They expected that publicity and education would arouse the public as the abolitionists had, and that voter outrage would force politicians to pass necessary legislation. Even when this process did not seem to be working, Blair retained his faith in the ultimate willingness of the American people to improve society.

## Chapter 9

# Foreign Policy

Like many senators who were elected to office because of their skill in domestic politics, Blair was a novice in the field of foreign policy. He was far more knowledgeable about tariffs, education, and voting rights than about foreign policy issues. The result was that he did not have the guiding principles or specific knowledge to play an important role in the debates on America's external affairs. His ignorance in this area led to his involvement in two of the most embarrassing episodes of his public career. The first was a possible conflict of interest involving a private claim in Peru, and the other came when China rejected him as the U.S. minister to that country. In both instances, a lack of foreign policy sophistication in the executive branch of the U.S. government contributed to his problems. Although these two episodes received national coverage, Blair suffered no real political damage. At this time, neither U.S. government officials nor the general public showed much concern about events beyond the nation's shores.

Despite his limited knowledge of foreign policy, Blair held some strong opinions. Singling out Great Britain as the greatest threat to the United States, he advocated for U.S. economic and military dominance in Latin America and declared that Canada and the United States were destined to become a single nation. He also called for the exclusion of Chinese labor from the United States under most circumstances. Although the roots of these attitudes were often obscure, Blair rarely deviated from them. His expectation that Canada and the United States would join under a single government appears to have been a common expectation of the people who lived in northern New Hampshire—I recall hearing this expressed in the 1950s. Without sensing the contradiction, Blair also called for tariff restrictions on Canadian products.[1] In particular, he was concerned that the potato farmers of Coos County would be driven out of business by Canadian exports.[2] He never sought to reconcile these inconsistent views, giving a further indication that he felt that foreign policy was unimportant.

These concerns about Britain and Latin America often fused into a single policy. During one congressional hearing, Blair testified: "English influence is very largely established in South America already. That increases very much the danger that her political influence will become predominant there. The existence of those facts has had great influence with my apprehensions that very soon South America will belong to Great Britain instead of the United States."[3] This fear of British power was one that he shared with many Americans. Perhaps, childhood stories about the Scots-Irish experience and the American Revolution made him even more sensitive to Britain's push for an empire in the 1880s. His close friendship with James G. Blaine may explain his special interest in Latin America. After leaving the Senate, Blair claimed that he had proposed the idea of commercial reciprocity with Latin America through an amendment to the Tariff of 1883 and that Blaine had taken the idea from him.[4]

Blair's concerns about Latin America and the British influence there, combined with a personal financial problem, led to his first major foreign policy debacle. Blair's finances had never been secure, and his election to the Senate only exacerbated the problem. Believing that he should live in a style befitting a member of that august body, Blair purchased a house within a block of the Capitol—where the Folger Library is now located—and had the residence suitably furnished.[5] Eliza dressed in fashionable clothing, and young Henry attended the best private schools available. All these expenses severely strained the small official income that Blair received as a senator.

Unexpected crises drained Blair's income even further. The most spectacular of these events took place in the spring of 1887 when a fire partially destroyed the family residence. One of the clerks of the Supreme Court spotted the fire and reported it to the fire department. The flames had started in an adjacent structure, allowing the firemen to arrive in time to save the Blair home from serious damage. In fact, the most dangerous part of the incident came when firefighters discovered that Eliza was confined to a bed and had to be carried out of the house.[6] Although most of the expense was covered by insurance, Blair observed: "Between the bane & the antidote—fire and water both we suffered somewhat of a loss."[7]

In an effort to achieve greater financial stability, Blair began to speculate in new industrial enterprises. Details on most of these transactions are missing, but apparently all of them failed.[8] One of the few surviving letters from this period amply documents Blair's plight. Writing to the attorneys representing the widow of a close friend, Blair explained the origin of a note of indebtedness found in the deceased's papers. After receiving strong assurances about a company from business friends, he had induced the man to invest in some mining stock. When the concern went bankrupt, all the speculators lost their entire investments. Blair claimed that he owed no legal obligation, noting, however: "I took the view that no friend should lose by me & gave him a note & an agreement to repay him. I have never yet been able to do it & have suffered to almost the last conceivable degree mentally & otherwise from my inability to do it. I have done the best so far that I can & hope to pay Mrs. Sanborn everything in due time but now it is impossible."[9] The failure of these speculative ventures may explain Blair's later attempt to recoup his fortune with a Latin American venture.

The venture started in New York City. On June 30, 1881, Blair was in the city on official business and visited his old New Hampshire political friend Aaron H. Cragin. Cragin introduced Blair to the businessman Jacob R. Shipherd.[10] Shipherd was president of an organization that claimed the right to mine nitrates in a guano-rich region of Peru. The French consortium previously asserting these rights had sold its claim to the Americans after failing to secure Peruvian recognition. The prostration of Peru in 1881 because of its reverses in a war with Chile offered Shipherd and his partners an opportunity to press their demands. Although weakened, the Peruvian government refused to deal with Shipherd's company. Recognizing that the only hope for success lay in receiving the backing of the American government, Shipherd sought to influence Secretary of State Blaine. According to his later testimony, Shipherd approached Blair because of the latter's well-known friendship with Blaine rather than the fact that Blair was a senator.[11]

Nothing of substance transpired at this first meeting, but at a meeting about two weeks later Blair and Shipherd reached an agreement. Disguising his intentions, Shipherd assured Blair that he was interested only in having him assess the legitimacy of the claim and the willingness of federal officials to support it. Two motivations seemed to influence Blair at this point. He was genuinely concerned that the United States needed to establish its presence in a region where British power seemed to be growing. At the same time, Shipherd indicated that he would pay Blair a fee to act as the private attorney for the firm. In accepting this position, Blair either did not think about the implications of his actions or convinced himself that he could separate his private and public lives. Shipherd offered Blair stock in the company as compensation for his services, but Blair indicated that he preferred a cash payment. Unable to resolve their differences, the two men agreed to settle that matter later, and Blair began working for the company.[12]

Under these dubious circumstances, Blair examined the documents pertaining to the claim and decided that the company was on strong legal ground. He then arranged for Shipherd to meet with Blaine on July 25 and 26, 1882. The exact content of their conversations is a matter of considerable dispute, but it is clear that Blair played no important role.[13] Apparently, Shipherd did not gain assurance of American intervention because he approached Blaine's son Walker, a State Department employee, to further influence the secretary. Blaine then summoned Blair, telling him to warn his client of the dangers of pursuing his case outside regular channels.[14] Shipherd subsequently wrote to the American ambassador to Peru in an effort to influence American policy on the scene. Although Shipherd later claimed that he had bribed the diplomat with $250,000 in Peruvian Company stock, the only tangible result was a letter from the ambassador to Blair demanding that Blair restrain his client's lobbying activities.[15]

Blair was hardly in a position to advise caution. Outraged by an incident in which he felt that Chile had humiliated the United States, he recommended that Shipherd "act as though the American ships of war were on their way to the Pacific coast. The policy of the Government has been exactly right and is now."[16] This was exactly what Shipherd wanted to hear and only increased his boldness. Pleased with his work, he sent Blair stock certificates that had a par value of $100,000 in October 1881.[17] Blair later claimed that he never intended to keep the certificates, but he admitted that he did not return them to Shipherd until November 25, 1881.[18] At that time, he told Shipherd that he was sure that the company's claims would come before Congress for action, placing him in a direct conflict of interest. His involvement with Shipherd's schemes ended at that point, and the senator felt confident that he had not violated his public trust.

Given the loose political morality of the time, Blair's activities might have gone unnoticed if Blaine had not been involved. As a persistent presidential candidate and the leading candidate for the Republican nomination in 1884, Blaine was a national personality. Already tainted by his involvement in past scandals, he was the target of efforts by Democratic and Republican opponents to prove further charges against him. In 1882, an investigating subcommittee of the House Foreign Affairs Committee was established to examine the impact of the Peruvian Company on American foreign relations. The Williams Committee, named for its chairman, the Alabama Democrat Thomas Williams, began its open sessions in March 1882. Shipherd proved to be the star witness, claiming to have bribed an ambassador, influenced the secretary of state, and duped a U.S. senator.[19] While Shipherd's testimony provided useful fodder for Blaine's opponents, even they recognized that there were important inconsistencies in the adventurer's story. The most glaring contradiction directly involved Blair. Shipherd first stated that Blair never knew of the attempt to bribe the ambassador. Later, he claimed that Blair was at a meeting when he mentioned the bribe to Blaine.[20]

Shipherd's allegation that Blair had witnessed the bribe discussion created pressures for public examination of Blair's role in the entire incident. Between April 21 and May 8, Blair had to drop all other matters to prepare himself for the confrontation with the House committee. Fortunately for him, Blaine preceded him as a witness and destroyed all suggestion that Shipherd had influenced American policy. Despite that fact, Blair spent an uncomfortable five days as a witness between May 1 and May 8. Maintaining that his relationship with Shipherd was that of a lawyer and his client, he claimed that certain information was confidential. The following exchange was typical of Blair's testimony:

Q. What was the amount of the certificate of stock sent to you by Mr. Shipherd in way of a retainer?
A. Do you think that essential to the investigation?
Q. I ask you the question.
A. I decline to state the amount. I have stated all in relation to my connection with Mr. Shipherd as counsel which I thought pertinent to the matter. I do not care to go further in that direction than the public interest requires.[21]

Although he later disclosed the value of the stock certificates, the Williams Committee made note of his reluctance to testify about matters involving his personal responsibility.[22]

Focused on investigating Blaine's role in the Peruvian venture, the Williams Committee was not really interested in Blair. Thus, it accepted at face value his claim that his sole motivation had been to counter growing British power in Latin America and to protect U.S. interests in Panama.[23] The *New York Times* subjected this defense to savage ridicule, emphasizing his complete lack of sophistication about foreign policy.[24] Other newspapers were more blunt, calling on Blair to resign from the Senate or to be censured if he did not.[25]

Blair's need to defend himself before the Williams Committee may have destroyed his best opportunity as a senator to enact the education bill into law. The legislation was reported out of the Senate Education and Labor Committee one day after the Williams Committee announced that it would call him to testify. His absence from the Senate for several weeks delayed debate on the bill until 1884, when the Democrats had won a majority in the House and could block its passage. In retrospect, three points seem clear: Blair had no influence on American policy toward Peru, he did not actually profit from the arrangement, and he used incredibly bad judgment throughout the entire affair. The comment of a New Hampshire newspaper undoubtedly captured the sentiments of his friends and political supporters: "We think that the Senator's friends wish he had kept out of this business."[26]

Chinese immigration was the next major foreign policy issue to capture Blair's attention. The Burlingame Treaty of 1868 had established the basis of international relations between the United States and China. This treaty provided for "the mutual advantage of the free migration and emigration of their citizens and subjects respectively from one country to the other for the purpose of curiosity, of trade or as permanent residents."[27] Additional provisions ensured that Chinese immigrants to the United States would receive substantial protection.

By 1870, opposition to Chinese workers was growing in many parts of the United States. Anti-Chinese feeling was particularly strong on the Pacific Coast and among important segments of organized labor. As a subtle way of limiting Chinese immigration, Republicans passed the Page Act in 1875, outlawing "the importation . . . of women for the purpose of prostitution."[28] In 1876, the Republican Party of California requested that the immigration sections of the Burlingame Treaty be renegotiated.[29] The 1876 appointment of a joint congressional committee to investigate the impact of immigration drew further attention to this issue.[30] The next year, a highly prejudiced congressional investigating committee produced a large volume of anti-Chinese testimony.[31] Maine senator James G. Blaine heightened tensions by characterizing Chinese immigrants as "vicious," "odious," "abominable," "dangerous," and "revolting" in a February 1879 letter to the *New York Tribune*.[32]

All this negative publicity encouraged the congressional majority to pass legislation further restricting Chinese immigration. In 1880, Congress passed an amendment to the Burlingame Treaty that limited the number of Chinese immigrants to fifteen per ship. Blaine defended this restriction by claiming that "China had violated the Treaty numerous times."[33] When President Rutherford B. Hayes vetoed the legislation, citing treaty obligations, the Senate was unable to override the veto. Hayes then sent James Angell to negotiate a revision of the treaty that would allow the United States to suspend Chinese immigration.

American representatives traveling with Angell found their Chinese hosts eager to please them and quickly concluded an agreement. This treaty dramatically altered the ability of Chinese nationals to live and work in the United States. The Chinese accepted the following change: "The coming of Chinese laborers to the United States, or their residence therein, affects the interests of that country. . . . [It has the] power to regulate, limit, or suspend such coming or residence, but not absolutely prohibit it."[34] The Senate approved the resulting agreement in 1880 by a 48–4 vote.[35] Two years later, Congress passed a bill to suspend Chinese immigration for twenty years. When President Arthur vetoed this bill, Congress passed legislation suspending Chinese immigration for ten years.[36]

A clause in an 1850 treaty allowed Chinese immigrants already living in the United States to reenter the country after visiting China. Increasing pressures on Congress to end this policy led to further negotiations between the two countries in 1888. Although the Chinese government protested the severe restrictions on the right of their nationals to return to the United States, the close presidential campaign of that year created a climate favorable for passage of such legislation. The resulting Scott Act directly violated the terms of previous treaties, but the Supreme Court did not overturn it.[37] Having no legal basis for defending this act, Secretary of State Blaine chose not to answer most of the protests forwarded by the Chinese legation.[38] The strong momentum in favor of immigration restrictions prompted passage of the Geary Act in 1892, which renewed the ban on Chinese immigration for ten more years.[39]

While influenced by Blaine's anti-immigrant stance, Blair's opposition to Chinese immigration primarily grew out of his political alliance with organized labor. For labor leaders, the possibility of a large migration of the world's most populous people to the United States was a matter of grave concern. Labor leaders blamed immigrants for flooding the labor market and keeping wages low. The inhumane labor contracts forced on Chinese workers before they left their homeland bolstered this argument. In New England and on the Pacific Coast, labor leaders' opposition to immigration revealed strong racial animus.[40]

Blair's 1878 trip to the Chinese ghetto in San Francisco reinforced his negative views of Chinese immigration. Ignoring the causes of the squalid scene, such as poverty, housing segregation, and the prohibition against the immigration of Chinese women, Blair became convinced that the Chinese were an immoral race.[41] Two years later, he voted in favor of a Senate proposal to limit the number of Chinese who could enter the country to fifteen passengers per ship.[42] He cited the Chinese government's refusal to control contract labor companies as the reason for his vote. He declared: "Men who are careful of human rights will do well to guard against introducing more slave systems into this country."[43] The irony of using abolitionist rhetoric to support another form of racism was lost on Blair. Still, he remained flexible enough on the immigration question to vote against the 1882 bill proposing a twenty-year suspension of Chinese immigration.[44]

By 1888, Blair fully embraced the idea that Chinese immigrants posed a threat to security. He was one of the leading speakers during the debate on the Scott Act—a proposal to ban Chinese laborers who revisited China from reentering the United States even if they held official documents permitting their return. Several of his comments revealed a strongly racist attitude. For example, in a Senate debate on September 7, 1888, he compared the Chinese by analogy to "yellow fever" and concluded: "I ask the Senator is it not in exact analogy to that power by which we exclude by national force pestilential disease from any portion of the country that we may undertake the prevention of the migration or immigration of the Chinaman to this country?"[45] Six days later, he again delivered a lengthy speech, referring to the Chinese in America as "evil" and "an adverse population."[46] He remarked: "My knowledge of the Chinese situation is of course comparatively slight but from the moment that I saw that seething, roaring, blood-curdling curse, Chinatown, in San Francisco, I felt as though there had been planted in the vitals of American civilization the seeds of death."[47] Despite these harsh comments, Blair proposed an amendment that would have delayed implementation of the Scott Act to allow further negotiation between the countries. Ultimately, he joined all but three members of Congress in voting for the Scott Act.[48] In a May 3, 1890, article in the *New York Mail and Express*, he warned that the United States faced "decivilization" because of its contact with the Chinese.[49]

This rhetoric might have escaped international attention if it had not been for the events of early 1891. Having been defeated for reelection to the Senate, Blair expected that President Harrison would find him an appropriate federal appointment. Providentially, the federal district judge Daniel Clark had died two weeks before the New Hampshire Senate election. Because Clark was a former U.S. senator from New Hampshire, the tradition of patronage distribution made Blair's nomination to the office likely. Blair recognized that the $5,000 salary—the same as his Senate pay—with accompanying restrictions on outside income would doom his family to the same financial instability they had endured for the past fifteen years. Accepting the judgeship also would have made it more difficult to return to elective politics, and he still believed that he could best achieve his goals in that forum. When Harrison offered to consider Blair for the position, Blair replied that he was too poor to become a federal judge.[50] He expressed concern that his financial situation would make him a target for bribery attempts that would undermine his effectiveness.

Harrison continued to look for a suitable appointment for Blair, and the two men agreed on a position in late February 1891. At that time, Harrison nominated Blair to be the new U.S. minister to China. Blair's colleagues quickly confirmed the nomination without serious debate.[51] Blair officially accepted the appointment the day his Senate term ended.[52] Neither Harrison nor the Senate members gave any thought to the Chinese reaction to Blair's appointment. Apparently, they viewed the appointment as a matter of internal politics. Even Blair, who had shown such hostility to the Chinese in this country, saw no problem. He had always welcomed opportunities to learn and expand his perspective, and this post promised to open up a new world to him. Even more important, the Chinese mission was regarded as one of the most desirable patronage prizes available in government service, giving Blair an opportunity to restore some of his lost prestige. His $12,000 annual salary would allow him to pay off his debts and provide for Eliza and Henry. Finally, this type of appointment would allow him to resume an active political career if he chose to do so.

Blair's appointment as the American minister to China came at a most inopportune time in the relationship between the two countries. By the middle of the 1880s, Chinese workers in the western states had been subjected to a virtual reign of terror. The worst incident in Wyoming left more than twenty dead.[53] Minister Chang Yin Hoon and other members of the Chinese legation expressed outrage at the refusal of American juries to convict the perpetrators. When Secretary of State Thomas F. Bayard challenged Chang's assertions, the Chinese minister replied with considerable heat and accuracy: "If there is any information at the Department of State that proper justice has been administered in a single case of the murder of Chinese in the territories of the United States, it will afford me great gratification to qualify my allegation on that subject."[54] Seeking to resolve the conflict between the two countries, the Chinese legation brought fewer cases of mistreatment before the State Department for a few years.

After the 1888 passage of the Scott Act, the Chinese put considerable pressure on the State Department to rescind this measure. Chang pointed out that the Scott Act voided the unrestricted travel privileges granted to Chinese residents of the United States by the treaty of 1880.[55] Chang's successor, Tsui Zwo Yin, noted that these illegal restraints were preventing more than twenty thousand Chinese with proper travel certificates from reentering the United States.[56] By the late fall of 1890, Tsui protested to Secretary of State Blaine: "Under the date of March 26 last I was impelled by an urgent sense of duty to send you a note of some length, . . . respecting the status of our treaty relations, as affected by the action of the last Congress of your country. . . . It has filled me with wonder that neither an acknowledgement of its receipt, nor a reply has up to this time been received."[57] Blaine having publicly opposed Chinese immigration for more than a decade, his lack of action reflected both the untenable diplomatic position of the United States and his personal bias. In follow-up correspondence, Tsui warned Blaine of his government's "disappointment" over the failure of Congress to conform to the provisions of the treaty.[58]

Under these very tense conditions, the appointment of any American minister to China would have been subject to a very careful review. While Blair basked in the glory of his appointment and rested for the long trip to China, Minister Tsui gathered evidence of Blair's anti-Chinese record in

Congress. Although Tsui spoke and read no English, he was a shrewd and sophisticated observer of the American scene. He was impressed with the achievements of American science and technology and was generally very favorably disposed toward the United States. After collecting information about Blair from newspapers, he sent it to the imperial government in Peking.[59] In late April 1891, unaware of the activities of the Chinese minister, Blair headed to San Francisco to board a ship to China. On April 25, Tsui asked Blaine for an emergency meeting to discuss the Blair appointment.[60] At that time, Tsui presented a translation of a cablegram from Viceroy Li Tieutsin that said in part: "Blair abused Chinese laborers too bitterly while in the Senate and was conspicuous in helping to pass the oppressive Exclusion Act. . . . The United States government . . . would do better not to appoint him as Minister Plenipotentiary to China. According to the usages of the Western nations and international law, China would also deem it inexpedient to receive him."[61] Blaine sent an immediate telegram to Blair in Chicago telling him not to proceed further.[62]

Blair responded with a long campaign to vindicate himself in the eyes of the Chinese. He first claimed that his support for the Scott Act was based on nothing more than acquiescence to a decision by the Republican Senate caucus. He then tried to explain why his comments in the 1888 Senate debate should not be offensive to the Chinese. Although his explanations further revealed his hostility to the rights of Chinese workers in the United States, he made one significant point. The entire apparatus of the American government—Congress, the Supreme Court, and the president—had approved the Scott Act. He was being punished more for the government's policy than for his own actions.[63] Acting Secretary of State William F. Wharton tacitly acknowledged the legitimacy of Blair's last point by requesting that the Chinese reconsider the Blair nomination.[64]

The Chinese government was more than willing to agree to Blair's interpretation of events. Lacking other pressure points, government officials had used Blair's anti-Chinese statements as a way to force reconsideration of restrictive immigration policies. Tsui pointed out in a June 23, 1891, note to Wharton: "The passing of the law while the treaty was being considered has had a very bad effect in China. If the President or the Secretary of State could do anything to repeal that law and to put in force again the treaties, the situation in China would be much changed; and then it would not make much difference what Mr. Blair had said, and he would be well received if the President asked for it."[65]

For Blair, the situation was confusing and dispiriting. On June 22, 1891, he submitted his resignation to the president, and then two weeks later he withdrew it.[66] His efforts to refute all the Chinese charges had no impact on developments.[67] Harrison accepted Blair's resignation on October 6, assuring the former senator that there was nothing in the entire episode that reflected poorly on him.[68] Blair's friends, including Frances Willard of the Women's Christian Temperance Union, tried to secure an appointment for him as minister to Japan, without success.[69] Blair blamed the Chinese for the entire episode, refusing to accept any responsibility for himself or his government.

Blair's remarks over the remainder of his political career left no doubt about the wisdom of the Chinese government's action. After returning to Congress in 1892, Blair delivered a major speech on the Chinese situation. He spoke at length in favor of an amendment to the Geary Act that would have required all Chinese in the United States to carry a validated entry form with their photograph on it. He rejected any suggestion that this last provision would be an unfair restriction of the rights of the Chinese in the United States. In a tirade undoubtedly fueled by the frustration and humiliation of the diplomatic episode, he lashed out at the Chinese in America. He called them "an alien race" and compared the Chinese section of San Francisco to "Sodom." Using an argument that must have sounded quite ironic to his southern listeners, he maintained: "God works in a different way. He does not intermingle civilizations. A great civilization, a higher civilization never yet was expanded, enlarged, or heightened by contact with, by infiltration of, a lower."[70] Applause greeted this outburst. In this instance, those who had opposed Blair on questions of black Americans' rights were his warmest supporters. Blair never recognized the inherent contradiction in his views of the rights of black and Chinese residents. If there ever was any question about his suitability to be the American envoy to China, this speech decisively answered the question.

In an 1894 congressional debate on the annexation of Hawaii, Blair again voiced his displeasure with the Chinese. He warned that, if the United States did not annex Hawaii, then China, Britain, and Japan would use this region against America's best interests.[71] In a later foreign policy debate, he took one last official jab at China. He opposed any new treaty with that country that did not close all the "loopholes" in immigration policy.[72] He preferred that the poor relations between the two countries continue rather than allowing any Chinese to come to the United States. The last major statement that Blair made on China was as a private citizen, but it showed that his views had not changed. In 1900, he called on President William McKinley to send fifty thousand American soldiers to China to punish the Boxers' declared war on foreign powers and to protect American interests.[73]

While Blair never displayed an understanding of foreign policy matters, his failures were part of a broader pattern. Like most Americans, he concentrated on domestic events. He spent months carefully investigating the need for education legislation, but he made no effort to understand the workings of international relations. He shared with his countrymen—both inside and outside government—certain assumptions about other nations and peoples. These ideas, often prejudices, seldom changed and did not in any way reflect the reality of the situations to which the United States had to frame diplomatic responses. Thus, he and other government officials often found themselves embarrassed by events and developments that they did not understand. At the same time, most Americans, including Blair, were not overly concerned by these setbacks because they did not view the world outside the United States as important.

*Chapter 10*

# New Hampshire Politics

Despite his national reputation, Henry Blair depended on political developments in New Hampshire to maintain himself in a position of power. Throughout the 1880s, economic developments in the state and Republican factionalism threatened to unseat him. He escaped defeat in 1885 but was overwhelmed by a strong opponent and changed conditions in 1891. After a brief return to Congress in an unexpected 1892 triumph, his electoral career was over. In the remaining twenty-five years of his life, he continued to advocate for political reform. He often worked as a lobbyist, maintaining contacts with such diverse individuals and groups as Booker T. Washington, William Howard Taft, and the National Association for the Advancement of Colored People. His later years proved fulfilling despite the absence of political success. At the time of his death in 1920, two of his major reform interests—women's suffrage and prohibition—were about to be added to the Constitution.

As a seasoned politician, Blair recognized that his career depended on the ongoing support of those who had lifted him to power. Although the reform element in the Republican Party was his most important national constituency, Civil War veterans were his most significant backers at state and local levels. Since every individual in this bloc was a voter and usually a Republican, veterans often had a disproportionate voice in New Hampshire politics. Blair had worked hard to earn a reputation as the champion of their interests. He defended their cause numerous times in Congress, maintaining that the government had an implied contract with the veterans to protect them from adverse outcomes of their national service.[1] He also showed his sure political instinct by appearing before a large number of veteran audiences in New Hampshire to share memories with his fellow comrades in arms and to keep alive old loyalties. He was a consistent speaker at the state Grand Army of the Republic encampments and was a widely sought after Memorial Day speaker.[2]

Despite the high visibility of these activities, Blair probably won more votes from his quiet work on individual pension cases. Because of the enormous backlog of pension requests, the claims of many New Hampshire soldiers were seriously delayed. Direct intervention with federal officials to request that a case receive special handling often was the only solution. Blair was especially diligent in this activity. In one four-month period, he processed more than one thousand of these requests—about six times more than the average member of Congress.[3] Having no professional office help until early 1884 and thereafter only the assistance of a single clerk, he made most of the trips to the pension office to check records and wrote most of the letters. When his personal intervention on behalf of individual veterans was not sufficient to secure the needed action, he introduced special bills into the Congress to secure the desired relief. During the Forty-eighth Congress, he introduced 139 individual veteran relief acts.[4] These tireless efforts created a large following of highly motivated partisans who would do anything in their power to assist him politically.

Beginning in the early 1880s, growing divisions within the New Hampshire Republican Party threatened Blair's chances of returning to the Senate. The party was plagued by two interrelated problems that came to a head in the early 1880s. An older leadership refused to step aside for a younger generation and used its control of the party machinery to try to thwart its youthful rivals. At the same time, New Hampshire was experiencing rapid industrialization and urban population growth. The businessmen associated with this changed economy demanded to be part of the Republican hierarchy. A series of crises resulting from competing interests seemed likely to split the party into factions too weak to prevent the Democrats from gaining control of state government.

The fight for the U.S. Senate seat during the June 1883 session of the legislature showed the shortsightedness of the traditional Republican leadership. For Blair, the situation seemed to be a rerun of the spring of 1878. Knowing that his seat would expire before the legislature met next in 1885, he tried to convince his U.S. Senate colleagues to pass a resolution requiring the New Hampshire legislature to elect his successor during the 1883 session.[5] Congressman James F. Briggs introduced similar legislation into the House.[6] Both initiatives failed, with Congress refusing to intervene in what members considered to be a local dispute.

New Hampshire Republicans refused to be discouraged by the failure of national legislation. Given the problems that the party had experienced over the past two years, they wanted to avoid controversy if at all possible. Many Republican newspapers and party members endorsed the election of two senators during the June 1883 session. They pointed out that the Republicans should take advantage of their present legislative majority and not risk losing a seat at the next election. Noting that Blair and Rollins were winning large numbers of supporters, most of these sources endorsed the reelection of both men.[7]

Several party leaders had their sights on the U.S. Senate seat. The early leads won by Blair and Rollins motivated them to prevent their election at all costs. The first strike came from Chandler, who announced that he was opposed to the selection of two senators during the session.[8] Blair announced his candidacy on the same day, denying rumors that he and Rollins had agreed to help each other win the Republican nominations.[9] There is every reason to accept Blair's announcement at face value. He and Rollins used entirely different campaign techniques and appealed to different elements in the party. Rollins was the organization man personified, with strong ties to local bosses and to individuals who sought and held patronage jobs. Blair, on the other hand, had a strong personal following among reform members of the party who had little interest in factional politics or patronage positions.

As the legislature prepared to meet, it became apparent that the opposition was prepared to adopt desperate measures to prevent the election of the two incumbents. Rumors began to circulate that the tactics used by Chandler and others to prevent Rollins's election in 1881 would be used again.[10] Republicans opposed to Rollins and Blair boycotted the Republican caucus held on June 14, 1883. One of the major reasons for their boycott was the perception that this would be the old guard's last opportunity to win a Senate seat. But there were other factors at work, including a strong feeling that Rollins had unfairly used patronage appointees to boost his campaign.[11] With only 134 of a total of 206 Republican legislators present, the caucus first agreed to elect two senators. Then Rollins and Blair were nominated on the first ballot in separate elections.

In the days before the state legislature's first official ballot, all candidates engaged in frantic maneuvering. When the first poll was taken, Rollins fell thirty-eight votes short of election.[12] This development changed the status of Blair's nomination entirely. The Rollins-dominated state Senate voted not to elect a second senator, casting Blair to the sidelines as the intraparty battle raged.[13] Democrats helped deepen this rift by charging that the Senate had betrayed Blair. Most Republicans condemned the caucus boycotters for throwing the party in turmoil. Speaking for many Republicans, the *Keene Sentinel* observed: "The caucus was called and conducted in the same manner that has marked these gatherings in the past. There was no 'packing,' no attempt to deprive any one of his rights, no unfairness of any kind. . . . By their course in this matter they have forfeited the respect of all true Republicans in the State and clouded their political future."[14] The editor of the Lebanon paper captured the frustration of the average Republican in the following: "As if the contest of last fall were not enough, we are treated to a contest equally as disgraceful, and for which there is no excuse. We are very, very, very sick of it."[15] By supporting the caucus, Blair avoided this criticism, strengthening his chances for election in 1885. Ironically, Chandler and other Republicans not directly opposing the caucus were hurt more than Blair.

Political developments at the national level heightened New Hampshire Republicans' awareness of the heavy price they had paid for their lack of unity. Because the winning party at the local, state, and national levels gained the power to appoint its own people to government positions, the rewards for victory were quite substantial. This drive for victory and jobs not only led to vigorous competition between the parties but also created factional and personal rivalries within parties.

The 1880s brought increased public pressure to reform what had become a well-entrenched patronage system. With the economy growing larger and more complex, corporations needed and demanded competent and dependable government officials to provide an adequate infrastructure for their enterprises. Political and social reformers sought honest administrators, and newspapers featured exposures of corruption that undercut popular support for the patronage system.[16]

The most formidable challenge to the patronage system came after the 1881 assassination of President James A. Garfield. A disappointed office seeker who expected Vice President Chester Arthur of New York to change appointment policies in favor of his political faction shot Garfield in a Washington railroad station. Popular revulsion at this deed and the system that lay behind it prompted Congress to create the Civil Service Commission in 1883, thus greatly reducing the number of federal patronage appointees. This tragedy and its aftermath confirmed the dangers of political factionalism.[17]

The presidential election of 1884 further demonstrated the perils of political factionalism. Although the Republican nominee, James G. Blaine, chose to emphasize the tariff question and the economy, other party leaders focused on southern Democrats' use of violence and intimidation to prevent blacks from voting. As a result, the divided party could not defeat the strong candidacy of the Democratic governor of New York, Grover Cleveland. One positive consequence of this defeat was that factions within the Republican Party would not be able to battle over patronage at the federal level for the next four years. However, they faced the prospect of running future campaigns without the assistance of campaign workers who were public officeholders or volunteers who aspired to hold one of these positions.[18] To restore the party to power, Blair had to center his attention on developments in New Hampshire and work to unify New Hampshire Republicans.

Despite Blair's failure to win immediate reelection in 1883, his national reputation encouraged Republicans in other states to request his services. In early September 1884, his speech in Maine helped the Republicans win some closely watched congressional races there.[19] Several weeks later, he campaigned for Republicans in the Midwest. In the closing week before the presidential election, he helped Blaine secure votes in the crucial state of New York.[20] Throughout this period, Blair never lost sight of the fact that he would be running for reelection to the Senate and that he needed to spend as much time as possible working with New Hampshire Republicans. In 1884, he was elected as a delegate to the state gubernatorial nominating convention, where he undoubtedly renewed acquaintances and made many useful contacts.[21] Later that year, he was a featured speaker at the First District congressional nominating convention, where he talked with many of his old allies.[22] He was also the major speaker following Republican torchlight parades in the cities of Portsmouth and Manchester.[23] In all these speeches, he emphasized the importance of the Republican reform tradition as a framework for legislation on education, labor, and personal equality.

Blair's efforts to identify legislators who would support his 1885 bid for a U.S. Senate seat began during the fall 1884 legislative campaign and quickly accelerated as a Republican victory seemed likely. Well aware that many candidates were trying to replace him, Blair remarked: "Everybody in New Hampshire runs for the senatorship."[24] Chandler was Blair's most active opponent, speaking every day during the last two weeks of the campaign.[25] When legislative candidates were nominated in late October, the U.S. Senate aspirants tried to get their friends selected to run in Republican districts.[26] It soon became apparent that Blair had more strength than any other candidate.[27] That fact encouraged other candidates to band together in an effort to prevent Blair from gaining too great a lead.[28] Unfortunately for this alliance, the still bitter Rollins refused to have anything to do with the men who he felt had betrayed him in 1883.[29]

Although Blair's campaign seemed to be going well, there was one troublesome consideration. With his term ending on March 4, 1885, and the legislature not reconvening until June, Governor Hale would have to name an interim senator. Blair was well aware that retaining his seat and the power and prerogatives of incumbency would greatly enhance his re-election chances.[30] Speculations about Hale's intentions were numerous, but they all included the names of someone other than Blair. One of the newspaper nominees, Orren C. Moore of Nashua, said that he would rather remain chairman of the state railroad commission than to have the dubious distinction of being senator for three months.[31] Chandler was another popular choice among political insiders, but the surviving correspondence indicates that Hale never offered the seat to him.[32]

While awaiting Hale's decision, Blair continued to perform his senatorial duties in Washington. Throughout the winter of 1885, his New Hampshire supporters remained extremely active, contacting every member of the Republican caucus even when a fatigued Blair had to be confined to bed.[33] One correspondent warned Chandler: "I hope you will come to Concord as early as possible for Blairs [sic] men are in camp all over the state. Durkee, Cheney & Co bivouac, they do not go to bed."[34] Prohibition supporters were particularly effective in winning support for Blair. One of Chandler's campaign workers reported: "The temperance cranks succeeded in turning Kimball and it was useless to talk with him. They made him believe that Blair is a Saint."[35] As his organization of reform Republicans gained momentum, Blair received the welcome news that Hale had reappointed him to the Senate.[36] The major reason for this decision appeared to be Hale's gratitude for Blair's assistance during the difficult 1882 gubernatorial campaign. When it was later revealed that Blair had invested in Hale's chair factory in Keene, none of Blair's opponents in either party suggested impropriety on his part.[37]

The reappointment made Blair the clear front-runner in the Senate race. As he gained popularity among Republican voters, the party newspapers around the state began to endorse him.[38] This praise and support extended beyond New Hampshire. Albion Tourgee, the liberal critic of the education bill, was particularly enthusiastic: "He is a great-hearted, ernest [sic] manly man, who bears about him a flavor of sincerity which it does one good to find in the midst of the flippancy and pessimism of the day. . . . [H]e is worth a ten-acre-lot full of the best of those who ridicule him. New Hampshire will show herself as dull as her granite hills themselves if she does not return him to the senate."[39] A number of prohibition groups, including the Temperance Alliance of the District of Columbia, actively supported Blair.[40] Forced to remain in Washington to participate in the new congressional session, he managed to retain the lead that these endorsements had helped build. Confident that he would win reelection, Senate leaders reappointed him as chairman of the Education and Labor Committee despite his temporary status and loss of seniority.[41]

Blair's Republican opponents began to seek any means available to defeat him. Former congressman Ossian Ray twice suggested to Chandler that the other candidates boycott the Republican caucus as the anti-Rollins group had done two years earlier, but that option no longer was viable.[42] Party newspapers endorsed the caucus as the final judge for the party, and one editor even called for a direct popular primary to end all the conflict.[43] When the legislature met in June 1885, most Republican members were determined not to repeat the spectacle of 1883.[44] Ray and Chandler recognized that, if they supported a caucus boycott, they would also have to contend with an enraged Rollins, who would, if necessary, join with Blair to support the caucus. Thus, politicians' concerns about their political futures significantly reduced Blair's chances of facing a revolt similar to the one that had defeated Rollins.

Recognizing that he needed to respond to his opponents' arguments, Blair returned to New Hampshire for the final weeks of the contest. As noted earlier, he was a tremendously persuasive campaigner, particularly when meeting with rural constituents. In a sarcastic but accurate tribute, the *Manchester Union* reported: "Blair can call on a man, and talk, or listen, for four hours, to the sheerest nonsense, without the slightest show of impatience, if necessary to his canvass."[45] This traditional style of campaigning still worked well in New Hampshire, and reports before the final vote indicated that Blair was in a very strong position. The caucus held on June 12, 1885, was a complete Blair triumph. With the exception of one person who was ill, every Republican legislator attended

The Honorable William E. Chandler of New Hampshire, secretary of the navy, Arthur cabinet. Courtesy Library of Congress Prints and Photographs Division.

| Table 2. 1885 Republican Caucus Vote for U.S. Senate Nomination | |
|---|---|
| Henry W. Blair | 108 |
| William E. Chandler | 37 |
| Charles H. Burns | 15 |
| Gilman Marston | 14 |
| Ossian Ray | 12 |
| Edward H. Rollins | 8 |
| James W. Patterson | 4 |
| Source: Portsmouth (NH) Daily Chronicle, June 13, 1885. | |

the meeting. The result of the first ballot is presented in table 2. The caucus declared Blair to be the party nominee and invited him to address its members. Blair thanked his opponents for their "courteous bearing" during the contest and called on the party to continue its moral crusade as the best means to serve the nation and to achieve electoral victory.[46]

Blair's success in 1885 was not repeated six years later when he ran for election for a third term in the U.S. Senate. He remained committed to his causes and constituents, but political leaders in New Hampshire were facing new demands. As was true in many parts of the country, business and financial institutions were gaining influence in both New Hampshire parties. Two railroad corporations emerged as the most powerful influences in the state legislature. The first was the Concord railroad, which dominated the traffic between the central part of the state and Boston. This relatively short line was somewhat unique in the United States during the 1880s. It was not in debt, and its stocks and bonds represented the true value of the land and equipment. The result was that the company paid substantial and regular dividends while providing consistently good but expensive service. Its great rival was the Boston and Maine Railroad (B&M), a company determined to establish a monopoly on rail transportation in northern New England. The B&M was a much more typical railroad business during this period. Management had expanded the original short line through sales and purchases of units that could not be profitable on their own. When these short lines proved unprofitable, the B&M Board of Directors resorted to the most often used financial tactic of the day, "watering" the stock by selling excessive shares to allow them to declare significant profits. This unsound business practice encouraged the corporation to avoid competition that would expose its weaknesses.[47]

Between 1880 and 1900, the two railroad corporations fought for control of railroad lines by increasing their involvement in New Hampshire politics. Both corporations intervened directly in the selection of delegates to the 1888 Republican gubernatorial convention.[48] The delegates became so inflamed that the voting lasted an unprecedented seven ballots before a candidate favored by neither line was selected.[49] When the state legislature met in June 1889, the railroads again vied for political advantage. In this heated atmosphere, it took eighty-two ballots to select a president of the state Senate.[50] Determined to establish the party's independence, the Republican leadership claimed that in its caucus the railroads played no role in the U.S. Senate nomination. However, there is considerable evidence that the railroads lent support to former party chairman Jacob Gallinger in his unsuccessful campaign for the U.S. Senate seat.[51] The successful U.S. Senate candidate was Chandler, who benefited from the antagonism between the two railroads.

Facing another long and unpredictable legislative battle, the executives and attorneys for the two railroad corporations got together and worked out a compromise bill. The seventeen sections of the measure completely divided up the short lines in the state between the two large railroads and settled other outstanding disputes. In return for allowing the B&M access to the northern New Hampshire market, the Concord was granted the power to water its stock with a new issue of securities valued at $1.8 million.[52] In just over a week, the compromise railroad bill was approved without change by both houses of the legislature and signed by the governor.[53] It was now clear that the railroads had enormous power in New Hampshire politics.

In this radically changed political atmosphere, Blair sought to retain his Senate seat. As expected, his major opponent was Gallinger. Born in Canada, Gallinger moved to the United States at an early age and later established a professional career in medicine. He was a widely respected political organizer. At one point, he boasted: "We have the name of *every voter in the state* returned to us, entered in one of four columns, designated, respectively, Republican, Democratic, Prohibitionist, or Doubtful. This involves a vast amount of labor, but our machinery is so perfect that it goes along without friction."[54] In addition to these numerous local

Jacob H. Gallinger, bust portrait, facing left. Courtesy Library of Congress Prints and Photographs Division.

contacts, Gallinger benefited from a close identification with the united power of the railroad lobbies. Like Blair, he had been very active in the prohibition and women's suffrage movements and could legitimately claim to be a reform advocate at this point in his career.[55] Although he could not attract any of Blair's committed allies, his reform record ensured that he would not lose the votes of Republicans committed to the party's reform tradition. Finally, he represented a new generation of Republican leadership. Blair's attendance at the funerals of his former New Hampshire U.S. Senate colleagues Edward Rollins and Gilman Marston marked him as a member of the "older generation" of leaders despite the fact that he was only two years older than Gallinger.[56]

The national political landscape also was changing. The Democratic political victory in the 1884 presidential election had convinced Republicans that they could no longer afford factionalism and that they needed to find new leaders. At the same time, the results emphasized the significance of the Democratic monopoly of southern electoral votes and the need to find a way to counteract it. Despite Republicans' efforts to make voting irregularities in the South a major issue in the 1886 congressional elections, Democrats retained control of the House of Representatives and made gains in the Senate. Fortunately for Republicans, President Grover Cleveland ordered the return of captured Confederate battle flags—an action that revived the Civil War antagonisms that had propelled Republicans to power.[57]

Republicans laid the groundwork for the 1888 presidential campaign by pressing for continued tariff protections and condemning Democrats for the physical intimidation and property destruction directed against southern Republicans. Seeking to attract businessmen, Upper South industrialists, and laborers concerned about the impact of foreign competition on their jobs, Republicans decried Cleveland's proposal to lower tariffs. At the same time, some Republicans continued to press for greater freedom of the ballot for blacks in the South. In December 1887, Blair's fellow New Hampshire Republican senator, William E. Chandler, introduced a bill to regulate federal elections in selected southern states. Outrages that occurred during the 1888 state elections in Louisiana and Arkansas before the presidential voting kept the issue in the forefront. Despite southern Democrats' use of violence to prevent black Republicans from voting, the Republican candidate, Benjamin Harrison, was elected president and the Republicans gained control of Congress.[58]

From Blair's perspective, the Republican victory proved to be barren of results. As described in chapter 7, the party failed to pass either Blair's education bill or the highly controversial federal elections bill sponsored by Congressman Henry Cabot Lodge of Massachusetts. Some Senate Republicans who placed a higher priority on financial matters than they did on issues raised by the Civil War and Reconstruction derailed these two pieces of legislation. These Republicans obtained a bill to increase silver coinage and passed the McKinley Tariff Act, which provided a high level of protection for American industry.[59] Blair was very upset by this turn of events, which signaled a movement away from issues he considered the most important.

To his dismay, Blair discovered that the desire for change in Republican leadership extended to New Hampshire as well. Blair, Gallinger, and several less prominent candidates began to line up support among members of the Republican caucus for the 1891 Senate contest. Using his traditional techniques of personal and issue-focused discussions, Blair met with most of the Republican legislators in his suite at the Eagle Hotel. A November 1890 poll of all Republican legislators claiming election to the legislature showed Blair with a 101–31 lead over Gallinger, with 29 votes for former governor Person C. Cheney.[60] Still, Blair's campaign appeals did not have the same claims on legislators' loyalty as in past elections, and Gallinger was steadily gaining adherents. Chandler, who had a truly irrational dislike of Gallinger, initially worked for Blair but, sensing the changing conditions, encouraged Cheney to become an active candidate.[61] Since Cheney and Blair were both from Manchester, Cheney's entrance in the contest weakened Blair considerably. Several of Blair's leading assistants went to work for Cheney, creating the perception that Blair could not win reelection on the first ballot. Despite the gradual erosion of Blair's position, the results of the January 16, 1891, Republican caucus (see table 3) surprised most observers. Reporters meeting with Blair in his suite after the contest found him quite composed and almost cheerful.[62] He may have recognized before the caucus that U.S. Senate elections were unpredictable and that he could lose his seat. There is also a strong probability that he recalled all the assistance Gallinger had extended to him in the past. Gallinger had played a major role in Blair's 1879 caucus victory and in the 1884 Republican state electoral victory that allowed him to be reelected to the Senate. In any case, Blair did not dwell on his loss, and his public remarks never revealed any harsh feelings.

| Table 3. 1891 Republican Caucus Vote for U.S. Senate Nomination | First Ballot | Second Ballot |
|---|---|---|
| Jacob H. Gallinger | 95 | 120 |
| Henry W. Blair | 62 | 48 |
| Person C. Cheney | 25 | 18 |
| Charles G. Burns | 5 | 4 |
| James F. Briggs | 5 | 1 |
| James W. Patterson | 1 | 0 |

Source: *Manchester (NH) Union*, January 16, 1891; William E. Chandler, *New Hampshire a Slave State* (Concord, NH: [Monitor], 1891, 31–43.

One of the standing political jokes during the Gilded Age concerned a politician who was dead but not yet aware of it. In early 1892, Blair seemed to fit this description. Although his political career appeared to be over, he found it impossible to abandon either his favorite causes or public life. While most observers ridiculed his reentry into politics, he eventually vindicated himself with a surprising congressional victory that once again established him as a force in state and national politics. This 1892 resurrection gave him a national platform from which to propound a modernized reform program that demonstrated his willingness to adjust to changing conditions. Although his 1895 attempt to reclaim a place in the Senate ultimately failed, the circumstances of his defeat did not destroy the renewed respect for him.

In late February 1892, Blair startled and amused the political world with the following announcement: "Twice I have declined . . . to allow the use of my name as that of a candidate for the Republican nomination for the presidency. Yesterday I was called upon in behalf of men from another part of the country who will be members of the next convention to consider the same question again, and I have decided that I shall accept and deeply appreciate the honor of any support which may be given me as a candidate for the Republican nomination at Minneapolis."[63] He apparently shared the widespread perception that Benjamin Harrison could not be reelected president. A Republican defeat meant that he would lose access to patronage, but he also was deeply concerned that the Republican Party was walking away from its traditional platform. The defeat of the education bill and the Lodge elections bill marked the end of Republican efforts to assist southern blacks. To Half-Breed Republicans like Blair, this change seemed to be a betrayal of traditional Republican principles. In a letter to the black leader Frederick Douglass, Blair explained why he had taken this uncharacteristically aggressive political step: "It must, I think, have become evident to all that there must be a return to the fundamental issues which stir the heart and touch the life of the Republic or there is nothing except assured defeat for us next autumn."[64] Blair may have been part of the movement that several state bosses started about this time to promote a favorite-son strategy to deny Harrison the nomination.[65] Even if he did not support this movement, his announcement played into the hands of the anti-Harrison coalition.

Blair's presidential campaign was a disaster from the very beginning. The *New York Times* description of his candidacy as "ludicrous" was widely shared.[66] Referring to his long speeches on the education bill, the *Buffalo Express* asked: "Would Mr. Blair be able to finish his inaugural before his term of office expired?"[67] Blair's attempts to secure the support of Senator Gallinger, Governor Hiram A. Tuttle, and other leading New Hampshire Republicans at a special meeting met with no success.[68] His failure was made more manifest when the New Hampshire Republican convention sent unpledged delegates to the national convention.[69] This vote reflected not only party members' lack of support for Blair's national aspirations but also their assessment that he did not need to be placated at the local level. A preconvention poll revealed that, while six of New Hampshire's eight national convention delegates opposed Harrison's nomination, none of them planned to vote for Blair.[70] At the national convention, even those people who had urged Blair to run deserted him. He was not nominated and did not receive a single vote.[71]

Although Blair appeared to be at the end of his political career, he was in fact on the verge of another successful campaign for public office. Later in 1892, an unusual set of circumstances led to his securing the Republican nomination for Congress in New Hampshire's First District. In two of the three previous elections, the popular Democratic candidate Luther McKinney of Manchester had carried the district. Forced to retire from Congress because of the rotation rule, McKinney was now the leading contender for the Democratic gubernatorial nomination. Recognizing that most people voted a straight ticket, local Republicans looked for a strong congressional candidate from Manchester to weaken McKinney's appeal to the voters in the gubernatorial race. The obvious choice was Cyrus Sulloway. Known as a political maverick who had supported the Greenback Party in 1878 and Grover Cleveland in 1884, Sulloway was now a Republican in good standing. However, a serious illness in Sulloway's family forced him to withdraw from active campaigning.[72] Desperate Republicans vetted several candidates and decided that none of them could carry Manchester—a necessity if the Republicans hoped to win back the congressional seat.

At this critical juncture, Blair announced that he was willing to accept the Republican nomination.[73] Despite his recent defeats, he remained popular in his adopted home city, and many local Republican leaders worked hard to gain delegates for him. The surviving evidence makes it clear that he did not personally canvass for votes or make any overt effort to gain the nomination.[74] At the same time, a number of Republicans in the district who were violently opposed to him continued to seek alternative candidates. Just before the convention, Blair's opponents brought forward Governor Tuttle as a candidate, but he quickly withdrew his name from consideration.[75] All the maneuvering by the competing interests produced the result displayed in table 4. Blair expressed his gratitude to the delegates in a short speech and pledged to work hard to bring a party victory in the coming campaign.[76] The convention had called Blair back from a political grave. Despite the expected difficulty of the coming canvass, he was delighted to resume activities that had been part of his life for four decades.

The Democrats campaigned primarily on the tariff reduction issue. Their congressional candidate was Charles F. Stone, a businessman and former member of the Republican Party from the small city of Laconia. Stone centered his canvass on opposition to the protective tariff and the Lodge elections bill.[77] He and other Democrats specifically charged that the McKinley tariff had lowered workers' wages by as much as 25 percent.[78] Perhaps hoping to attract some Republican voters, Stone was careful not to offer detailed information on how he would reform the McKinley tariff. Claiming that the depressed economic conditions were due to general Republican policies, he urged all dissatisfied voters to support him. The enthusiasm and cohesiveness of Democratic voters seemed to make this an ideal strategy for Stone and his allies. They hoped to hold their own followers in a district they had carried in the last election while gaining the support of anti-Blair Republicans. In addition, they expected

| Table 4. 1892 Republican Congressional Nomination, First District | |
|---|---|
| | **First Ballot** |
| Henry W. Blair | 174 |
| Hiram A. Tuttle | 68 |
| Cyrus A. Sulloway | 56 |
| Henry B. Burnham | 18 |
| Source: Manchester (NH) Union, September 8, 1892. | |

the nomination of McKinney for governor to greatly strengthen the party in every contest.

Appeals to ethnic voters whose numbers were rapidly growing in New Hampshire cities became even more important in this campaign. The Democrats conducted extensive outreach in ethnic communities because as a French language newspaper charged: "Le parti republican est essentiellement hostile a l'element etranger."[79] The Stone organization was especially active in Manchester's French, German, and Irish communities. Stone even visited Blair's home territory of Ward 5 in Manchester, where he praised the largely Irish population for its contributions during the Civil War.[80]

Believing that ethnic voters would no longer be intimidated by Republican election officials and businessmen, the Democrats assumed that these constituencies would provide enough votes to defeat Blair.[81] However, since the labor investigation of 1883, Blair had demonstrated greater sensitivity to the concerns of his French constituents. French Democrats refused to criticize him directly, and he did not seem badly hurt by the Stone organization's outreach efforts. Refusing to concede the French vote, the Republicans supported another French-language newspaper. With the backing of this newspaper, Blair was able to retain a significant proportion of the French community's vote.[82]

Blair actively campaigned in all the major communities in the district, emphasizing the role that the tariff had played in preserving jobs and maintaining high wages.[83] Refusing to answer most partisan charges made against him, he generally conducted a positive canvass. He joked about his rejection by China—his audiences were always sympathetic—and downplayed his favorite reform measures.[84] In late October 1892, he was forced to deal directly with a campaign crisis. Without consulting Blair or the state leadership, Portsmouth Republicans had gone to court seeking federal supervision of local elections.[85] Recognizing that federal intervention would be more likely to alienate voters than to prevent fraudulent ballots from being cast, Blair and other Republicans were able to cancel it.[86] Despite this incident and the fact that he had not campaigned for himself in a general election in fifteen years, Blair ran an effective canvass. The enthusiasm and good humor in his presentations suggest he was enjoying his reentry into the political arena.

As Blair had suspected, Harrison proved to be a weak presidential candidate. Sensing a national victory, Democrats redoubled their efforts to defeat Blair. The Democrats had carried the First District in two of the last three congressional elections, and the successful candidate was their gubernatorial candidate in 1892. They were convinced that Harrison's unpopularity would drag down all the other Republican candidates.[87] The outcome of the vote remained unclear until several days after the balloting. Complete results are shown in table 5. While Blair did not win an absolute majority, he did much better than most observers had expected. Considering the obstacles he had faced just six months earlier, any kind of victory was worth celebrating. The key to his success was the 3,838–3,468 margin he won in the city of Manchester. Blair later claimed that he had carried the district when the party feared its certain loss, an assessment shared by most political observers.[88]

Although the election victory wiped away much of the disappointment of the previous two years, it did not restore Blair to his previous position of political power. No longer was he a committee chairman with the authority to move his favorite bills directly to the floor for debate. Instead, he was a freshman congressman—albeit with more prestige than most—and a member of the minority party. His appointment to the Pacific Railroad and Foreign Affairs Committees rather than to the Education Committee ensured that his reform proposals would not have friendly sponsors in crucial committee debates.[89] Resigned to his new role as commentator, Blair actively participated in House debates and focused House attention on a variety of reform proposals. His familiarity with parliamentary tactics and his willingness to act as party spokesman for lost causes contributed to his success. Also, his name recognition among House members made it easier for him to command attention.

Soon after his election to the House, rumors began to circulate that

| Table 5. 1892 Vote for Congress, First District | |
|---|---|
| Henry W. Blair | 21,031 |
| Charles F. Stone | 20,412 |
| Others | 735 |
| *Source:* Federal Election Returns, New Hampshire Department of Records Management and Archives. | |

he would be a candidate in the 1895 U.S. Senate race.[90] While these statements probably were based on speculation, Blair was thinking very seriously about succeeding Chandler. A January 1893 conversation between the two men later became the subject of considerable controversy. During a carriage ride to the Washington railroad station, and in the presence of a third person, Chandler confided that his health was not good and that he would probably not seek another term in the Senate. He encouraged Blair to consider taking his place, assuring Blair that he would welcome him into the race even if he—Chandler—decided to run again.[91] Convinced that Chandler's last-minute intervention had cost him the Senate seat in 1891, Blair believed that Chandler owed him the chance to return to the Senate. Because Chandler's health was quite poor, Blair assumed that Chandler would step aside in his favor. Chandler, on the other hand, thought Blair understood that Chandler was leaving his options open and that he might run again. By April 1893, it became clear that, regardless of Chandler's plans, Blair would seek election to the Senate.[92]

National developments greatly influenced the contest between Blair and Chandler. In the spring of 1893, the U.S. economy was shaken by one of its periodic stock market panics and the deep recession that followed. Industrial unemployment reached catastrophic levels, and the entire nation faced financial ruin. At the same time, the Democrats who controlled Congress and the presidency dismantled the election laws that Republicans had created to protect black voters in the South. Given the choice between two viable strategies to appeal to voters, Republicans chose to emphasize economic issues. The Republican leadership was rewarded for its decision when voters overwhelmingly blamed Democrats for the hard times. Starting with elections in 1893, the Republicans won sweeping victories in the northern states. This development ensured that New Hampshire Republicans with commitments to economic growth policies would elect Chandler's successor to the Senate after the 1894 election.[93]

For the remainder of 1893, Blair and Chandler attended to their legislative duties, keeping in close touch and on friendly terms.[94] Early in 1894,
the pace of the Senate campaign began to accelerate. Blair planned strategy and began to form campaign organizations for the coming contest.[95]
His canvass prompted considerable favorable comment. The *Manchester
Union* pointed out that since he had no money and owned no newspaper
he had to go directly to the people. Noting that Blair was the only candidate in the field who had recently been elected to high office by popular
vote, the reporter opined that he would be more responsive to the feelings of the people.[96] On March 17, 1894, Blair formally announced that
he would not seek a second term in the House and would instead attempt
to return to the Senate. In his announcement, he once again called for
more federal aid to southern schools. Maintaining that greater assistance
to southern schools would protect northern workers from uneducated and
poorly paid southern workers, he warned: "The country has been in no
such peril since the rebels fired on Fort Sumter."[97]

At this point, Chandler started his own campaign for reelection. He
and Blair may have been encouraged by the overwhelming Republican
victories in the March 1894 township elections. If this momentum could
be maintained in the fall legislative elections, a Republican would be
elected to the U.S. Senate seat. Chandler's contacts with local leaders
and friends throughout the state must have been quite reassuring.[98] In the
northern third of the state, where Blair had first won elective office, Chandler appeared to have overwhelming support owing to his strong personal
organization and Blair's failure to stay in contact with the new Republican leaders in these communities. Assuming that he would be reelected
as long as no outside forces intervened, Chandler moved quickly to neu-
tralize threats. He served notice on Gallinger that he would run against
him two years later if Gallinger interfered in this contest.[99] Gallinger must
have taken this point quite seriously because he soon announced that he
would play no part in the Senate campaign.[100]

Chandler recognized that his tenuous relationship with the B&M
Railroad posed the greatest threat to his reelection. Aided by two Maine
politicians, he obtained an interview with Lucius Tuttle, the railroad corporation's president. This was the first of five such meetings that took
place during the battle for the Senate seat. Tuttle promised Chandler
that the railroad would not attack him or aid his opponents. When some

of Chandler's friends complained that the railroad men were working against them, Tuttle assured the agitated senator: "Explicit instructions have been given and, I believe, are being carefully followed, that the B. & M. R. R. shall not be complicated with any of the political fights in New Hampshire."[101] The veracity of Tuttle's statement was soon proved when the candidacy of a railroad attorney collapsed because of a lack of support from the corporation. According to Chandler's biographer, the B&M adopted an attitude of "benevolent neutrality" toward Chandler that bordered on an endorsement of his candidacy.[102]

During the summer of 1894, as Blair and Chandler tried to perfect their campaign organizations, the American Protective Association (APA) unexpectedly intervened on Blair's behalf. This nativist, anti-Catholic organization first appeared in New Hampshire in 1894. The formation of its first lodge in Portsmouth brought an immediate negative response from the community in the form of a boycott.[103] Led by J. M. Ropes, the director of the YMCA in Laconia, the APA soon had chapters in several industrial cities in the state.[104] In September 1894, the national secretary of the APA spoke in Manchester on the topic "the A.P.A. and Romanism compared."[105] Other than conducting a small and peaceful parade in Franklin Falls in December, the APA made little effort to recruit large numbers of followers.[106]

If APA members had limited their involvement in New Hampshire politics to these few episodes, no one would have been concerned about their activities. However, in the midst of the fall 1894 campaign, the APA endorsed Blair for the U.S. Senate. Having concentrated its strength in Manchester, it designated A. M. Wilson of that city to direct the campaign. The order instructed local units to attend Republican caucuses and work for candidates favorable to Blair.[107] Chandler immediately confronted this new threat by persuading the APA national council to prevent local implementation of the plan.[108] In addition, he went on the offensive. He wrote to New Hampshire Republicans who supported some of the APA's positions, strenuously defending religious liberty in politics.[109]

Blair's opponents in Portsmouth charged that Blair endorsed the APA, but there is no evidence to support that claim.[110] On the other hand, there is no record that he directly repudiated the organization's backing. He may have believed that the group was so insignificant that it could be ignored. It is also possible that he was insensitive to the issues raised by the APA and the necessity to take a stand on them. He never expressed opposition to Catholic officeholding, but his remarks about Jesuits during discussions of the education bill marked him as someone who might be sympathetic to the APA cause. The entire episode brought little credit to Blair and gave him no discernible political advantage.

As if Blair did not have enough difficulties at this point, Chandler was able to arrange a formal political alliance with the B&M Railroad. Why the railroad chose to join ranks with its most consistent antagonist instead of Blair is something of a mystery. What is clear is that by early December 1894 Lucius Tuttle was actively involved in Chandler's canvass.[111] Surviving correspondence indicates that the relationship between the volatile senator and the imperious businessman was not a smooth one.[112] Nevertheless, the bargain was sealed, and the strange alliance held up throughout the entire caucus campaign. For many young New Hampshire politicians already aware of the political clout of the railroad, this was the final push necessary to place them in Chandler's camp.

Faced with this formidable alliance, Blair continued to labor in his traditional campaign style. He inundated legislators with documents and appeals for assistance.[113] He argued that he was entitled to the Senate seat on several counts. First, Chandler's machinations in 1891 had caused Blair's loss to Gallinger. Second, Blair had rescued the First Congressional District from Democratic control in 1892 at great personal sacrifice. Third, during the January 1893 carriage ride, Chandler had allegedly agreed to withdraw in Blair's favor. For the first time in his political career, Blair's tone became one of self-pity. In one of his appeals, he observed: "Meanwhile times have changed. I am older. Business opportunities have disappeared."[114] Although Blair was seeking support from people who were often unaware of his full political career, he did not emphasize his reform record. Concerned about the potency of Blair's arguments, Chandler issued one of his typical philippics against Blair. Like his earlier attacks against Blair, this one was political rather than personal. He simply disputed Blair's interpretation of the 1891 Senate contest and the 1893 conversation.[115] The two men apparently had too much respect for each other's integrity to indulge in the types of recrimination common to the politics of the times.

Surviving correspondence in the Chandler papers gives a clear indication why Chandler felt compelled to reply to Blair. Despite the overwhelming odds, Blair's old-fashioned personal style of campaigning was proving to be remarkably effective. A number of correspondents warned

| Table 6. 1895 Republican Caucus Vote for U.S. Senate | |
|---|---|
| | **First Ballot** |
| William E. Chandler | 224 |
| Henry W. Blair | 56 |
| John B. Smith | 2 |
| Charles H. Burns | 1 |
| Source: Manchester (NH) Union, January 11, 1895. | |

Chandler that Blair was unexpectedly winning the support of significant numbers of caucus members.[116] In an effort to blunt Blair's gains, the Chandler supporter Charles Marseilles called on Blair to withdraw from a hopeless contest.[117] Blair replied that he had entered the campaign at Chandler's invitation.[118] Unfortunately for Blair, the regular congressional session began in early December, forcing him to leave the direction of his canvass to others.[119] Although his absence had not been a handicap in past caucus battles, the Chandler organization was too powerful to overcome without his personal direction.

Sensing the weakness of Blair's candidacy, his campaign managers arranged a test vote that they might win. They came out in support of the candidacy of James O. Lyford for speaker of the New Hampshire House of Representatives. Since Lyford's opponent, Stephen S. Jewett, was closely associated with Chandler, this vote would be a strong indicator of how well Blair would fare in the Senate race. With strong support from Chandler's backers, Jewett was easily elected speaker by a 171–56 vote.[120] Despite the discouraging outlook, Blair remained in the contest until the end. Although he won 21 of Manchester's 28 votes at the January 1895 Republican caucus, Chandler drew the vast majority of the votes from the rest of the state (see table 6). With Gallinger assured of reelection in 1897, Blair now faced a bleak political future. The conditions necessary for his success had disappeared: a segment of voters committed to the reform programs and principles of the 1850s, a large and powerful group of Civil War veterans, and a political system that emphasized personal contacts and a willingness to work within the party structure. His consistent stands on issues—a virtue in earlier times—had become a liability that Blair could not escape. He was neither willing nor able to shape himself into the new style of political leader. Still, he must have felt much better about his situation than he had in the spring of 1892. His election to the House in 1892 had restored his reputation as a knowledgeable statesman, and he had demonstrated his continuing commitment to reform in the congressional sessions that followed. In the contest against Chandler, he had challenged the personal machine of the incumbent and the growing power of the B&M Railroad corporation with some success. Despite these achievements, Blair spent the remaining twenty-five years of his life as a spectator and commentator rather than as a direct participant in American politics and reform movements.

*Chapter 11*

# Later Years

Blair's last twenty-five years were a time of continued activity and interest in public life. Incomplete manuscript sources prevent a total reconstruction of this period, but it is possible to trace the broad outlines of these later years. While he had no major impact on national or state policies, Blair continued to take part in political events that were of interest to him. At the same time, he opened a law office in Washington, where he used his many personal contacts to become a successful lobbyist. As a former senator, he found that he had ready access to the Congress and executive branch. Many of his legal cases grew out of reform interests that he had championed earlier. While he was carving out a satisfying and financially rewarding existence for himself, Eliza and his son, Henry, were making major contributions of their own. These achievements helped buffer him against the death of friends and relatives that occurred throughout the period. Despite the loss of public office, the last years of Blair's life were a fitting conclusion to his political reform career.

After losing to Chandler, Blair continued to draw his congressional salary for the three remaining months of his term. This financial cushion gave him time to decide whether to set up his law practice in Washington or Manchester. The decision to practice in Washington must have been difficult because Eliza remained behind in Manchester. The reason for this separation is not clear except that she apparently found Washington life too taxing and Blair felt that he had the greatest opportunity for financial success in the nation's capital. Their surviving correspondence shows that the long distance between them was not the result of an estrangement and was deeply regretted by both. With his son living in Washington, Blair had an additional incentive to practice there. Henry had graduated from Columbian—now George Washington—University Law School in 1892 and had passed the bar in Washington.[1]

Another reason that Blair stayed in Washington was that the New

Henry W. Blair in retirement. Courtesy New Hampshire Historical Society, Giles Low II Collection, F2183.

Hampshire political landscape was becoming increasingly foreign to him. A group of energetic young reformers—known as Progressives—was challenging established Republican leaders like U.S. senator Jacob Gallinger for control of the New Hampshire Republican Party. Convinced that the older leadership had aligned itself with powerful economic entities to retain power, these new reformers ignored many of the issues addressed in the Civil War era and concentrated on the problems created by industrialization and urbanization. They openly condemned the close relations between the state Railroad Commission and the Boston and Maine Railroad and the rapid deforestation of the northern part of the state by large lumber companies. As automobiles became a major part of the transportation system, the Progressives demanded that the state improve its highway system. The final break between the old and the new Republican leadership occurred in 1903, when the state legislature passed a local option liquor bill ending the statewide prohibition that Blair had championed.[2] Clearly, there was no comfortable place for Henry Blair in this new Republican Party.

On August 9, 1895, Blair delivered a long address entitled "The Future of Temperance Reform" in Ocean Grove, New Jersey. He called for churches to become more directly involved in the battle to secure a national prohibition amendment. Taking a stance quite different from his complaints about Catholic Church interventions during the education bill debate, he asserted: "But it will be said that this is interfering with politics. Of course it is, and there is no way to advance the Temperance cause further without interfering in politics. The Christian religion has always been meddling in politics. The clergy have always led in the important politics of every great Christian country."[3] Despite the appearance of inconsistency, Blair firmly believed that politics was the proper arena for reformers, including clergymen.

Although the political realities of the 1890s precluded the revival of the education bill, Blair refused to accept final defeat. In a long letter to the black leader Booker T. Washington in early 1896, he urged the Alabama educator to support the concept of federal aid to southern schools. He noted that, as president of Tuskegee Institute, Washington was the leader of his race. With the disfranchisement movement rapidly gaining strength in the South, Blair maintained that the education bill offered the only hope of saving black political power.[4] While Washington may have agreed with Blair, his reply—if there was one—has not been preserved.

Following McKinley's election in 1896, Frances Willard and the Women's Christian Temperance Union urged McKinley to appoint Blair to some appropriate office.[5] While Blair undoubtedly would have been pleased by a suitable appointment, there is no record that he actively tried to secure a place. In any event, no appointment was forthcoming. Blair subsequently acted as an agent for a New Hampshire native seeking a presidential appointment as a customs collector in Alaska.[6] In another instance, he attempted to secure a favor for a former comrade from the Fifteenth Regiment.[7] These activities were very similar to what he had previously done as a member of Congress. Although Blair often used his past connections to secure a hearing for his cases, there is no evidence that he tried to secure an unfair or illegal advantage for his clients.

Blair's ability to blend reform interests with patronage work is illustrated by his strong advocacy for the appointment of Marilla Ricker as envoy to Colombia. Ricker was an extraordinary individual who became, by her action, the first woman to seek a diplomatic post in American history. Born in Durham, New Hampshire, she married a wealthy older man when she was quite young. He died, leaving her with a substantial estate. This financial independence allowed her to pursue her career interests without reference to prevailing ideas about the proper role of women in American society. Encouraged by her father and her late husband, both of whom believed that women should have full legal rights, Ricker began blazing new trails for American women. In 1870, she demanded the right to vote as a taxpayer under the Fourteenth Amendment. Starting the next year, she was allowed to vote in the state elections in New Durham Township. In 1872, she left for Europe to study at several universities and to learn a number of languages. On her return, she studied law and passed the District of Columbia bar examination in 1882. She was admitted as a recognized attorney before the Supreme Court, and, in 1890, she became the first woman allowed to practice law in New Hampshire. While forging this remarkable career, Ricker learned the full extent of discrimination directed toward women. In her application to McKinley, she not only stated her qualifications but also went on to say: "There is no gender in brain, and it is time to do away with the silly notion that there is."[8]

Blair pressed Ricker's candidacy with a vigor that indicated more than just a personal interest. He, like Ricker, saw this application as an opportunity to expand the horizons of American women. In a letter to McKinley, he said that he had known Ricker for many years. After reviewing her linguistic, legal, and even physical qualifications, he asserted: "In short, Mr. President, unless women are to be forever excluded from the diplomatic service, there can never be a more fortunate opportunity than this to take the advanced step . . . and . . . establish the great truth that the soul and not the sex of the applicant is the true test of the qualification for public service."[9] He followed this letter to McKinley with one to Chandler asking that the New Hampshire congressional delegation endorse Ricker's candidacy.[10] Blair continued to press McKinley on the matter by using the techniques that he had used during the fight for the education bill. He created the appearance of strong public support for the Ricker candidacy by securing an impressive number of endorsements and petitions.[11] Despite Blair's efforts, Ricker was passed over for a West Virginia newspaper editor who had helped McKinley carry that previously Democratic state. Blair's inability to obtain presidential appointments for Ricker or himself indicated that he could expect little patronage from the new Republican administration.

Regarding the education bill as his benchmark legislation, Blair continued to judge the value of his former associates on the basis of their stand on that one issue. Each time one of the bill's supporters died, he was reminded of the finality of the measure's defeat. After attending the funeral of one Senate colleague, he commented: "He was a great & good man and profoundly & powerfully for the education bill, making a very strong speech for it."[12]

On a more positive note, Blair became deeply involved in writing the history of his Civil War regiment. He spent much of his time between April and June 1899 looking for old records and photographs and composing autobiographical materials.[13] While writing *History of the Fifteenth Regiment, New Hampshire Volunteers, 1862–1863*, Charles McGregor heavily relied on Blair's research for certain types of information. The result was an unusually frank assessment of the regiment's record interspersed with flattering accounts of Blair's heroic actions.

During these years, Blair continued his career as an active lobbyist in Washington. With Chandler and most of his other contemporaries no longer in Congress, he became much more dependent on Gallinger to expedite matters for him.[14] Clients familiar with his past record continued to call on him, and he became one of the most active lobbyists for black interests. During the debate on the Hepburn Railway Regulation Act of 1906, Booker T. Washington hired him to try to protect black rights in interstate transportation.[15] As late as 1914, National Association for the Advancement of Colored People minutes indicate that Blair performed some services for that organization.[16]

Although Blair recognized that he was not in step with the dominant reform movement of the new century, he continued to pursue his dream of ensuring that every child in America had an opportunity to attend school. In 1902, he published an article entitled "The Negro Problem" in the *Independent*, using this forum to vindicate the education bill. He must have felt some satisfaction as well as frustration when he wrote: "Twenty years ago, and for ten years thereafter, incessantly, *I told you so.*"[17] Taking a somewhat different tack than he had in the 1880s, he urged: "Take care of the white race. . . . As their intelligence increases their prejudices will disappear, and in self-defense they will see to it that colored people have the same schools and opportunities, and the enjoyment of the same rights before the law which they possess themselves. To educate the white man is the negro's [*sic*] only hope."[18] He went on to suggest that private gifts could create an educational foundation large enough to carry out the work contemplated by the education bill. He called on the wealthy businessmen of the North to contribute to this fund.[19]

In May 1899, chronic illness forced Eliza into inactivity. Thereafter, her condition deteriorated to such an extent that Blair was forced to bring her to Washington, where he and Henry could care for her. Her suffering came to an end when she died in Washington on January 2, 1907.[20] Blair took her back to Campton, where she was buried in the Blair family plot in the public cemetery. While there is no record of his reaction to the loss of his wife of forty-seven years, circumstantial evidence suggests that Blair was momentarily overwhelmed. Composing a letter of condolence to Gallinger, whose wife had died a month later, he showed in his shaky writing the impact of emotional stress more than at any other time in his life. He may have been trying to console himself when he wrote: "I know your tender and generous nature must be crushed by this dreadful blow, and I also know how helpless mere words are in such distress."[21]

Eliza's death could have rendered the seventy-two-year-old Blair passive and started him on a swift emotional and physical decline. This did not happen in large part because of his relationship with his son. Young Henry proved to be the type of son that Blair hoped he would be. As a student at Exeter, he assumed a leadership position with student publications and made a number of close friendships.[22] During the summer of

Henry P. Blair in the 1890s. Courtesy New Hampshire Historical Society, Giles Low II Collection, F2204.

1887, he served as a camp counselor at Camp Chocorua in the lakes region of central New Hampshire. Young Blair appeared to be ideally suited for this position. He was the leading hitter and the catcher on the staff softball team, a song leader, and a hiking guide. As editor of the camp newsletter, he informed his youthful readers that their camp life was not just a way to "pass a pleasant summer: it has a higher purpose."[23] This echo of his father's thinking must have been particularly welcome to his parents. Even the drudgery of some camp responsibilities did not seem to destroy his enthusiasm.[24] One of his primary motivations for working at the camp was to earn monies that could be applied toward his college expenses at Dartmouth.

Young Henry's college years appear to have been quite successful and well-rounded. He and a partner won the college tennis championship in the spring of his senior year, and he was one of the class orators at graduation in June 1889.[25] The older Blair undoubtedly felt great pride in the fact that his son had not experienced the hardships he had endured and that the young man had fulfilled his one great and uncompleted ambition—to attend and graduate from Dartmouth. After graduating from law school in 1892, young Henry shared accommodations with his father in Washington for the next three decades.

Sharing accommodations with his son provided both companionship and financial security for Blair. In sharp contrast to his father, Henry proved to be a successful businessman. The younger Blair also achieved recognition as a sound scholar and legal advocate. From 1901 to 1909, he served on the faculty of the Columbian and George Washington University Law School. He also served as the first assistant corporation counsel for the city of Washington and maintained a flourishing private partnership. In 1914, Henry left his legal career to become president of the Equitable Life Insurance Company. President Calvin Coolidge later offered him a U.S. Supreme Court appointment that he declined. However, Henry continued the family tradition of public service by serving as president of the Washington Board of Education from 1913 to 1916. He also served as a member of several hospital boards, the Boy Scouts, and Saint Mark's Episcopal Church.[26] Having fulfilled his father's hopes, Henry was a source of great pride to Blair in his final years.

Following the death of his younger sister Esther in 1910, Blair spent considerable time with her children in Passaic, New Jersey. Family tradition remembers "Uncle Henry" as a stern patriarch who stayed with the family during a number of periods of illness.[27] He reportedly took a great interest in the younger members of the group and thoroughly enjoyed being the source of information about family history and tradition.[28] He was delighted when a grandnephew, Giles Low, moved back to Campton and settled on one of the two Beech Hill farms near where Blair had been raised by the Bartletts. He wanted to know everything about the old place: "I want you to write me about . . . every square foot of the farm, wood land, and all exterior boundaries, fences, the growth of wood and timber. . . . How about the cutting of the hay . . . and all of the particulars of the grasshoppers or their remains, if they are stored away in the catacombs of the old place."[29]

Blair did not completely ignore political matters after 1895. After receiving some assistance from William Howard Taft while the latter was secretary of war, he became a devoted follower. He also was impressed by Taft's administration of the Philippines.[30] The result was that he felt free to offer gratuitous advice to the future president. Counseling against a proposed plan to sell the Philippines to Japan, he ironically observed: "I don't believe that Japan will attempt to destroy us from off the face of the earth any way."[31] When the Republicans nominated Taft for president in 1908, Blair threw himself into the campaign, later claiming that he was partially responsible for the Republican victory.[32] After Taft's election, he felt free to request favors for the interests he represented. These groups often were businesses needing government assistance.[33] This new class of clients suggests that the growing perception of Blair as a relative conservative was making his financial situation more secure. Also, his increasingly successful son and old friends like Chandler may have been directing business to him.[34]

At the beginning of Taft's administration, Blair had warned him to appoint only Taft loyalists to the cabinet.[35] Blair's worst fears were realized when Theodore Roosevelt announced his candidacy for the 1912 Republican nomination. Blair, acting as an unofficial spokesman for Taft in New Hampshire, sought to return the campaign to "true issues" as he saw them. Writing to Taft, Taft's associates, and to newspapers, he urged Republicans to defend the protective tariff against "free trade" Democrats rather than fighting over "irrelevant" issues like primaries, initiative, referendum, and recall.[36] Consistent with Taft's campaign strategy, Blair believed that discussion should center around matters of substance like the tariff, the education bill, or granting suffrage for blacks and women rather than trying to change the rules of the game. After Progressives nominated Roosevelt, Blair formed the National Anti–Third Term League and acted as its president.[37] This paper organization, directed against Roosevelt, called for a constitutional amendment to limit presidents to two four-year terms. The league had no real impact on the campaign and marked the last contact between Taft and Blair.

In later years, Blair became involved in public affairs one last time. The debate over the peace treaty at the end of World War I stirred him to write a long letter to New Hampshire senator George H. Moses. He took the orthodox Republican position that the treaty should be amended before approval. What distinguished his position was the unique solution he offered to the treaty's shortcomings. He explained to Moses: "The proposed treaty has no foundation stone. It is built upon the sand and shall fail because it is not founded upon the rock of education of the masses of the people, without which democratic government is impossible. Such a peace is active preparation for final slavery or still greater wars. The education of the masses of the people is the supreme issue in the whole world."[38] More than six decades after failing to fulfill his own education ambitions, and nearly three decades after the defeat of the education bill, Blair continued to view universal education as the key to societal advancement and world peace.

On March 14, 1920, Blair's struggle to improve American society ended. He died at age eighty-five in a Washington hospital after a long and productive life.[39] His body was returned to Campton, and he was buried beside Eliza in the family plot. The grave site sits on a little hill in the Blair section of Campton overlooking the Blair covered bridge across the Pemigewasset River.

For most of his life, Blair placed higher priority on a political career than financial security. In most cases, the legislation that he introduced was derivative. Someone else provided the original inspiration, and he provided the practical details. Yet he was tremendously successful in creating coalitions to support reform legislation. While his beliefs did not affect personal relationships, he shared with many Protestant Americans a deep distrust of the Catholic Church. His response to the Chinese immigration bordered on the irrational. He never developed a clear understanding of how industrialization was changing the U.S. economy or of its pervasive influence on politics. Nonetheless, the events of 1920 demonstrate that his proposed reforms did not fail. It was in that year that two of his most "visionary schemes"—national prohibition and women's suffrage—became part of the U.S. Constitution. Two decades later, Congress approved federal funding for public education.

Blair's virtues and accomplishments were far greater than his shortcomings. He overcame enormous hardships in his youth and gained high public office despite being unable to complete his formal education. During the Civil War, he displayed great physical and moral courage. He was the finest popular politician and legislator in New Hampshire for two decades when the competition from other highly skilled politicians was intense. In a period of overwhelming materialism, Blair stood for reforms that he believed would advance the public interest. He had a vision of an America where women, blacks, and industrial workers would have greater legal and political rights and where social evils like ignorance and drunkenness would be abolished like slavery. While his poor personal finances sometimes led to unwise financial arrangements, he never knowingly betrayed the public trust in a period when many of his colleagues did. He was a good husband and father who encouraged his son to work for the good of society. He did all this with general good humor and with an optimistic frame of mind that encouraged others to persist in the face of great odds.

Blair's greatest contribution was his success in keeping alive the early Republican reform tradition. Like other Half-Breed Republicans, he refused to abandon blacks after Reconstruction. Lincoln's call for a government for and by the people remained a guiding principle throughout his life. But, like Lincoln and the early Republicans, Blair envisioned all this within a partisan political context. To him, reform outside the political system was an exercise in futility. Why should reformers abandon a process that had helped end slavery and that embodied Lincoln's vision of constructive and peaceful change? Although Blair's faith in the common people had boundaries, it was nevertheless genuine. His reform platform may have been more limited than later generations would have liked, but public wariness of federal interventions made incremental change the only viable option. In his own way, Blair shepherded essential American reforms through a hostile environment so that they could be reinterpreted and applied in more favorable political climates. This is a record that any public official would cherish. In Blair's case, the recognition of these accomplishments has been too long delayed.

# Notes

## Introduction

1. Henry Adams, *Democracy: An American Novel* (New York: New American Library, 1961), 90.

2. Matthew Josephson, *The Politicos: 1865–1896* (New York: Harcourt, Brace, 1938); William F. Gillette, *Retreat from Reconstruction: 1869–1879* (Baton Rouge: Louisiana State University Press, 1979).

3. John G. Sproat, *"The Best Men": Liberal Reformers in the Gilded Age* (New York: Oxford University Press, 1965), 70–93, 112–41; John M. Dobson, *Politics in the Gilded Age: A New Perspective on Reform* (New York: Praeger, 1972), 108–20, 161–70.

4. Ari Hoogenboom, *Outlawing the Spoils: A History of the Civil Service Reform Movement, 1865–1883* (Urbana: University of Illinois Press, 1961), 252–67; Gabriel Kolko, *Railroads and Regulation, 1877–1916* (New York: Norton, 1970), 45–83.

5. Richard E. Welch, *George Frisbee Hoar and the Half-Breed Republicans* (Cambridge, MA: Harvard University Press, 1971), 99–168.

6. Daniel W. Rowe, "American Victorianism as a Culture," *American Quarterly* 27 (December 1975): 515–17.

7. Ibid., 522–27.

8. Eric Foner, *Free Soil, Free Labor, Free Men: The Ideology of the Republican Party before the Civil War* (New York: Oxford University Press, 1970).

9. Lawrence A. Cremin, ed., *The Republic and the School: Horace Mann on the Education of Free Men* (New York: Columbia University Teachers College Bureau of Publications, 1957), 91.

10. Ferenc M. Szasz, "Daniel Webster—Architect of America's 'Civil Religion,'" *Historical New Hampshire* 34 (Fall–Winter 1979): 223–43.

11. See Henry W. Blair, *The Temperance Movement; or, The Conflict between Man and Alcohol* (Boston: William B. Smythe, 1888), 372–96.

## 1. Early Years

1. Alice Felt Tyler, *Freedom's Ferment: Phases of American Social History from the Colonial Period to the Outbreak of the Civil War* (New York: Harper & Bros., 1952), 70–78.

2. This account was related to me as part of the family's oral history by Giles Low II, a grandnephew of Henry Blair's, in June 1980.

3. Timothy L. Smith, *Revivalism and Social Reform: American Protestantism on the Eve of the Civil War* (New York: Harper & Row, 1957), 114–34; Charles W. Kern, *God, Grace, and Granite: The History of Methodism in New Hampshire, 1768–1988* (New York: Phoenix, 1988).

4. Stephen J. Stein, *The Shaker Experience in America: A History of the United Society of Believers* (Westport, CT: Praeger, 2003).

5. Newell G. Bringhurst, *Brigham Young and the Expanding American Frontier* (Boston: Little, Brown, 1986), 20–26; Claudia Lauper Bushman and Richard Lyman Bushman, *Building the Kingdom: A History of the Mormons in America* (New York: Oxford University Press, 2001); Works Progress Administration (WPA), *New Hampshire: A Guide to the Granite State* (Boston: Houghton Mifflin, 1938), 219.

6. George Wallingford, *John Humphrey Noyes, the Putney Community* (n.p., 1931).

7. WPA, *New Hampshire*, 408.

8. Emily W. Leavitt, *The Blair Family of New England* (Boston: David Clapp & Son, 1900), 22–23, 151–55.

9. Peter Blair et al., Agreement, Campton Congregational Church Records, New Hampshire Historical Society, Concord.

10. Quincy Blakely, *A Historical Discourse Delivered at the Centennial Celebration of the Congregational Church in Campton, N.H., October 20, 1874* (Boston: Alfred Mudge & Son, 1876), 21.

11. Leavitt, *Blair Family*, 155–56; Eben Little, Davy Baker, and Jacob Giddings, Statement, December 11, 1826, Henry William Blair Papers, New Hampshire Historical Society; Blakely, *Historical Discourse*, 65.

12. Blakely, *Historical Discourse*, 65; P. C. Headley, *Public Men of Today* (Hartford: S. S. Scranton, 1882), 94.

13. Henry W. Blair to Blanche L. Baker, April 6, 1911, Blair Papers.

14. Ibid.

15. Ibid.

16. Henry W. Blair, "Memoir of Gen. John Leverett Thompson," *Grafton and Coos Bar Association Proceedings* 3 (1895–1898): 156.

17. Henry W. Blair to Blanche L. Baker, April 6, 1911, Blair Papers.

18. Ibid.

19. Ibid.

20. Henry W. Blair, Memorandum, April 15, 1914, Blair Papers.

21. Eliza N. Blair, *'Lisbeth Wilson: A Daughter of New Hampshire Hills* (Boston: Lee & Shepard, 1895), 95–108.

22. James O. Lyford, *Life of Edward H. Rollins* (Boston: Dana Estes, 1906), 310.

23. Henry W. Blair, Memorandum, April 15, 1914, Blair Papers.

24. Henry W. Blair to Charles McGregor, June 19, 1899, in Charles McGregor, *History of the Fifteenth Regiment, New Hampshire Volunteers* (Concord, NH: Fifteenth Regiment Association, 1900), 124; "Hon. Henry William Blair," *Granite Monthly* 6 (April 1883): 194.

25. Blair to McGregor, June 19, 1899, in McGregor, *Fifteenth Regiment*, 124.

26. Henry W. Blair to Charles Marseilles, April 28, 1878, Charles Marseilles Papers, New Hampshire Historical Society.

27. Henry W. Blair to Blanche L. Baker, April 6, 1911, Blair Papers.

28. Campton School District Papers, New Hampshire Historical Society.

29. *Catalogue of the New Hampshire Conference Seminary and Female College, 1858–9* (Concord, NH: Fogg, Hadley, 1859).

30. Henry W. Blair to Charles McGregor, June 19, 1899, in McGregor, *Fifteenth Regiment*, 124.

31. Ibid.

32. Henry W. Blair, Biographical Sketch, March 5, 1867, Jonathan Eastman Pecker Papers, New Hampshire Historical Society; McGregor, *Fifteenth Regiment*, 125.

33. Joseph F. Kett, *Rites of Passage: Adolescence in America, 1790 to the Present* (New York: Basic, 1977), 29, 45. See also J. M. Opal, *Beyond the Farm: National Ambitions in Rural New England* (Philadelphia: University of Pennsylvania Press, 2008).

34. McGregor, *Fifteenth Regiment*, 125.

35. Charles H. Bell, *The Bench and Bar of New Hampshire* (Boston: Houghton Mifflin, 1894).

36. Ibid., 484; Blair, "Memoir of Gen. John Leverett Thompson," 156.

37. U.S. Bureau of the Census, Manuscript, 1860, Grafton County, New Hampshire, Reel 750, National Archives, Washington, DC.

38. Henry W. Blair, Report, January 15, 1857, and Alson L. Brown Petition, December 10, 1857, May 20, 1858, Blair Papers.

39. Ezra S. Stearns, *History of Plymouth, New Hampshire* (Cambridge, MA: Harvard University Press, 1906), 457–59, 573.

40. *New Hampshire Women: A Collection of Portraits and Biographical Sketches* (Concord: New Hampshire Publishing Co., 1895), 215.

41. Henry W. Blair to Albert S. Batchellor, August 31, 1908, Blair Papers.

42. "Hon. Henry William Blair," 196.

## 2. Colonel

1. James M. McPherson, *Battle Cry of Freedom: The Civil War Era* (New York: Ballantine, 1988), 213–33; Doris Kearns Goodwin, *Team of Rivals: The*

*Political Genius of Abraham Lincoln* (New York: Simon & Schuster, 2005), 260–78; David Herbert Donald, *Lincoln* (New York: Simon & Schuster, 1995), 250–56.

2. McPherson, *Battle Cry*, 234–59.

3. Goodwin, *Rivals*, 323–29; Donald, *Lincoln*, 285–92.

4. Goodwin, *Rivals*, 335–46.

5. Phillip Shaw Paludan, *The Presidency of Abraham Lincoln* (Lawrence: University Press of Kansas, 1994), 58–66.

6. Herman Hattaway and Archer Jones, *How the North Won: A Military History of the Civil War* (Urbana: University of Illinois Press, 1991), 41–45.

7. McPherson, *Battle Cry*, 418–21.

8. Ibid., 396–402, 415–18.

9. Hattaway and Jones, *North*, 176–81.

10. McPherson, *Battle Cry*, 491.

11. McGregor, *Fifteenth Regiment*, 125.

12. Stearns, *Plymouth*, 499.

13. Henry W. Blair to Anthony Colby, September 29, 1862, New Hampshire Adjutant General's Correspondence, New Hampshire Division of Records Management and Archives.

14. Muster Roll, November 12, 1862, Miscellaneous Regimental Papers, Fifteenth New Hampshire Infantry Regiment Volunteers, National Archives.

15. McGregor, *Fifteenth Regiment*, 125.

16. Ibid., 125.

17. Anthony Colby to John W. Kingman, November 7, 1862, Adjutant General's Correspondence; McGregor, *Fifteenth Regiment*, 143–44, 199.

18. McGregor, *Fifteenth Regiment*, 151–95.

19. Ibid., 195–200.

20. McPherson, *Battle Cry*, 577–79, 586–88, 626–29.

21. James G. Hollandsworth Jr., *Pretense to Glory: The Life of General Nathaniel P. Banks* (Baton Rouge: Louisiana State University Press, 1998), 89–101.

22. Hattaway and Jones, *North*, 376–78, 391–97.

23. Oren E. Farr to Nellie Farr, February 21, 1863, Oren E. Farr Papers, David M. Rubenstein Rare Book and Manuscript Library, Duke University Library.

24. U.S. War Department, *The War of the Rebellion: A Compilation of the Official Records of the Union and Confederate Armies*, ser. 1, vol. 15 (Washington, DC: U.S. Government Printing Office, 1882), 649.

25. McGregor, *Fifteenth Regiment*, 201.

26. Ibid., 234.

27. John W. Kingman to Nathaniel S. Berry, February 23, 1863, Governor's Records, and Muster-Out Roll, Miscellaneous Regimental Papers, New Hampshire Division of Records Management and Archives.

28. McGregor, *Fifteenth Regiment*, 274.

29. William Marvel, "Back from the Gates of Hell: The Deadly Campaign of the Drafted Militia," *Historical New Hampshire* 44 (Fall 1989): 105, 113–15.

30. McGregor, *Fifteenth Regiment*, 263.

31. Ibid., 320.

32. Curtis T. Cook, "The Siege of Port Hudson" (M.A. thesis, Louisiana State University, 1934), 78–79.

33. Hollandsworth, *Banks*, 118–33.

34. Cook, "Siege," 79–81; Frank L. Byrne, *Prophet of Prohibition: Neal Dow and His Crusade* (Madison: University of Wisconsin Press, 1961), 95–96; Edward Cunningham, *The Port Hudson Campaign, 1862–1863* (Baton Rouge: Louisiana State University Press, 1963), 56–58.

35. Cunningham, *Port Hudson*, 58.

36. Cook, "Siege," 57.

37. Lawrence Lee Hewitt, *Port Hudson: Confederate Bastion on the Mississippi* (Baton Rouge: Louisiana State University Press, 1987), 159–60.

38. McGregor, *Fifteenth Regiment*, 437–41.

39. Henry W. Blair, Biographical Sketch, March 5, 1867, Pecker Papers.

40. McGregor, *Fifteenth Regiment*, 437.

41. Ibid., 442n.

42. Ibid., 458.

43. Ibid., 482.

44. Ibid.

45. Ibid., 489–91.

46. Ibid., 523–24.

47. Ibid., 533.

48. Ibid., 590, 592.

49. Peter Eltinge to —— Eltinge, May 30, 1863, Eltinge-Lord Papers, Duke University Library.

50. *Congressional Record*, 51st Cong., 1st Sess., March 20, 1888, 2432.

51. James G. Hollandsworth, *The Louisiana Native Guards: The Black Military Experience during the Civil War* (Baton Rouge: Louisiana State University Press, 1995), 48–69.

52. *Congressional Record*, 51st Cong., 1st Sess., March 20, 1888, 2250.

53. Ibid., 2246.

54. *Congressional Record*, 51st Cong., 1st Sess., September 4, 1888, 8246.

55. McGregor, *Fifteenth Regiment*, 587.

56. "Hon. Henry William Blair," 195.

57. Hattaway and Jones, *North*, 375–416.

58. McPherson, *Battle Cry*, 670–81.

59. Ibid., 724–43.

60. Ibid., 743–56.

61. John C. Waugh, *Reelecting Lincoln: The Battle for the 1864 Presidency* (Cambridge, MA: Da Capo, 1997), 295–361; William C. Harris, "Conservative Unionists and the Presidential Election of 1864," *Civil War History* 38 (December 1992): 298–318; Paludan, *Presidency*, 285–93.

62. Hattaway and Jones, *North*, 629–74.

## 3. Apprentice Lawyer and Politician

1. Henry W. Blair, Biographical Sketch, March 5, 1867, Pecker Papers.

2. Donald B. Cole, *Jacksonian Democracy in New Hampshire, 1830–1851* (Cambridge, MA: Harvard University Press, 1970).

3. Francis E. Robinson, "Isaac Hill" (M.A. thesis, University of New Hampshire, 1933).

4. Roy F. Nichols, *Franklin Pierce: Young Hickory of the Granite Hills* (Philadelphia: University of Pennsylvania Press, 1931).

5. Richard H. Sewell, *John P. Hale and the Politics of Abolition* (Cambridge, MA: Harvard University Press, 1965), 51–54; Lucy M. Lowden, "Black as Ink, Bitter as Hell: John P. Hale's Mutiny in New Hampshire," *Historical New Hampshire* 27 (Spring 1972): 32–35.

6. Franklin Pierce to John P. Hale, January 24, 1845, Franklin Pierce Papers, Dartmouth College Library.

7. Nichols, *Pierce*, 133–34; Sewell, *Hale*, 57–58.

8. John H. White et al. to John Atwood, November 20, 1850, George S. Fogg Papers, New Hampshire Historical Society; Nichols, *Pierce*, 182–85; Lucy M. Lowden, "The People's Party: 'The Heirs of Jackson' and the Rise of the Republican Party in New Hampshire, 1845–1860" (M.A. thesis, Western Illinois University, 1971), 47–50.

9. Thomas R. Bright, "The Anti-Nebraska Coalition and the Emergence of the Republican Party in New Hampshire, 1853–1857," *Historical New Hampshire* 27 (Summer 1972): 69–70; *Portsmouth (NH) Daily Chronicle*, February 4, 7, 16, 25, March 3, 7, 1854; William Kent et al. to William Plummer Jr., February 11, 1854, William Plummer Papers, New Hampshire Historical Society.

10. *Portsmouth (NH) Daily Chronicle*, September 1, 1854, March 15, 1855, March 13, 1856; Lyford, *Rollins*, 39–46, 49–50.

11. William E. Gienapp, *The Origins of the Republican Party, 1852–1856* (New York: Oxford University Press, 1987), 103–47.

12. Ibid., 413–48.

13. Lex Renda, *Running on the Record: Civil War Era Politics in New Hampshire* (Charlottesville: University Press of Virginia, 1997), 11, 35–36, 51.

14. Ibid., 55.

15. Ibid., 56.

16. *Portsmouth (NH) Daily Chronicle*, July 13, 1854.

17. Gustavus Myers, *History of Bigotry in the United States* (New York: Random House, 1943), 221–22.

18. *Portsmouth (NH) Daily Chronicle*, May 8, 10, 1856.

19. Lyford, *Rollins*, 53–55, 69–70; Leon B. Richardson, *William E. Chandler, Republican* (New York: Dodd, Mead, 1940), 29–31.

20. Renda, *Record*, 69–132.

21. McPherson, *Battle Cry*, 170–233, 490–510, 698–717, 751–73, 803–6.

22. Richard Merrill Jr. to Leverett and Blair, November 16, 1865, and William Gordon to William Leverett and Henry W. Blair, November 28, 1865, Blair Papers.

23. State Election Returns, New Hampshire Department of Records Management and Archives, Concord, NH.

24. *Journal of the House of Representatives of the State of New Hampshire, June Session, 1866* (Concord, NH: George E. Jenks, 1866), 56.

25. *Manchester (NH) Union*, June 15, 1866; Henry W. Blair to Edward H. Rollins, April 26, 1870, Blair Papers.

26. *Journal of the House, 1866*, 232.

27. Ibid., 315.

28. Ibid., 317–19.

29. Ibid., 279, 300.

30. Ibid., 133.

31. Ibid., 329.

32. Lyford, *Rollins*, 200–203.

33. State Election Returns, New Hampshire Department of Records Management and Archives.

34. *Journal of the Honorable Senate of the State of New Hampshire, June Session, 1867* (Manchester, NH: John B. Clarke, State Printer, 1867), 49–50; *Manchester (NH) Union*, June 27, 1867.

35. *Journal of the Senate, 1867*, 43.

36. Charles W. Calhoun, *Conceiving the New Republic: The Republican Party and the Southern Question, 1869–1900* (Lawrence: University Press of Kansas, 2006), 7–89.

37. A. Burfree to Henry W. Blair, February 14, 1868, Blair Papers.

38. State Election Returns, New Hampshire Department of Records Management and Archives.

39. Ibid.

40. Henry W. Blair to Edward H. Rollins, April 26, 1870, Blair Papers.

41. George R. Fowler to Henry W. Blair, March 13, 1868, J. E. Pecker to Blair, March 30, 1868, and Levi W. Burton to Blair, April 8, 1868, Blair Papers.

42. *Journal of the Honorable Senate of the State of New Hampshire, June Session, 1868* (Manchester, NH: John B. Clarke, State Printer, 1868), 41, 44, 57, 66, 56, 91–92, 93, 98, 108.

43. D. L. Burnham to Henry W. Blair, February 10, 28, 1868, Blair Papers.

44. William E. Chandler to Henry W. Blair, February 9, 1868, Edward H. Rollins to Blair, February 17, 1868, and B. B. Huse to Blair, March 6, 1868, Blair Papers.

45. Sam B. Page to Blair, March 11, 1868, and "Eastern Grafton Educational Association," March 12, 13, 1868, Blair Papers.

46. *Journal of the Senate, 1868,* 91.

47. Ward A. McAfee, "Reconstruction Revisited: The Republican Education Crusade of the 1870s," *Civil War History* 42 (June 1996): 133–53, and *Religion, Race, and Reconstruction: The Public School in the Politics of the 1870s* (Albany: State University of New York Press, 1998), 79–149.

48. McAfee, *Public School,* 57–78.

49. Lyman D. Stevens to Henry W. Blair, December 6, 13, 1869, May 19, 1870, A. H. Cragin to Blair, July 5, 1870, and James W. Patterson to Blair, July 8, 1870, Blair Papers.

50. John C. Page, Statement, May 24, 1873, Hannah Ladd to Henry W. Blair, January 7, 1874, and Blair to A. H. Cragin, January 24, 1874, Blair Papers.

51. Hannah Ladd to Henry W. Blair, February 17, March 24, May 25, 1874, Blair Papers.

52. Horace S. Cummings to William E. Chandler, May 26, 1885, William Eaton Chandler Papers, New Hampshire Historical Society; Pamphlet (May 1885), Blair Papers.

53. Henry W. Blair to Second Auditor, Treasury Department, August 5, 1872, Blair Papers.

54. Henry W. Blair to William E. Chandler, August 13, 1872, Chandler Papers.

55. Henry W. Blair to William E. Chandler, February 8, April 14, 1873, Chandler Papers; George P. Folsom, Open Letter, April 4, 1873, and Blair to Nicholas Vedder, April 14, 1873, Blair Papers.

56. A. H. Cragin to Henry W. Blair, March 22, 1870, and Blair to Edward H. Rollins, April 26, 1870, Blair Papers.

57. *Journal of the House of Representatives of the State of New Hampshire, June Session, 1870* (Nashua, NH: Orren C. Moore, State Printer, 1870), 147, 178; *Journal of the Honorable Senate of the State of New Hampshire, June Session, 1870* (Nashua, NH: Orren C. Moore, State Printer, 1870), 61, 75, 84.

58. *New Hampshire Sentinel* (Keene), September 29, 1870.

59. A. C. Hardy to Henry W. Blair, October 24, 1871, Blair Papers.

60. H. P. Warren, "The New Hampshire State Normal School," *Granite Monthly* 5 (October 1881): 53.

61. Giles Low II, interview by the author, June 1980.

62. Lyford, *Rollins*, 243–44; *Manchester (NH) Union*, March 1, 1871.

63. *Portsmouth (NH) Daily Chronicle*, November 28, December 6, 1872.

64. L. B. Hoskins to Henry W. Blair, October 31, 1870, Ossian Ray to Blair, December 4, 1870, and Evarts Farr to Blair, December 13, 1870, Blair Papers.

65. Chester Pike to Henry W. Blair, December 30, 1870, Blair Papers.

66. Dexter F. White, "Senator James W. Patterson: Villain or Victim" (M.A. thesis, University of New Hampshire, 1956), 1–21.

67. Ibid., ii–iii; James W. Patterson, *Influence of Education upon Labor* (Springfield, MA: C. W. Bryan, 1873), and *The Relations of Education to Public Questions* (Hanover, NH: J. B. Parker, 1875).

68. James W. Patterson to Henry W. Blair, April 25, 1868, Blair Papers.

69. James W. Patterson to Henry W. Blair, August 12, 1870, Blair Papers.

70. James W. Patterson to Henry W. Blair, March 22, 1871, Blair Papers.

71. James W. Patterson to Henry W. Blair, August 8, 1868, Blair Papers.

72. James W. Patterson to Henry W. Blair, March 22, 1870, Blair Papers.

73. White, "Patterson," 21–33.

74. *New Hampshire Sentinel* (Keene), February 6, 1873.

75. James W. Patterson to William E. Chandler, February 23, 1879, Chandler Papers.

76. *New Hampshire Sentinel* (Keene), December 19, 26, 1872; *Granite State Free Press* (Lebanon, NH), December 20, 1872.

77. Henry W. Blair to William E. Chandler, January 14, 1873, Chandler Papers.

78. *New Hampshire Sentinel* (Keene), January 23, 1873.

79. Henry W. Blair to William E. Chandler, February 8, 1873, Chandler Papers.

80. *New Hampshire Sentinel* (Keene), February 20, 1873.

81. *Manchester (NH) Union*, January 16, 1873.

82. State Election Returns, New Hampshire Department of Records Management and Archives.

83. *Manchester (NH) Union*, January 8, 1874.

84. Lyford, *Rollins*, 309–10.

85. *Manchester (NH) Union*, February 27, 1874.

86. State Election Returns, New Hampshire Department of Records Management and Archives.

87. Edward Dow to Henry W. Blair, August 26, 1873, Blair Papers.

88. *Manchester (NH) Union*, February 23, 1874.

89. C. K. Kelley to Henry W. Blair, September 9, 1870, and J. L. Mesuries to Blair, February 17, 1871, Blair Papers.

90. "Hon. Henry William Blair," 195–96.

91. *Portsmouth (NH) Daily Chronicle*, December 20, 1873, June 19, 1874.

## 4. Congressman

1. Calhoun, *Southern Question*, 68–76.
2. *Portsmouth (NH) Daily Chronicle*, October 13, 1874.
3. Henry W. Blair to William E. Chandler, December 3, 1874, Chandler Papers.
4. *Granite State Free Press* (Lebanon, NH), January 15, 1875.
5. Ibid.
6. *Manchester (NH) Union*, January 5, 1875; *Portsmouth (NH) Daily Chronicle*, January 7, 1875.
7. Lyford, *Rollins*, 328–29; *Manchester (NH) Union*, January 13, 1875.
8. *Portsmouth (NH) Daily Chronicle*, January 8, 1875; Amos Newton Somers, *History of Lancaster, New Hampshire* (Concord, NH: Rumford, 1899), 239.
9. *Manchester (NH) Union*, January 8, 1875.
10. *New Hampshire Sentinel* (Keene), January 18, February 18, 1875.
11. Henry W. Blair to William E. Chandler, January 29, 1875, Chandler Papers.
12. *Portsmouth (NH) Daily Chronicle*, February 12, 1875.
13. *New Hampshire Sentinel* (Keene), March 4, 1875.
14. Henry W. Blair to William E. Chandler, February 1, 1875, Chandler Papers.
15. *Granite State Free Press* (Lebanon, NH), February 19, 1875; *White Mountain Republic* (Littleton, NH), February 25, 1875; *New Hampshire Sentinel* (Keene), March 4, 1875.
16. *Manchester (NH) Union*, February 24, 1875.
17. J. E. Rider to William E. Chandler, November 15, 1875, Chandler Papers.
18. William E. Chandler to Henry W. Blair, January 24, 1875, Chandler Papers.
19. *New Hampshire Sentinel* (Keene), March 4, 1875.
20. Henry W. Blair to Eliza N. Blair, February 24, 1875, Blair Papers.
21. State Election Returns, Federal Election Returns, New Hampshire Department of Records Management and Archives.
22. *Congressional Record*, 44th Cong., 1st Sess., December 20, 1875, 250.
23. *Congressional Record*, 44th Cong., 1st Sess., December 17, 1875, 241.
24. *Congressional Record*, 44th Cong., 1st Sess., index, 204–5, and 44th Cong., 2nd Sess., index, 115.
25. *Congressional Record*, 44th Cong., 1st Sess., January 21, 1876, 550–51.
26. *Congressional Record*, 44th Cong., 1st Sess., January 22, 1876, 576.
27. *Congressional Record*, 44th Cong., 1st Sess., May 18, 1875, 3165.
28. Ibid., 3170.
29. Ibid.
30. Ibid., 3171.
31. McAfee, *Public School*, 114–42.
32. *Congressional Record*, 44th Cong., 1st Sess., July 29, 1876, app., 235.

33. Ibid., 236.

34. Ibid., 236–43.

35. Henry W. Blair to Eliza N. Blair, July 30, 1876, Blair Papers.

36. Henry W. Blair to Eliza N. Blair, August 10, 1876, and J. M. Edmunds to Blair, August 24, 1876, Blair Papers.

37. *Congressional Record*, 44th Cong., 2nd Sess., December 12, 1876, 145.

38. *Congressional Record*, 44th Cong., 2nd Sess., December 27, 1876, app., 9.

39. Ibid., 9–10.

40. Ibid., 11–12, 16.

41. Ibid., 17.

42. Henry W. Blair to Eliza N. Blair, June 13, 1876, Blair Papers.

43. J. M. Edmunds to Henry W. Blair, August 24, 1876, and A. J. Huntoon to Blair, September 4, October 31, 1876, Blair Papers; *New Hampshire Sentinel* (Keene), September 25, 1876.

44. Daniel Hall to Henry W. Blair, August 26, September 11, 1876, Blair Papers; *Manchester (NH) Union*, September 25, 1876.

45. Henry S. Hilliard to Henry W. Blair, October 8, 1876, Blair Papers.

46. *Manchester (NH) Union*, February 5, 1877; W. Cone Mahurin to Henry W. Blair, February 16, 1877, Blair Papers.

47. *Granite State Free Press* (Lebanon, NH), January 26, 1877; *New Hampshire Sentinel* (Keene), February 1, 1877; Alfred H. Brown to Henry W. Blair, January 25, 1877, Samuel Nims to Blair, January 29, February 3, 1877, Leonard A. Maurin to Blair, February 15, 1877, and H. M. Putney to Blair, February 22, [1877], Blair Papers.

48. Charles A. Bridges to Henry W. Blair, November 16, 1876, and C. A. Field to Blair, December 9, 1876, Blair Papers; *New Hampshire Sentinel* (Keene), December 21, 1876.

49. *Granite State Free Press* (Lebanon, NH), January 12, 1877.

50. *New Hampshire Sentinel* (Keene), January 18, 1877.

51. Lyford, *Rollins*, 371.

52. J. I. Parsons to Henry W. Blair, March 4, 1877, Blair Papers.

53. W. Cone Mahurin to Henry W. Blair, February 16, 1877, and Charles A. Bridges to Blair, February 12, 1877, Blair Papers.

54. Edward H. Rollins to Henry W. Blair, January 4, 1877, Blair Papers.

55. Edward H. Rollins to Henry W. Blair, January 12, 1877, Blair Papers.

56. Henry W. Blair to William E. Chandler, March 12, 1877, Chandler Papers.

57. Federal Election Returns, New Hampshire Department of Records Management and Archives.

58. *New Hampshire Sentinel* (Keene), May 24, 1877; *Portsmouth (NH) Daily Chronicle*, June 20, 1877.

59. *Granite State Free Press* (Lebanon, NH), August 14, September 7, 1877.

60. *Manchester (NH) Union*, August 27, 1877.

61. *New York Times*, December 8, 1877.

62. See Vincent P. DeSantis, "President Hayes's Southern Policy," *Journal of Southern History* 12 (November 1955): 476–96.

63. *New Hampshire Sentinel* (Keene), October 25, 1877.

64. Henry W. Blair to William E. Chandler, April 8, 1877, Chandler Papers; *Manchester (NH) Union*, April 20, 1877.

65. *New Hampshire Sentinel* (Keene), December 6, 1877.

66. *Manchester (NH) Union*, December 14, 1877.

67. *New Hampshire Sentinel* (Keene), December 6, 1877.

68. *Congressional Record*, 45th Cong., 3rd Sess., February 14, 1879, app., 233.

69. Ibid.

70. *Congressional Record*, 45th Cong., 2nd Sess., June 13, 1878, app., 438.

71. Ibid., 440–41.

72. Ibid., 442.

73. *Congressional Record*, 45th Cong., 3rd Sess., February 28, 1879, 2124–25.

74. Ibid., 2219–22.

75. *New Hampshire Sentinel* (Keene), May 3, 1875.

76. *Granite State Free Press* (Lebanon, NH), May 3, 1878.

77. *New Hampshire Sentinel* (Keene), May 9, 1878.

78. Henry W. Blair to Charles Marseilles, January 6, March 12, 1878, Marseilles Papers.

79. *Congressional Record*, 44th Cong., 3rd Sess., January 18, 1879, app., 18.

80. *Congressional Record*, 45th Cong., 1st Sess., November 7, 1877, 258–59.

81. *Congressional Record*, 45th Cong., 2nd Sess., January 17, 1878, 399.

82. Ibid., 400.

83. *New Hampshire Sentinel* (Keene), January 2, 1879.

84. *New Hampshire Sentinel* (Keene), August 1, 1878.

85. Aaron F. Stevens to Henry W. Blair, December 14, 1878, Blair Papers.

86. Edgar H. Woodman to Henry W. Blair, December 11, 1878, Blair Papers.

87. William A. Willis to Henry W. Blair, December 19, 1878, E. G. Peirce to Blair, April 3, 1879, C. H. Thurston to Blair, April 21, 1879, J. W. Wheeler to Blair, April 25, 1879, and J. Frank Seavey to Blair, April 29, 1879, Blair Papers.

88. John B. Flanders to Henry W. Blair, December 23, 1878, Blair Papers. See also A. B. Stearns to Blair, December 18, 1878, and N. B. Prescott to Blair, February 17, 1879, Blair Papers.

89. John G. Cashman to Henry W. Blair, April 28, 1879, Blair Papers.

90. Joseph B. T. Graves to Henry W. Blair, December 24, 1878, Charles E. Campbell to Blair, December 1878, and T. A. Barker to Blair, March 29, 1879, Blair Papers.

91. James M. Lovering to William E. Chandler, December 31, 1878, Chandler Papers.

92. J. A. Wood to William E. Chandler, January 17, 1879, Chandler Papers.

93. J. A. Wood to William E. Chandler, February 28, 1879, Chandler Papers; J. T. S. Libbey to Henry W. Blair, February 28, 1879, Blair Papers.

94. J. T. S. Libbey to Henry W. Blair, December 20, 1878, and Hiram Hodgdon to Blair, January 27, 1879, Blair Papers.

95. Clipping, *Boston Advertiser*, June 14, 1879, Blair Papers; Lyford, *Rollins*, 414–15.

96. Aaron F. Stevens to William E. Chandler, May 25, 1879, Chandler Papers.

97. J. A. Wood to William E. Chandler, February 6, 1879, Chandler Papers.

98. J. T. S. Libbey to Henry W. Blair, December 20, 1878, February 28, 1879, W. R. Shepard to Blair, December 23, 1878, Charles E. Campbell to Blair, December 1878, February 5, 1879, J. E. French to Blair, February 20, May 31, 1879, D. J. Spinney to Blair, April 1, 1879, C. L. Chapman to Blair, April 3, May 16, 24, 1879, Albert Wallace to Blair, April 8, 1879, Alexander Warden to Blair, April 9, 1879, D. E. Willard to Blair, April 11, 1879, C. R. Thurston to Blair, April 21, 1879, J. W. Wheeler to Blair, April 25, 1879, B. F. Rackley to Blair, April 28, 1879, John G. Chapman to Blair, April 28, 1879, J. Frank Seavy to Blair, April 29, 1879, J. J. Merrow to Blair, May 24, 1879, and E. B. Philbrick to Blair, May 29, 1879, Blair Papers.

99. W. E. Stevens to William E. Chandler, February 14, 1879, and James W. Patterson to Chandler, February 23, 1879, Chandler Papers; *New Hampshire Sentinel* (Keene), March 6, 1879.

100. H. Wayne Morgan, *From Hayes to McKinley: National Party Politics, 1877–1896* (Syracuse, NY: Syracuse University Press, 1969), 32–39.

101. W. E. Stevens to William E. Chandler, February 14, 1879, Chandler Papers.

102. E. H. Rollins to William E. Chandler, April 25, May 3, 1879, Chandler Papers.

103. D. J. Spinney to Henry W. Blair, April 1, 1879, Blair Papers.

104. Clipping, *Boston Advertiser*, June 14, 1879, Blair Papers.

105. William E. Chandler, *Reply of Mr. Wm. E. Chandler to the Slanders of Honorable Bainbridge Wadleigh, Lately U.S. Senator* (Concord, NH: n.p., 1879), 16.

106. Ibid., 13–14.

107. Ibid., 16–21.

108. Ibid., 23.

109. Eugene Hale to William E. Chandler, June 14, 1879, and James T. Beach to Chandler, June 16, 1879, Chandler Papers.

110. *New York Times*, June 13, 1879.

111. William E. Chandler, *Mr. Chandler's Rejoinder to Mr. Wadleigh* (n.p., 1879).

112. *Portsmouth (NH) Daily Chronicle*, June 14, 1879.

113. Tally Sheet, [June 12, 1879], Clipping, *Boston Herald*, June 14, 1879, Blair Papers.

114. Clipping, *Boston Advertiser*, June 14, 1879, Blair Papers.

115. *New York Times*, June 13, 1879.

116. *Portsmouth (NH) Daily Chronicle*, June 13, 1879.

117. *New York Times*, June 13, 1879.

118. Clipping, *Boston Herald*, June 14, 1879, Blair Papers.

119. Lyford, *Rollins*, 412.

120. Clipping, *Boston Globe*, June 14, 1879, Blair Papers.

121. *Journal of the Honorable House of Representatives of the State of New Hampshire, June Session, 1879* (Manchester: John B. Clarke, State Printer, 1879), 304–5.

122. Clipping, *Boston Journal*, [June 1879], Blair Papers; *New Hampshire Sentinel* (Keene), June 19, 1879.

123. Eugene Hale to William E. Chandler, June 14, 1879, Chandler Papers.

## 5. Origin of the Education Bill

1. Henry W. Blair to Eliza N. Blair, June 19, 20, 1879, Blair Papers.

2. Henry W. Blair to Eliza N. Blair, July 4, 1879, and Mrs. R. S. Kimball to Eliza N. Blair, July 18, 1879, Blair Papers.

3. Henry W. Blair to Eliza N. Blair, July 4, 1879, Blair Papers.

4. David J. Rothman, *Politics and Power: The United States Senate, 1869–1900* (New York: Atheneum, 1969), 111–19.

5. Ibid., 120–36.

6. *Congressional Record*, 45th Cong., 1st Sess., June 27, 1879, 2383.

7. Clipping, August 12, 1879, Blair Papers.

8. Henry W. Blair to Eliza N. Blair, July 4, 1879, Blair Papers.

9. *New Hampshire Sentinel* (Keene), August 28, 1879.

10. Henry W. Blair to Eliza N. Blair, July 31, August 18, 1879, Blair Papers.

11. Henry W. Blair to Eliza N. Blair, August 10, 1879, Blair Papers.

12. Henry W. Blair to James A. Garfield, July 5, 1880, James Abram Garfield Papers, Library of Congress, Washington, DC.

13. Henry W. Blair to Eliza N. Blair, September 6, 1879, Blair Papers.

14. Henry W. Blair to William E. Chandler, November 20, 1879, Chandler Papers.

15. G. A. Ruby to Henry W. Blair, May 15, 1880, and —— Brady to Blair, June 2, 1879, Blair Papers.

16. *Congressional Record*, 46th Cong., 3rd Sess., February 20, 1880, 1326.

17. Henry W. Blair to Eliza N. Blair, August 21, 1879, September 23, [1879], Blair Papers.

18. *New Hampshire Sentinel* (Keene), April 29, 1880.

19. *Congressional Record*, 46th Cong., 3rd Sess., December 7, 1880, 14–15.

20. M. Gabrielene Wagener, "A Study of Catholic Opinion on Federal Aid to Education, 1870–1945" (Ph.D. diss., University of Notre Dame, 1963), 54.

21. Daniel W. Crofts, "The Blair Bill and the Elections Bill: The Congressional Aftermath to Reconstruction" (Ph.D. diss., Yale University, 1968), 33.

22. Gordon C. Lee, *The Struggle for Federal Aid, First Phase: A History of the Attempts to Obtain Federal Aid for Common Schools, 1870–1890* (New York: Bureau of Publications, Teachers College, Columbia University, 1949), 89.

23. *Congressional Record*, 46th Cong., 3rd Sess., December 17, 1880, 217.

24. Ibid., 219.

25. McAfee, *Public School*, 105–13.

26. Wagener, "Catholic Opinion," 49–50; John W. Evans, "Catholics and the Blair Education Bill," *Catholic Historical Review* 46 (October 1960): 276–78.

27. James B. Clyne, "The Catholic Attitude towards Federal Aid in Education in the United States: 1870–1892" (M.A. thesis, Catholic University, 1952), 28–36.

28. Crofts, "Blair Bill and Elections Bill," 10–16; McAfee, *Public School*, 114–16.

29. Crofts, "Blair Bill and Elections Bill," 20.

30. William Mahone to Harrison E. Riddleberger, August 31, 1877, Letterbook No. 27, 303, and R. T. Thorp to Mahone, November 6, 1879, William Mahone Papers, Duke University Library; *Bristol News*, November 13, 1877, November 6, 1879; Elizabeth A. Hancock, ed., *Autobiography of John E. Massey* (New York: Neale, 1909), 147; William C. Pendleton, *Political History of Appalachian Virginia, 1776–1927* (Dayton, VA: Shenandoah, 1927), 334–36; Jack P. Maddux Jr., *The Virginia Conservatives, 1867–1879: A Study in Reconstruction Politics* (Chapel Hill: University of North Carolina Press, 1970), 273; Charles E. Wynes, *Race Relations in Virginia, 1870–1902* (Charlottesville: University Press of Virginia, 1961), 19.

31. T. J. Kilpatrick to William Mahone, October 29, 1881, Mahone Papers; *Woodstock Virginian*, May 19, 1882.

32. Henry W. Blair to William Mahone, December 7, 1881, Mahone Papers.

33. *Congressional Record*, 46th Cong., Special Session, March 18, 1881, 33.

34. *New Hampshire Sentinel* (Keene), April 21, 1881.

35. Henry W. Blair to J. Ambler Smith, June 25, 1881, Mahone Papers.

36. Henry W. Blair to William E. Chandler, September 28, 1881, Chandler Papers.

37. Ibid.

38. Rothman, *Politics and Power*, 26–36.

39. Crofts, "Blair Bill and Elections Bill," 23–28.

40. J. L. M. Curry to Rutherford B. Hayes, April 14, 1882, in *Teach the Freeman: The Correspondence of Rutherford B. Hayes and the Slater Fund for Negro Education*, ed. Louis Rubin (Baton Rouge: Louisiana State University Press, 1959), 33; Jessie P. Rice, *J. L. M. Curry: Southerner, Statesman, and Educator* (New York: King's Crown, 1949), 116–18.

41. Crofts, "Blair Bill and Elections Bill," 35–37.

42. Ibid., 45–46.

43. Gladys V. King, "The Blair Education Bill with Special Reference to Southern Attitudes" (M.A. thesis, University of North Carolina, 1943), 10–11.

44. King, "Blair Education Bill," 59–65.

45. Crofts, "Blair Bill and Elections Bill," 46.

46. Ibid., 46–47.

47. Ibid., 47–49.

48. *Congressional Record*, 47th Cong., 1st Sess., December 6, 1881, 21.

49. *Congressional Record*, 47th Cong., 1st Sess., June 13, 1882, 4833.

50. Ibid., 4520–33.

51. *Manchester (NH) Union*, June 14, 1882.

52. *Congressional Record*, 47th Cong., 1st Sess., June 13, 1882, 4820–22.

53. Rush Welter, *Popular Education and Democratic Thought in America* (New York: Columbia University Press, 1952), 152.

54. *Congressional Record*, 47th Cong., 1st Sess., June 13, 1882, 4523–33.

55. Ibid., 4833.

56. Crofts, "Blair Bill and Elections Bill," 53.

57. *New Hampshire Sentinel* (Keene), December 6, 1882.

58. *Congressional Record*, 45th Cong., 1st Sess., March 18, 1884, 2008; Lee, *Federal Aid*, 106.

59. *Congressional Record*, 45th Cong., 1st Sess., March 18, 1884, 2008; Crofts, "Blair Bill and Elections Bill," 53–54.

60. Rice, *Curry*, 116–18.

61. Crofts, "Blair Bill and Elections Bill," 60–61.

62. The most complete study of black support is Daniel W. Crofts, "The Black Response to the Blair Education Bill," *Journal of Southern History* 37 (February 1971): 41–65.

63. Allen J. Going, "The South and the Blair Bill," *Mississippi Valley Historical Review* 44 (September 1957): 273.

64. *Congressional Record*, 47th Cong., 2nd Sess., January 15, 1883, 1446–47.

65. *Congressional Record*, 47th Cong., 2nd Sess., January 9, 1883, 1015.

66. Crofts, "Blair Bill and Elections Bill," 55–56.

67. Ibid., 58–59.

68. Ibid., 60–61.

69. Ibid., 61–62.

70. *Congressional Record*, 48th Cong., 1st Sess., December 5, 1883, 36.

71. J. L. M. Curry to Robert C. Winthrop, April 10, 1884, and Winthrop to Curry, April 15, 1884, Jabez Lamar Monroe Curry Papers, Library of Congress.

72. *Congressional Record*, 48th Cong., 1st Sess., March 18, 1884, 1999.

73. *New Hampshire Sentinel* (Keene), January 30, 1884.

74. Ibid.

75. *Congressional Record*, 48th Cong., 1st Sess., March 18, 1884, 1999.

76. Ibid.

77. Ibid., 2000.

78. Ibid., 2000–2001.

79. Ibid., 2008–9.

80. Ibid., 2013–29.

81. Ibid., 2030–31.

82. *Congressional Record*, 48th Cong., 1st Sess., March 19, 1884, 2061.

83. Ibid., 2061.

84. Ibid., 2066.

85. Ibid., 2069–70.

86. *Congressional Record*, 48th Cong., 1st Sess., March 21, 1884, 2147–48.

87. Crofts, "Blair Bill and Elections Bill," 64.

88. Ibid., 65–66.

89. Ibid., 67–69.

90. *Congressional Record*, 48th Cong., 1st Sess., April 7, 1884, 2724.

91. J. L. M. Curry to Robert C. Winthrop, April 10, 1884, Curry Papers.

92. Henry W. Blair to William M. Evarts, April 29, 1884, William Marwell Evarts Papers, Library of Congress.

93. Crofts, "Blair Bill and Elections Bill," 103–4.

94. Ibid., 104–5.

95. James A. Barnes, *John G. Carlisle, Financial Statesman* (New York: Dodd, Mead, 1931), 152–53.

96. Henry W. Blair to Grover Cleveland, November 26, 1884, Series 2, Reel 2, Grover Cleveland Papers, Library of Congress.

97. Crofts, "Blair Bill and Elections Bill," 107; *Portsmouth (NH) Daily Chronicle*, December 10, 1884.

98. Crofts, "Blair Bill and Elections Bill," 107.

99. Ibid., 105.

100. Ibid., 109–10.

101. *Manchester (NH) Union*, August 2, 1884.

102. "Aspects of National Education," *Catholic World* 31 (June 1880): 398–409;

Isaac T. Hecker, "Catholics and Protestants Agreeing on the School Question," *Catholic World* 32 (February 1881): 699–713, "A New but False Plea for the Public Schools," *Catholic World* 36 (December 1882): 412–22, and "The Impending Issue of the School Question," *Catholic World* 36 (March 1883): 849–52; Bernard J. McQuaid, "The Other Side of the Story as Told by an American," *Journal of Education* 17 (March 15, 1883): 163–64; J. F. Slattery, "Some Aspects of the Negro Problem," *Catholic World* 38 (February 1884): 604–13.

103. Crofts, "Black Response," 55.

104. See *Richmond (VA) Planet*, February 21, 1885.

105. Crofts, "Blair Bill and Elections Bill," 83–86.

## 6. A Sense of Place

1. John William Ward, *Andrew Jackson: Symbol for an Age* (New York: Oxford University Press, 1962).

2. Kevin T. Barksdale, *The Lost State of Franklin: America's First Secession* (Lexington: University Press of Kentucky, 2009), and "Our Rebellious Neighbors: Virginia's Border Counties during Pennsylvania's Whiskey Rebellion," *Virginia Magazine of History and Biography* 111 (2003): 5–32; Jeffrey J. Crow, "The Whiskey Rebellion in North Carolina," *North Carolina Historical Review* 66 (January 1989): 1–28; Burt Feintuch and David Watters, eds., *The Encyclopedia of New England* (New Haven, CT: Yale University Press, 2005), 671; Edwin Arzo Charlton, *New Hampshire as It Is: A Historical Sketch of New Hampshire; A Gazetteer of New Hampshire; A General View of New Hampshire* (Whitefish, MT: Kessinger, 2008), 348; WPA, *New Hampshire*, 335.

3. Kenneth W. Noe and Shannon Wilson, eds., *The Civil War in Appalachia: Collected Essays* (Knoxville: University of Tennessee Press, 1997); Noel C. Fisher, *War at Every Door: Partisan Politics and Guerrilla Violence in East Tennessee, 1860–1869* (Chapel Hill: University of North Carolina Press, 1997); W. Todd Groce, *Mountain Rebels: East Tennessee and the Civil War, 1860–1870* (Knoxville: University of Tennessee Press, 1999); John C. Inscoe and Gordon B. McKinney, *The Heart of Confederate Appalachia: Western North Carolina in the Civil War* (Chapel Hill: University of North Carolina Press, 2000); Martin Crawford, *Ashe County's Civil War: Community and Society in the Appalachian South* (Charlottesville: University Press of Virginia, 2001); Brian D. McKnight, *Contested Borderland: The Civil War in Appalachian Kentucky and Virginia* (Lexington: University Press of Kentucky, 2006); Jonathan Dean Sarris, *A Separate Civil War: Communities in Conflict in the Appalachian South* (Charlottesville: University Press of Virginia, 2006).

4. Charlton, *New Hampshire*, 237; James B. Vickery, Richard E. Judd, and Sheila McDonald, "Maine Agriculture, 1783–1861," in *Maine: The Pine Tree*

*State from Prehistory to the Present,* ed. Richard E. Judd, Edwin A. Churchill, and Joel W. Eastman (Orono: University of Maine Press, 1995), 243, 246; Paul W. Gates, "Two Hundred Years of Farming in Gilsum," *Historical New Hampshire* 33 (Spring 1978): 6; Alonzo J. Fogg, *Statistics and Gazetteer of New Hampshire* (Concord, NH: D. L. Guernsey, 1874), 82.

5. Feintuch and Watters, eds., *Encyclopedia,* 571.

6. Lynn A. Bonfield and Mary Morrison, "'Tell us all the news': Letters from Peacham, Vermont, at Mid-Nineteenth Century," *Vermont History* 48 (Summer/Fall 2000): 182.

7. Feintuch and Watters, eds., *Encyclopedia,* 548.

8. Jesse H. Shera, *Foundations of the Public Library: The Origins of the Public Library Movement in New England, 1629–1855* (Chicago: University of Chicago Press, 1949), 69–186.

9. William J. Gilmore, *Reading Becomes a Necessity: Material and Cultural Life in Rural New England* (Knoxville: University of Tennessee Press, 1989), 82.

10. Fogg, *Gazetteer,* 307.

11. Wilson Smith, "Purity and Progress in New Hampshire: The Role of Charles B. Haddock," *New England Quarterly* 28 (December 1956): 463–64, 467–68, 470.

12. Gilmore, *Reading,* 119.

13. Fogg, *Gazetteer,* 98–99, 121, 185, 316, 339, 350–51; Charlton, *New Hampshire,* 128, 257.

14. Robert L. Ferm, "Seth Storrs, Congregationalism, and the Founding of Middlebury College," *Vermont History* 64 (January 2001): 258.

15. Feintuch and Watters, eds., *Encyclopedia,* 30, 874. For example, the small city of Claremont, New Hampshire, contained extensive farmland and a company that manufactured lathes and planers, two shoe factories, a cotton cloth mill, a woolen cloth mill, a cutlery company, a paper and book maker, two banks, and forty-six stores. See Charlton, *New Hampshire,* 150–53.

16. Eric Purchase, *Out of Nowhere: Disaster and Tourism in the White Mountains* (Baltimore: Johns Hopkins University Press, 1999), 26, 117; [Lucy Crawford], *Lucy Crawford's History of the White Mountains* (1846; Boston: Appalachian Mountain Club, 1970); James L. Garvin, "Early White Mountain Taverns," *Historical New Hampshire* 50 (Spring/Summer 1995): 23–37; Dona Brown, *Inventing New England: Regional Tourism in the Nineteenth Century* (Washington, DC: Smithsonian Institution Press, 1995), 43–74; Robert L. McGrath and Barbara J. MacAdam, *"A Sweet Foretaste of Heaven": Artists in the White Mountains, 1830–1930* (Hanover, NH: University Press of New England, 1988).

17. F. Allen Burt, *The Story of Mount Washington* (Hanover, NH: Dartmouth Publications, 1960); Purchase, *Disaster,* 44, 50.

18. McGrath and MacAdam, *Artists*.

19. Nathaniel Hawthorne, *Twice-Told Tales* (New York: Modern Library, 2001); Purchase, *Disaster*, 110.

20. Brown, *Tourism*, 52, 61–68, 80–81.

21. Feintuch and Watters, eds., *Encyclopedia*, 461, 474, 504; Ernest L. Scott, "Sarah Josepha Hale's New Hampshire Years," *Historical New Hampshire* 49 (Summer 1994): 96.

22. *Manchester (NH) Union Leader*, September 24, 1885.

23. Ibid.

24. *Congressional Record*, 47th Cong., 2nd Sess., January 10, 1883, 1184–85.

25. *Congressional Record*, 51st Cong., 1st Sess., September 5, 1890, 9716.

26. *Congressional Record*, 48th Cong., 1st Sess., March 19, 1884, 2070.

27. *Congressional Record*, 48th Cong., 1st Sess., March 18, 1884, 2029–30.

28. *Congressional Record*, 51st Cong., 1st Sess., August 12, 1890, 8405.

29. *Congressional Record*, 46th Cong., 3rd Sess., February 8, 1881, 1352.

30. *Mountain Echo* (London, KY), December 23, 1881, September 8, 1882.

31. *Congressional Record*, 51st Cong., 1st Sess., February 19, 1890, 1493.

32. Noe and Wilson, eds., *Civil War in Appalachia*; Fisher, *War at Every Door*; Groce, *Mountain Rebels*; Inscoe and McKinney, *Confederate Appalachia*; Crawford, *Ashe County's Civil War*; McKnight, *Contested Borderland*; Sarris, *Separate Civil War*.

33. Gordon B. McKinney, *Southern Mountain Republicans, 1865–1900: Politics and the Appalachian Community* (Chapel Hill: University of North Carolina Press, 1978).

34. McKinney, *Mountain Republicans*, 146–81; Richard D. Starnes, "The Stirring Strains of Dixie: The Civil War and Southern Identity in Haywood County, North Carolina," *North Carolina Historical Review* 74 (July 1997): 237–59.

35. Ronald D. Eller, *Miners, Millhands, and Mountaineers: Industrialization of the Appalachian South, 1880–1930* (Knoxville: University of Tennessee Press, 1978), 39–85.

36. Henry D. Shapiro, *Appalachia on Our Mind: The Southern Mountains and Mountaineers in the American Consciousness, 1870–1920* (Chapel Hill: University of North Carolina Press, 1978), 15–26, 60–80.

37. Anthony Harkins, *Hillbilly: A Cultural History of an American Icon* (New York: Oxford University Press, 2004), 49; J. W. Williamson, *Hillbillyland: What Movies Did to the Mountains and What the Mountains Did to the Movies* (Chapel Hill: University of North Carolina Press, 1995), 1–20.

38. Shannon H. Wilson, *Berea College: An Illustrated History* (Lexington: University Press of Kentucky, 2006), 78–80.

39. Nancy F. Elkins, "Seventh-Day Adventists: A Study of Home Mission

Work in Western North Carolina," *Appalachian Journal* 5 (Winter 1981): 119–25; Mark Andrew Huddle, "Soul Winner: Edward O. Guerrant, the Kentucky Home Missions, and the 'Discovery' of Appalachia," *Ohio Valley History* 5 (2005): 47–64.

40. Mary Breckinridge, *Wide Neighborhoods: A Story of the Frontier Nursing Service* (Lexington: University Press of Kentucky, 1981); Gene Wilhelm Jr., "Folk Settlements in the Blue Ridge Mountains," *Appalachian Journal* 5 (Winter 1978): 204–45.

41. Shapiro, *Appalachia*, 32–58.

42. John Alexander Williams, *West Virginia and the Captains of Industry* (Morgantown: West Virginia University Library, 1976).

43. Richard D. Starnes, *Creating the Land of the Sky: Tourism and Society in Western North Carolina* (Tuscaloosa: University of Alabama Press, 2005).

44. *Congressional Record*, 51st Cong., 1st Sess., February 5, 18, 19, 1890, 1075, 1439, 1443–44, 1480–81, 1493.

45. *Congressional Record*, 51st Cong., 1st Sess., February 10, 1890, 1164–66.

46. *Portsmouth (NH) Daily Chronicle*, November 2, 1889.

47. *Congressional Record*, 51st Cong., 1st Sess., February 18, 1890, 1440.

48. *Congressional Record*, 51st Cong., 1st Sess., February 17, April 24, 1890, 1395, 3756.

49. Willard B. Gatewood, "North Carolina and Federal Aid to Education: Reaction to the Blair Bill, 1881–1890," *North Carolina Historical Review* 40 (October 1963): 470–72; Scrapbook, 1883, William O'Connell Bradley Papers, University of Kentucky Library; William Lamb to Henry W. Blair, November 24, 1888, Series 1, Reel 13, Benjamin Harrison Papers, Library of Congress; Going, "South," 278.

50. King, "Blair Education Bill," 82–83.

51. U.S. Senate Committee on Education and Labor, *Report on the Relations between Labor and Capital*, 4 vols. (Washington, DC: U.S. Government Printing Office, 1885), 4:1; *Congressional Record*, 47th Cong., 2nd Sess., February 2, 1883, 1976–77.

52. W. David Lewis, *Sloss Furnaces and the Rise of the Birmingham District: An Industrial Epic* (Tuscaloosa: University of Alabama Press, 1994), 41–42, 46–61, 66, 69; U.S. Senate Committee on Education and Labor, *Report on Labor and Capital*, 4:27, 29, 34, 133–35, 169–70, 193, 234, 247, 250–65, 347–49, 361.

53. Derrell Roberts, "Joseph E. Brown and the Convict Lease System," *Georgia Historical Quarterly* 44 (December 1960): 399–410; Allen Johnston Going, *Bourbon Democracy in Alabama, 1874–1890* (University: University of Alabama Press, 1951), 181–83; Daniel A. Novak, *The Wheel of Servitude: Black Forced Labor after Slavery* (Lexington: University Press of Kentucky, 1978), 23–33; Robert David Ward and William Warren Rogers, *Convicts, Coal, and the Banner Elk*

*Tragedy* (Tuscaloosa: University of Alabama Press, 1987); A. C. Hutson, "The Overthrow of the Convict Lease System in Tennessee," *East Tennessee Historical Society's Publications* 51 (1979): 92–113; Karin A. Shapiro, *A New South Rebellion: The Battle against Convict Labor in the Tennessee Coalfields, 1871–1896* (Chapel Hill: University of North Carolina Press, 1998); Gordon B. McKinney, "Zeb Vance and the Construction of the Western North Carolina Railroad," *Appalachian Journal* 29 (Fall 2001–Spring 2002): 58–67.

54. U.S. Senate Committee on Education and Labor, *Report on Labor and Capital*, 4:301–9, 356–67.

55. Ibid., 427–35, 441–42.

56. Ibid., 361, 404.

57. Ibid., 43–44, 148–49, 189, 487.

58. *Congressional Record*, 51st Cong., 1st Sess., February 10, 1890, 1164.

59. *Congressional Record*, 51st Cong., 1st Sess., February 19, 1890, 1492.

60. *Congressional Record*, 51st Cong., 1st Sess., February 18, 1890, 1443.

## 7. Debate and Defeat of the Education Bill

1. Crofts, "Blair Bill and Elections Bill," 110–11.

2. *Congressional Record*, 49th Cong., 1st Sess., December 8, 1885, 130.

3. *Congressional Record*, 49th Cong., 1st Sess., December 9, 1885, 117.

4. *Congressional Record*, 49th Cong., 1st Sess., December 18, 1885, 310.

5. King, "Blair Education Bill," 106.

6. H. Martin Williams to Henry W. Blair, January 11, 1886, and Logan McKee to Blair, January 23, 1886, Blair Papers.

7. *Congressional Record*, 49th Cong., 1st Sess., February 9, 1885, 1238–83.

8. [Edward P. Clark], "Connecticut's Warning against Blair Educational Bill," *The Nation* 42 (February 11, 1886): 121.

9. [Edward P. Clark], "A Bill to Promote Mendicancy," *The Nation* 42 (February 18, 1886): 143.

10. Crofts, "Blair Bill and Elections Bill," 149.

11. *Congressional Record*, 49th Cong., 1st Sess., February 16, 1886, 1482.

12. *Congressional Record*, 49th Cong., 1st Sess., February 24, 1886, 1731–33.

13. Ibid., 1726–27.

14. Ibid., 1726–27.

15. Crofts, "Blair Bill and Elections Bill," 112–13.

16. Ibid., 113–16; *Congressional Record*, 49th Cong., 1st Sess., February 26, 1886, 1820.

17. *Congressional Record*, 49th Cong., 1st Sess., February 26, 1886, 1820.

18. *Congressional Record*, 49th Cong., 1st Sess., March 2, 1886, 1952.

19. Ibid., 1951.

20. Crofts, "Blair Bill and Elections Bill," 119.

21. Ibid., 116–17.

22. Henry W. Blair to Rutherford B. Hayes, March 7, 1886, Rutherford Birchard Hayes Papers, Library of Congress.

23. Crofts, "Blair Bill and Elections Bill," 119.

24. *Congressional Record*, 49th Cong., 1st Sess., March 4, 1886, 2063.

25. Crofts, "Blair Bill and Elections Bill," 119.

26. *Congressional Record*, 49th Cong., 1st Sess., March 5, 1886, 2104–5.

27. Henry W. Blair to Frederick Douglass, March 13, 1886, Reel 4, Frederick Douglass Papers, Library of Congress.

28. Henry W. Blair to Frederick Douglass, March 20, 1885, Reel 4, Douglass Papers.

29. Crofts, "Blair Bill and Elections Bill," 123–25.

30. *Congressional Record*, 49th Cong., 1st Sess., March 29, 1886, 2582.

31. Henry W. Blair to Rutherford B. Hayes, March 29, 1886, Hayes Papers.

32. Crofts, "Blair Bill and Elections Bill," 127; Evans, "Catholics," 259n.

33. Crofts, "Blair Bill and Elections Bill," 128–29.

34. Henry W. Blair to Rutherford B. Hayes, January 22, 1887, Hayes Papers.

35. Crofts, "Blair Bill and Elections Bill," 131.

36. Ibid., 145.

37. Ibid., 134–35.

38. Ibid., 137.

39. Edward Clark, *A Bill to Promote Mendicancy* (New York: Evening Post Publishing Co., 1890), 23–25.

40. Ross B. Paulson, *Women's Suffrage and Prohibition: A Comparative Study of Equality and Social Control* (Glenview, IL: Scott, Foresman, 1973), 141–42.

41. Evans, "Catholics," 288–89.

42. *Manchester (NH) Union*, June 1, 1886.

43. *Congressional Record*, 50th Cong., 1st Sess., February 15, 1886, 1218.

44. Ibid.

45. John G. Shea, "Federal Schemes to Aid Common Schools in the Southern States," *American Catholic Quarterly Review* 13 (April 1888): 348–49, 356.

46. Ibid., 347.

47. August D. Small, "Send the Whole Boy to School," *Catholic World* 17 (August 1888): 589–600.

48. See "The Blair Education Bill," *Critic* 7 (June 1886): 265–66; and King, "Blair Education Bill," 135.

49. Henry W. Blair to John F. Crowell, January 8, 1888, John Franklin Crowell Papers, Duke University Library.

50. Going, "South," 282–83.

51. *Granite State Free Press* (Lebanon, NH), December 23, 1887.

52. *Congressional Record*, 50th Cong., 1st Sess., January 17, 1888, 512–17.

53. *Congressional Record*, 50th Cong., 1st Sess., January 26, 1888, 734–38.

54. Ibid., 744, 746.

55. *Congressional Record*, 50th Cong., 1st Sess., February 15, 1888, 1232.

56. Crofts, "Blair Bill and Elections Bill," 164.

57. *Manchester (NH) Union*, March 22, 1888.

58. Crofts, "Blair Bill and Elections Bill," 167.

59. Ibid., 137–38, 168, 173.

60. Ibid., 173.

61. *Granite State Free Press* (Lebanon, NH), October 5, 1888.

62. William Lamb to Henry W. Blair, November 24, 1888, Series 1, Reel 13, Harrison Papers.

63. See *New York Mail and Express*, May 1, 6, 1889.

64. *New York Mail and Express*, August 2, 1890.

65. Henry W. Blair to Benjamin Harrison, November 10, 28, 1888, Series 1, Reel 13, Harrison Papers.

66. *Manchester (NH) Union*, July 22, 1889.

67. *Manchester (NH) Union*, July 15, 1890.

68. Elizabeth L. Meriam to Ellen P. Meriam, July 14, 1889, Meriam-Adams Papers, Duke University Library.

69. *Portsmouth (NH) Daily Chronicle*, January 7, 1890.

70. *Manchester (NH) Union*, November 2, 1889.

71. Crofts, "Blair Bill and Elections Bill," 230–31.

72. William E. Chandler, "National Control of Elections," *Forum* 9 (August 1890): 705–18; Henry C. Lodge, "The Coming Congress," *North American Review* 119 (September 1889): 298–99.

73. Crofts, "Blair Bill and Elections Bill," 239–40.

74. Thomas Adams Upchurch, *Legislating Racism: The Billion Dollar Congress and the Birth of Jim Crow* (Lexington: University Press of Kentucky, 2004), 212.

75. H. A. Herbert to Zebulon B. Vance et al., April 8, [1889], Zebulon Baird Vance Papers, North Carolina Department of Archives and History.

76. Rothman, *Politics and Power*, 81–83; William G. Shade, Stanley D. Hopper, David Jacobson, and Stephen E. Moiles, "Partisanship in the United States Senate: 1869–1901," *Journal of Interdisciplinary History* 4 (Autumn 1973): 155–205.

77. *Congressional Record*, 51st Cong., 1st Sess., February 5, 1890, 1067–69.

78. *Congressional Record*, 51st Cong., 1st Sess., February 6, 1890, 1092–1102.

79. *New York Mail and Express*, March 22, 1890.

80. *New York Mail and Express*, February 10, 1890.

81. Henry W. Blair to Benjamin Harrison, February 10, 1890, Series 1, Reel 25, Harrison Papers.

82. *Congressional Record*, 51st Cong., 1st Sess., February 10, 1890, 1163–64.

83. *Congressional Record*, 51st Cong., 1st Sess., February 11, 1890, 1201–3.

84. Henry W. Blair to Benjamin Harrison, February 10, 1890, Series 1, Reel 25, Harrison Papers.

85. *New York Mail and Express*, March 22, 1890.

86. *New York Mail and Express*, February 15, 1890.

87. *Congressional Record*, 51st Cong., 1st Sess., February 17, 1890, 1396.

88. *Portsmouth (NH) Daily Chronicle*, February 19, 1890.

89. *Congressional Record*, 51st Cong., 1st Sess., February 18, 1890, 1422.

90. *Congressional Record*, 51st Cong., 1st Sess., February 19, 1890, 1489–90.

91. *Portsmouth (NH) Daily Chronicle*, February 19, 1890.

92. *Littleton Courier*, March 19, 1890.

93. *Portsmouth (NH) Daily Chronicle*, February 20, 1890.

94. Crofts, "Blair Bill and Elections Bill," 204–6.

95. *New York Mail and Express*, March 22, 1890.

96. *Congressional Record*, 51st Cong., 1st Sess., March 20, 1890, 2436.

97. Crofts, "Blair Bill and Elections Bill," 220.

98. Crofts, "Black Response," 60.

99. Henry W. Blair, *Address Delivered at the American Federation of Labor Convention at Philadelphia* (Washington, DC: American Federation of Labor, 1892), 5.

100. *New York Mail and Express*, April 12, 1890.

## 8. General Reformer

1. *New York Times*, September 24, 1899, 22.

2. U.S. Senate Committee on Education and Labor, *Report on Labor and Capital*, 1:1.

3. *Congressional Record*, 47th Cong., 2nd Sess., February 2, 1883, 1976–77.

4. Samuel Gompers, *Seventy Years of Life and Labor: An Autobiography*, 5 vols. (New York: E. P. Dutton, 1943), 1:234–37.

5. U.S. Senate Committee on Education and Labor, *Report on Labor and Capital*, 1:1–41.

6. Ibid., 8.

7. *New Hampshire Sentinel* (Keene), March 3, 1883.

8. Atherton Noyes to [Henry P. Blair], October 20, 1885, Herbert H. Balch to Henry P. Blair, October 26, 1885, and W. U. Walther to Henry P. Blair, October 28, [1885], Blair Papers.

9. U.S. Senate Committee on Education and Labor, *Report on Labor and Capital*, 1:93–101.

10. Ibid., 270–301, 361–86.

226                                                    Notes to Pages 134–140

11. Ibid., 279–82.
12. Ibid., 449–46.
13. Ibid., 460.
14. Ibid., 466–525.
15. Ibid., 1057.
16. Ibid., 1062–94.
17. Ibid., 1091–94.
18. Ibid., 1072–73.
19. Ibid., 1090–91.
20. *New Hampshire Sentinel* (Keene), May 16, 1883.
21. U.S. Senate Committee on Education and Labor, *Report on Labor and Capital*, 2:596–605.
22. Ibid., 619–21.
23. Ibid., 627.
24. Ibid., 598–600, 606, 608, 612, 616–17, 619, 627–30, 632–33.
25. Ibid., 3:184.
26. Ibid., 195–202.
27. Ibid., 4:820.
28. Ibid., 427–36.
29. Ibid., 427–41.
30. Ibid., 434.
31. Ibid., 452.
32. Ibid., 610.
33. Ibid., 813, 819.
34. Ibid., 459–60, 462–65, 613–16, 620, 633–34, 666–69, 815–16.
35. *Congressional Record*, 48th Cong., 1st Sess., February 12, 1883, 2472.
36. *Congressional Record*, 48th Cong., 1st Sess., February 13, 1883, 2595.
37. *Congressional Record*, 48th Cong., 1st Sess., December 4, 1883, 16; March 10, 1884, 1746–50; May 19, 1884, 4285–86; and May 23, 1884, 4427.
38. *Manchester (NH) Union*, February 2, 16, 1886.
39. *Manchester (NH) Union*, February 20, 1885.
40. *Congressional Record*, 49th Cong., 1st Sess., March 1, 1886, 1900.
41. *Granite State Free Press* (Lebanon, NH), April 9, 1886.
42. *New Hampshire Sentinel* (Keene), April 21, 1886.
43. *Congressional Record*, 51st Cong., 2nd Sess., February 5, 1891, 2191–93.
44. Blair, *Address*, 2.
45. Ibid., 4.
46. Ibid.
47. Ida H. Harper and Susan B. Anthony, *History of Woman Suffrage*, 6 vols. (New York: Fowler & Wells, 1881–1922), 4:47.
48. *Manchester (NH) Union*, August 29, 1873.

49. *Manchester (NH) Union*, February 17, 1879.

50. *Congressional Record*, 49th Cong., 2nd Sess., December 2, 1886, 36.

51. *Congressional Record*, 49th Cong., 2nd Sess., January 25, 1887, 991–1003.

52. Gaines M. Foster, *Moral Reconstruction: Christian Lobbyists and the Federal Legislation of Morality, 1865–1920* (Chapel Hill: University of North Carolina Press, 2002), 4–6, 29, 225–26.

53. Ibid., 49–56.

54. Ibid., 78.

55. Ibid., 98.

56. Ibid.

57. Ibid.

58. Ibid., 99–100.

59. Ibid.

60. Ibid., 100.

61. Ibid., 100–101, 106.

62. Ibid., 40.

63. *New Hampshire Sentinel* (Keene), October 4, 1882; *Congressional Record*, 48th Cong., 1st Sess., January 30, 1884, 748–49.

64. *Congressional Record*, 47th Cong., 2nd Sess., December 23, 1882, 630, and December 2, 1882, 653.

65. *Manchester (NH) Union*, July 7, 1883.

66. *Congressional Record*, 48th Cong., 1st Sess., December 5, 1883, 37.

67. Henry W. Blair, "Alcohol in Politics," *North American Review* 138 (January 1884): 50–59.

68. Ibid., 59.

69. Foster, *Christian Lobbyists*, 42–43.

70. *Congressional Record*, 49th Cong., 1st Sess., April 20, 1885, 3822.

71. Ibid., 3823.

72. *Manchester (NH) Union*, September 17, 1886.

73. *New Hampshire Sentinel* (Keene), September 22, 1886.

74. Foster, *Christian Lobbyists*, 41–42, 166.

75. *Manchester (NH) Union*, August 2, 1882.

76. Crofts, "Blair Bill and Elections Bill," 71.

77. Henry W. Blair to William E. Chandler, July 19, 1887, Chandler Papers.

78. *Granite State Free Press* (Lebanon, NH), February 20, 1888.

79. *Portsmouth (NH) Daily Chronicle*, January 11, 1889.

80. *Manchester (NH) Union*, February 11, 1889.

81. Paul Kleppner, *The Third Electoral System, 1853–1892: Parties, Voters and Political Cultures* (Chapel Hill: University of North Carolina Press, 1979), 336–37.

82. Howard S. Russell, *A Long Deep Furrow: Three Centuries of Farming in New England* (Hanover, NH: University Press of New England, 1976), 432–33.

83. State Election Returns, New Hampshire Department of Records Management and Archives. All computation is mine.

84. *Portsmouth (NH) Daily Chronicle*, March 5, 1889.

85. *New York Mail and Express*, May 6, 1889.

86. *Manchester (NH) Union*, November 2, 1889.

87. *New York Mail and Express*, July 26, 1890.

88. *New York Mail and Express*, August 16, 1890.

89. Henry W. Blair, "The Race Problem: A Problem in Civilization," *National Education Association Proceedings* 19 (1890): 282.

90. *New York Mail and Express*, March 22, 1890.

91. *Congressional Record*, 53rd Cong., 1st Sess., September 30, 1893, 2040.

92. *Congressional Record*, 51st Cong., 1st Sess., January 16, 1890, 630–31.

93. *Congressional Record*, 53rd Cong., 2nd Sess., August 3, 1894, 8182.

94. Ibid.

95. Blair to Douglass, August 14, 1894, Reel 8, Douglass Papers.

96. *Manchester (NH) Union*, September 8, 1894.

## 9. Foreign Policy

1. *Congressional Record*, 50th Cong., 1st Sess., January 11, 22, 1889, 668, 1083–84.

2. *New Hampshire Sentinel* (Keene), March 7, 1878.

3. *New York Times*, May 7, 1882, 10.

4. *Manchester (NH) Union*, August 31, 1891.

5. Henry W. Blair to Eliza N. Blair, July 1, 31, August 19, 1879, Blair Papers.

6. *Manchester (NH) Union*, April 5, 1887.

7. Henry W. Blair to William E. Chandler, April 10, 1887, Chandler Papers.

8. Pamphlet, [May 1885], Blair Papers; *Portsmouth (NH) Daily Chronicle*, June 10, 1885.

9. Henry W. Blair to Bingham, Mitchell, and Fletcher, October 14, 1888, Blair Papers.

10. *New York Times*, May 5, 1882.

11. *Manchester (NH) Union*, March 22, 1882.

12. *Manchester (NH) Union*, April 11, 1882.

13. *Manchester (NH) Union*, May 23, 1882.

14. Ibid.

15. Ibid.

16. *New York Times*, May 2, 1882.

17. *New York Times*, May 9, 1882.

18. *New York Times*, May 2, 1882.

19. *Manchester (NH) Union*, March 22, 23, 27, April 6, 8, 11, 12, 14, 1882.

20. *Manchester (NH) Union*, April 12, 14, 1882.

21. *New York Times*, May 6, 1882.

22. *New York Times*, May 9, 1882.

23. *New York Times*, May 5, 1882.

24. Ibid.

25. *Manchester (NH) Union*, March 31, 1882.

26. *Granite State Free Press* (Lebanon, NH), May 12, 1882.

27. Tyler Dennett, *Americans in Eastern Asia: A Critical Study of the Policy of the United States with Reference to China, Japan and Korea in the 19th Century* (New York: Barnes & Noble, 1941), 540.

28. Andrew Gyory, *Closing the Gate: Race, Politics and the Chinese Exclusion Act* (Chapel Hill: University of North Carolina Press, 1998), 71.

29. Dennett, *Eastern Asia*, 541.

30. Gyory, *Chinese Exclusion*, 77, 85, 93.

31. Dennett, *Eastern Asia*, 542.

32. Gyory, *Chinese Exclusion*, 3–4.

33. Ibid., 142.

34. David M. Pletcher, *The Awkward Years: American Foreign Relations under Garfield and Arthur* (Columbia: University of Missouri Press, 1962), 294–95.

35. Gyory, *Chinese Exclusion*, 166–67, 215–16, 218.

36. Pletcher, *Awkward Years*, 299–300.

37. Ibid., 302–3.

38. Tsui Kwo Yin to James G. Blaine, October 1, 1890, Notes from the Chinese Legation in the United States to the Department of State, 1868–1906, vol. 2, National Archives.

39. Upchurch, *Legislating Racism*, 181–85.

40. See Frederick Rudolph, "Chinamen in Yankeedom: Anti-Unionism in Massachusetts in 1870," *American Historical Review* 53 (October 1947): 1–29.

41. *Congressional Record*, 50th Cong., 1st Sess., September 13, 1888, 8567.

42. *Manchester (NH) Union*, March 20, 1879.

43. *New Hampshire Sentinel* (Keene), March 20, 1879.

44. Henry W. Blair to William F. Wharton, June 22, 1891, Series 1, Reel 31, Harrison Papers.

45. *Congressional Record*, 50th Cong., 1st Sess., September 7, 1888, 8376–77.

46. *Congressional Record*, 50th Cong., 1st Sess., September 13, 1888, 8568.

47. Ibid., 8567.

48. Henry W. Blair to William F. Wharton, June 22, 1891, Series 1, Reel 31, Harrison Papers.

49. *New York Mail and Express*, May 3, 1890.

50. McGregor, *Fifteenth Regiment*, 121–22.

51. *Manchester (NH) Union*, February 28, 1891.

52. Henry W. Blair to Benjamin Harrison, March 5, 1891, Series 1, Reel 30, Harrison Papers.

53. *Manchester (NH) Union*, September 7, 1885; *New Hampshire Sentinel* (Keene), September 16, 1885.

54. Chang Yin Hoon to Thomas F. Bayard, October 12, 1886, Chinese Legation Notes, National Archives.

55. Chang Yin Hoon to Thomas F. Bayard, January 26, 1889, Chinese Legation Notes.

56. Tsui Zwo Yin to James G. Blaine, March 26, 1890, Chinese Legation Notes.

57. Tsui Zwo Yin to James G. Blaine, October 1, 1890, Chinese Legation Notes.

58. Tsui Zwo Yin to James G. Blaine, December 4, 1890, Chinese Legation Notes.

59. Kenneth W. Rea, ed., *Early Sino-American Relations, 1841–1912: The Collected Articles of Earl Swisher* (Boulder, CO: Westview, 1977), 191–93.

60. Tsui Zwo Yin to James G. Blaine, April 25, 1891, Chinese Legation Notes.

61. Li Tieutsin, Cablegram, April 24, 1891, Chinese Legation Notes.

62. James G. Blaine to Henry W. Blair, April 29, 1891, Series 1, Reel 31, Harrison Papers.

63. Henry W. Blair to William F. Wharton, June 22, 1891, Series 1, Reel 31, Harrison Papers.

64. William F. Wharton Memorandum, June 15, 1891, Chinese Legation Notes.

65. Tsui Zwo Yin to William F. Wharton, June 23, 1891, Chinese Legation Notes.

66. Henry W. Blair to Benjamin Harrison, June 22, 1891, Series 1, Reel 31, and Blair to Harrison, July 9, 1891, Series 1, Reel 32, Harrison Papers.

67. Henry W. Blair to William F. Wharton, July 15, 1891, Series 1, Reel 32, Harrison Papers.

68. Benjamin Harrison to Henry W. Blair, October 6, 1891, Series 1, Reel 33, Harrison Papers.

69. William E. Chandler to Benjamin Harrison, June 18, 1891, Chandler Papers; Frances Willard to Harrison, July 4, 1891, Henry W. Blair File, Department of State, General Record: Applications and Recommendations for Public Office, Cleveland, Harrison Administrations, 1885–1893, National Archives.

70. *Congressional Record*, 53rd Cong., 1st Sess., October 16, 1893, 2551–58.

71. Ibid.

72. *Congressional Record*, 53rd Cong., 2nd Sess., April 25, 1894, 4090.

73. Clipping, *Army and Navy Journal* (New York), July 28, 1900, Blair Papers.

## 10. New Hampshire Politics

1. *Congressional Record*, 48th Cong., 1st Sess., June 20, 1884, 5394.

2. For the text of one of his Memorial Day speeches, see *Manchester (NH) Union*, June 1, 1885.

3. *Portsmouth (NH) Daily Chronicle*, March 28, 1885.

4. *Portsmouth (NH) Daily Chronicle*, May 5, 1885.

5. *Congressional Record*, 47th Cong., 2nd Sess., February 17, 1883, 2837–43.

6. *Granite State Free Press* (Lebanon, NH), December 15, 1882.

7. *Manchester (NH) Union*, April 5, 1883; *New Hampshire Sentinel* (Keene), April 18, 25, 1883; *Granite State Free Press* (Lebanon, NH), May 18, 1883.

8. *Manchester (NH) Union*, March 16, 1883.

9. *New York Times*, March 16, 1883; *New Hampshire Sentinel* (Keene), March 21, 1883.

10. *Granite State Free Press* (Lebanon, NH), June 1, 1883.

11. *Manchester (NH) Union*, June 15, 1883.

12. *Journal of the Honorable House of Representatives of the State of New Hampshire, June Session, 1883* (Concord, NH: Parsons B. Cogswell, Public Printer, 1884), 437–39 (June 19, 1883).

13. *Manchester (NH) Union*, June 15, 1883.

14. *New Hampshire Sentinel* (Keene), June 20, 1883.

15. *Granite State Free Press* (Lebanon, NH), June 22, 1883.

16. Calhoun, *Southern Question*, 169–93.

17. Ibid., 190–200.

18. Ibid., 208–11.

19. James Morrison Jr. to Blair, September 27, 1884, Blair Papers.

20. *Manchester (NH) Union*, October 3, 28, 1884.

21. *Manchester (NH) Union*, August 23, 1884.

22. *Portsmouth (NH) Daily Chronicle*, September 12, 1884.

23. *Portsmouth (NH) Daily Chronicle*, October 3, 1884; *Manchester (NH) Union*, November 4, 1884.

24. *Manchester (NH) Union*, August 15, 1884.

25. Richardson, *Chandler*, 353.

26. *Manchester (NH) Union*, October 30, 1884.

27. A. F. Howard to William E. Chandler, November 13, 1884, Ossian Ray to Chandler, November 23, 1884, James A. Briggs to Chandler, November 24, 1884, and J. P. Whittle to Chandler, December 10, 1884, Chandler Papers.

28. Ossian Ray to William E. Chandler, November 15, 1884, Chandler to Gilman Marston, December 15, 1884, and Charles H. Burns to Chandler, December 17, 1884, Chandler Papers.

29. J. A. Wood to William E. Chandler, December 29, 1884, Chandler Papers.

30. A. F. Howard to William E. Chandler, November 18, 1884, Chandler Papers.

31. *Portsmouth (NH) Daily Chronicle*, December 15, 1884.

32. A. F. Howard to William E. Chandler, November 18, 1884, and Daniel Hall to Chandler, December 17, 1884, Chandler Papers; *Manchester (NH) Union*, December 16, 1884.

33. Ossian Ray to William E. Chandler, January 24, 1855, Chandler Papers; *Granite State Free Press* (Lebanon, NH), February 13, 1885.

34. Charles R. Corning to William E. Chandler, January 22, 1885, Chandler Papers.

35. A. F. Howard to William E. Chandler, June 17, 1885, and "Citizen" to Chandler, May 6, 1885, Chandler Papers.

36. *Manchester (NH) Union*, March 6, 1885.

37. *Portsmouth (NH) Daily Chronicle*, June 10, 1885.

38. *Portsmouth (NH) Daily Chronicle*, January 22, March 28, 1885; *Granite State Free Press* (Lebanon, NH), January 30, 1885.

39. *Portsmouth (NH) Daily Chronicle*, February 4, 1885.

40. *Granite State Free Press* (Lebanon, NH), January 30, 1885.

41. *Congressional Record*, 49th Cong., 1st Sess., March 12, 1885, 37.

42. Ossian Ray to William E. Chandler, April 20, May 10, 1885, Chandler Papers.

43. *New Hampshire Sentinel* (Keene), May 6, 1885; *Portsmouth (NH) Daily Chronicle*, May 25, 1885; *Granite State Free Press* (Lebanon, NH), March 27, 1885.

44. *New Hampshire Sentinel* (Keene), June 10, 1885.

45. *Manchester (NH) Union*, May 2, 1885.

46. *New Hampshire Sentinel* (Keene), June 17, 1885.

47. Richardson, *Chandler*, 276–77.

48. *Portsmouth (NH) Daily Chronicle*, September 6, 1888.

49. Ibid.

50. *Manchester (NH) Union*, June 5, 1889.

51. Richardson, *Chandler*, 404.

52. *Manchester (NH) Union*, July 12, 1889.

53. *Manchester (NH) Union*, July 19, 24, 25, 1889.

54. Jacob H. Gallinger to William Mahone, March 31, 1888, Mahone Papers.

55. *Granite State Free Press* (Lebanon, NH), October 17, 1894; *Manchester (NH) Union*, May 30, 1889.

56. *Manchester (NH) Union*, August 3, 1889, July 8, 1890.

57. Calhoun, *Southern Question*, 211–17.

58. Ibid., 217–25.

59. Ibid., 226–59.

60. *Manchester (NH) Union*, January 12, 1891.

61. Clipping, January 9, 1891, Scrapbook, vol. 2, Jacob Harold Gallinger Papers, New Hampshire Historical Society.

62. *Manchester (NH) Union*, January 16, 1891.

63. *New Hampshire Sentinel* (Keene), February 24, 1892.

64. Blair to Douglass, February 25, 1892, Reel 6, Douglass Papers.

65. See Donald M. Dozer, "Benjamin Harrison and the Presidential Campaign of 1892," *American Historical Review* 54 (October 1948): 49–77.

66. *New York Times*, February 23, 1892.

67. *Granite State Free Press* (Lebanon, NH), March 11, 1892.

68. *Manchester (NH) Union*, February 26, 1892.

69. *Manchester (NH) Union*, April 28, 1892.

70. *Manchester (NH) Union*, June 7, 1892.

71. *Manchester (NH) Union*, June 11, 1892.

72. *Manchester (NH) Union*, September 7, 1892.

73. *New Hampshire Sentinel* (Keene), August 17, 1892.

74. *Granite State Free Press* (Lebanon, NH), September 16, 1892.

75. *Manchester (NH) Union*, September 8, 1892.

76. Ibid.

77. *Manchester (NH) Union*, October 4, 1892.

78. *Manchester (NH) Union*, September 28, 1892.

79. *Le National* (Manchester, NH), October 25, 1892.

80. *Manchester (NH) Union*, October 1, 1892.

81. William E. Chandler to Henry W. Blair, March 24, 1893, Chandler Papers.

82. *Manchester (NH) Union*, October 1, 1892.

83. *Manchester (NH) Union*, October 6, 1892.

84. Ibid.

85. *Manchester (NH) Union*, October 28, 1892.

86. *Manchester (NH) Union*, November 1, 1892.

87. *Manchester (NH) Union*, November 8, 1892.

88. See Richardson, *Chandler*, 444.

89. *Congressional Record*, 53rd Cong., 1st Sess., August 21, 1893, 554.

90. *Manchester (NH) Union*, January 19, 1893.

91. See Henry W. Blair to William E. Chandler, January 19, 1893, Chandler Papers; *Manchester (NH) Union*, January 8, 1895.

92. *New Hampshire Sentinel* (Keene), April 5, 1893.

93. Calhoun, *Southern Question*, 260–76.

94. Henry W. Blair to William E. Chandler, July 24, November 16, 1893, March 21, 1894, and Chandler to Blair, June 15, 1894, Chandler Papers.

95. Charles H. Burns to Frank Parsons, January 24, 1894, Frank Parsons Papers, New Hampshire Historical Society; *Manchester (NH) Union*, February 26, 1894.

96. *Manchester (NH) Union*, February 26, 1894.

97. *Granite State Free Press* (Lebanon, NH), March 23, 1894.

98. William E. Chandler to Frank Parsons, April 3, 1894, Parsons Papers; George A. Moses to Chandler, April 3, 9, 22, 1894, George Higgins Moses Papers, New Hampshire Historical Society.

99. *Manchester (NH) Union*, April 10, 1894.

100. Richardson, *Chandler*, 490.

101. Ibid.

102. Ibid.

103. *New Hampshire Sentinel* (Keene), July 25, 1894.

104. J. Davis to William E. Chandler, November 23, 1894, Chandler Papers.

105. *Manchester (NH) Union*, September 7, 1894.

106. *Manchester (NH) Union*, December 18, 1894.

107. A.P.A. *Instructions*, [October 1894], Chandler Papers.

108. P. A. Smith to William E. Chandler, December 14, 26, 1894, and Joseph R. McCready to Chandler, December 17, 1894, Chandler Papers.

109. William E. Chandler to Lewis Kimball, November 17, 1894, Chandler Papers.

110. *Portsmouth (NH) Daily Chronicle*, January 2, 1895.

111. [Lucius Tuttle] to William E. Chandler, December 7, 1894, Chandler Papers.

112. David R. Pierce to William E. Chandler, December 4, 1894, Chandler to Lucius Tuttle, December 8, 1894, J. H. Manley to Chandler, December 17, 20, 1894, and Tuttle to Chandler, December 20, 1894, January 7, 10, 1895, Chandler Papers.

113. William J. Reed to William E. Chandler, November 13, 1894, J. T. Twombly to Chandler, December 1, 1894, Louis G. Hoyt to Chandler, December 4, 1894, and H. H. Wanser to Chandler, December 11, 1894, Chandler Papers.

114. Henry W. Blair, *Letter to Republican Legislators* (n.p., [1894]).

115. William E. Chandler, Circular Letter, November 28, 1894, Chandler Papers.

116. E. Gustine to William E. Chandler, November 14, 1894, Charles W. Talpey to Chandler, November 15, 1894, C. B. Hopkins to Chandler, November 15, 1894, J. B. Rider to Chandler, November 17, 1894, A. Render to Chandler, November 23, 1894, C. D. McDuffie to Chandler, November 26, 1894, William Sinclair to Chandler, November 27, 1894, E. Carrier to Chandler, November 29, 1894, Louis G. Hoyt to Chandler, December 4, 1894, and George A. Hill to Chandler, December 14, 1894, Chandler Papers.

117. Charles Marseilles to Henry W. Blair, December 18, 1894, Marseilles Papers.

118. *Manchester (NH) Union*, January 8, 1895.

119. Clipping, December 5, 1894, Marseilles Papers.

120. *Manchester (NH) Union*, January 2, 1895.

## 11. Later Years

1. Clipping, October 4, 1948, Blair Papers.

2. James Wright, *The Progressive Yankees: Republican Reformers in New*

*Hampshire, 1906–1916* (Hanover, NH: University Press of New England, 1987), xxi, 21, 26, 28–30, 64.

3. Henry W. Blair, *The Future of Temperance Reform* (n.p., 1895), 28.

4. Henry W. Blair to Booker T. Washington, February 21, 1896, in *The Booker T. Washington Papers*, ed. Louis R. Harlan, 14 vols. (Urbana: University of Illinois Press, 1972–1989), 4:119–21.

5. Mrs. H. C. McCabe to Frances E. Willard, January 13, 1897, Willard to Elisa N. Blair, January 16, 26, 1897, James H. Potts to Willard, January 22, 1897, John P. Newman to Willard, January 26, 1897, and John M. Walden to Willard, January 28, 1897, Blair Papers.

6. Henry W. Blair to William McKinley, June 9, 1898, copy, Chandler Papers.

7. Thomas S. Clark to Henry W. Blair, February 10, 1898, in McGregor, *Fifteenth Regiment*, 453–54.

8. Bennie L. DeWhitt, "A Wider Sphere of Usefulness: Marilla Ricker's Quest for a Diplomatic Post," *Prologue* 5 (Winter 1973): 203–5.

9. Henry W. Blair to William McKinley, March 8, 1897, Marilla Ricker File, Applications and Recommendations for Office, 1897–1901, General Records of the State Department, National Archives.

10. Henry W. Blair to William E. Chandler, March 10, 1897, Chandler Papers.

11. Henry W. Blair to William McKinley, March 24, April 10, May 3, June 25, 1897, Ricker File.

12. Henry W. Blair to Eliza N. Blair, January 28, 1899, Blair Papers.

13. Henry W. Blair to Eliza N. Blair, April 6, 1899, C. W. Nelson to Blair, May 6, 1899, and Blair to Charles McGregor, May 16, 1899, Blair Papers; Blair to Charles McGregor, June 19, 1899, in McGregor, *Fifteenth Regiment*, 124.

14. Henry W. Blair to Jacob H. Gallinger, September 7, 11, 1905, Gallinger Papers.

15. Kelly Miller to Booker T. Washington, February 6, 1906, and Washington to Whitefield McKinlay, March 3, 1906, in Harlan, ed., *Washington Papers*, 8:517–18, 536–37.

16. Minutes of the Board of Directors, February 6, July 7, 1914, National Association for the Advancement of Colored People Papers, Library of Congress.

17. Henry W. Blair, "The Negro Problem," *The Independent* 54 (February 20, 1902): 444.

18. Ibid., 443.

19. Ibid.

20. Harper and Anthony, *Woman Suffrage*, 6:402–3.

21. Henry W. Blair to Jacob H. Gallinger, February 3, 1907, Gallinger Papers.

22. Herbert H. Balch to Henry P. Blair, October 26, 1895, Blair Papers.

23. *The Camp Fire*, August 13, 22, 27, 1887, Blair Papers.

24. Henry P. Blair to Henry W. and Eliza N. Blair, June 25, 1887, Blair Papers.

25. *Manchester (NH) Union*, June 18, 28, 1889.

26. Clipping, October 4, 1948, Blair Papers.

27. Giles Low II, interview by the author, June 1980.

28. Henry W. Blair to Blanche K. Baker, April 6, 1911, Blair Papers.

29. Henry W. Blair to Giles Low, July 8, 1910, Blair Papers.

30. Henry W. Blair to William Howard Taft, May 8, 1905, Series 3, Reel 50, and Blair to Fred C. Carpenter, January 15, 1909, Series 3, Reel 118, William Howard Taft Papers, Library of Congress.

31. Henry W. Blair to William Howard Taft, June 17, 1905, Series 3, Reel 51, Taft Papers.

32. Henry W. Blair to Fred C. Carpenter, January 15, 1909, Series 3, Reel 118, Taft Papers.

33. Ibid.; and Henry W. Blair to William Howard Taft, December 12, 1912, Series 6, Reel 432, Taft Papers.

34. Jonathan C. Reiff to William E. Chandler, April 8, 1907, Chandler to Reiff, April 12, 1907, Henry W. Blair to Chandler, April 12, 1907, and Reiff to Blair, April 15, 1907, Chandler Papers.

35. Henry W. Blair to Fred C. Carpenter, January 15, 1909, Series 3, Reel 118, Taft Papers.

36. *Manchester (NH) Union*, March 23, 1912.

37. See enclosure in Henry W. Blair to Woodrow Wilson, May 5, 1914, Woodrow Wilson Papers, Library of Congress.

38. "Letter of Ex-Senator Henry W. Blair," [September 22, 1919], Wilson Papers.

39. *New York Times*, March 15, 1920.

# Index

237

CPSIA information can be obtained at www.ICGtesting.com
Printed in the USA
BVOW041107211212

308274BV00002B/4/P